Reflections on Africa and Global Affairs

Other titles

Reflections on Industry and Economy
Reflections on Media and Gender Issues
Reflections on Good Governance and Democracy
Reflections on Labour and Trade Unions
Reflections on Friends, Comrades and Heroes

Reflections on Africa and Global Affairs

Issa Aremu

Lagos, Benin, Ibadan, Jos, Port-Harcourt, Zaria

First published 2015
ISBN 978-978-53321-1-7

Malthouse Press Limited
43 Onitana Street, Off Stadium Hotel Road,
Off Western Avenue, Lagos Mainland
E-mail: malthouse_press@yahoo.com
malthouselagos@gmail.com
Tel: +234 (01) 0802 600 3203

Foreword

In the years as a weekly columnist, Issa Aremu has competently covered a truly astonishing range of issues, persons and events, criss-crossing continents with such remarkable ease without any loss in incisiveness and clarity of thought. Such effort undoubtedly requires being constantly abreast of global socio-economic and political developments, not a mean feat itself and which explains the choice of each topic as events unfolded across the world.

In these sixty-seven chapters, Issa probes, argues and draws attention to lessons and possible consequences of various issues and developments for the future. In West Africa, falling within his critical radar are politics in Liberia, salutary effects of elections in Ghana, constitutional manipulations in Niger, canons of Kwame Nkrumah to sobering reflections on Nigeria, what he dubbed the rise and fall of Nigeria's diplomacy, and import of Hilary Clinton's assessment of state of governance.

In East Africa, those violent elections in Kenya, complexities of the Zimbabwe situation, and the person of Robert Mugabe himself come under focus. Southern Africa was dominated by events in South Africa, from the shocking wave of explosive manifestations of xenophobia, the inauguration of President Zuma, the centenary of the ANC, useful lessons from the life and times of Nelson Mandela, to bilateral relations with Nigeria after the politics of yellow fever which involved both sides denying entry to each other's visitors for some weeks.

North Africa and the Middle East understandably, too, attracted attention: the return of Libya after abandoning its nuclear programme, Gaddafi political moves and antics, downfall and early post-Gaddafi developments; anti-democratic reactions to democratic victory of Hamas at elections, Iranian elections, the Iraq imbroglio,

Israel's badly-managed flotilla operation and self-image, Obama's speech in Cairo, Mubarak's manoeuvres and eventual displacement, to a wholesale review of Arab protest in favour good governance.

For the African continent, Issa turned his attention to the significance of a variety of events, from developments in European Union, Margaret Thatcher, lessons from Davos, American foreign policy, to the indiscretions of Horowitz and World Bank's policies and ethical standards it advocates, to the dominance of the CNN. Running through all these are concern for proper governance and development that should eliminate mass poverty, relative lack of critical and thinking and thus poverty of ideas among African political and bureaucratic policy makers.

His reflections on the "Asian crisis" is quite intriguing, wondering whether the "miracle" was over as most Asian economies seemed to be in trouble, and arguing that the World Bank and the IMF have been neck-deep in damage control there; urging Nigerians and Africans to copy and not beg China for aid; discussing developments in the India subcontinent and the crucial role of Sonia Ghandi and the Congress Party in the process; the paradox of two systems in one- booming, capitalist Hong Kong within China; and impact of ethnic divisions in Singapore.

Predictably for the North American subcontinent, the United States of America threw up more issues that drew comments from Issa Aremu: from Reaganomics, issues dominating George W. Bush's election; the suspect reliability of American intelligence reports over the years; the election of Obama, inauguration and first 100 days of his administration; and message carried by Hillary Clinton in her visit to several African countries.

On reading the book, I find that one need not agree with positions canvassed and arguments put forward by Issa Aremu to appreciate his perspectives. Indeed, some are outrightly provocative, writing tongue-in-cheek, as it were, and designed to provoke reaction! The second and which is more important, for every faraway development discussed, he displays the commendable knack for drawing on local similarities or relating such to local developments and goes on to prescribe some policy outcomes or directions. It is easy to see from evident thorough research and facts and arguments presented, the events, issues and persons discussed here, are a world away from usual self-interested ramblings and self-validated half-truths of partisan columnists who dominate the mass media in Nigeria. I recommend this book and should be a useful addition to any library.

Professor Ibrahim Gambari

Table of Contents

About the Author

Comrade Issa Obalowu Aremu, NPOM, mni, was born in 1961 to the extended family of Mallam Mahmood Aremu and Hadjia Afusat Amoke of Alapata and Kasandubu compounds of Ilorin respectively. He attended Ansar Ud Deen primary school, Ijagbo. He had his secondary education at Ilorin Grammar School before moving to School of Basic Studies, Ahmadu Bello University, ABU, Zaria in 1977.

Issa's passion for organizing and activism started in the late 1970s and early 80s, decades of progressive and radical ideas in ABU. He was an active member of ABU students' unionism and rose to become the Secretary General of the reputable radical Marxist-Leninist Movement for Progressive Nigeria (MPN). He was among the score of students' leaders repressed with expulsion by Ango Abdullahi Vice Chancellorship in 1981 at his final year. He eventually obtained his BSc (Hons) degree in Economics from University of Port Harcourt in 1985 with Second Class Upper. He has his Master degree in Labour and Development studies from the prestigious Institute for Social Studies (ISS), The Hague, The Netherlands, in 1991. He is an alumnus of George Meany Labour Centre, Maryland, Washington, USA (1987 and 2003). He joined the labour movement as the Head, Economic/Research department of Nigeria Labour Congress (NLC) between 1987 and 1989. He later moved to the National Union of Textile Garment and Tailoring Workers of Nigeria (NUTGTWN), a private sector affiliate union of NLC in 1989. After 20 years of active union carrier, he rose from an organizing Secretary to become the General Secretary of the union in March 2000. He took over as the General Secretary of the union from Comrade Adams Oshiomhole mni, the Comrade governor of Edo State and two times former President of Nigeria Labour Congress (NLC).

Comrade Issa Aremu is currently one of the Vice-Presidents of the Nigeria Labour Congress (NLC). In 2013 In Johannesburg, South Africa, he was elected the Chairman, new IndustriALL Global Union, Africa Region with more than 50 million members in 165 countries with headquarters in Geneva, Switzerland making an Executive African Member of IndustriALL Global Union. Having attended Senior Executive Course 27 of the National Institute (mni) for Policy and Strategic Studies, Kuru, Jos in 2005, Comrade Issa Aremu is a Member of the National Institute.

In 2013 he was elected the Secretary-General of the Alumni Association of the National Institute for Policy & Strategy Studies, AANI.

He is currently the Chairman of the Interim Management Committee of First Guarantee Pension Limited and a member of the tripartite National Labour Advisory Committee (NLAC) made up of government, employers and trade unions. He also serves in the Board of Labour City Transport Service (LCTS). He is the Chairman, International Committee of Nigeria Labour Congress (NLC).

Comrade Issa Aremu, mni has served on the Board of Michael Imoudu National Institute of Labour Studies (MINILS) and Nigeria Social Insurance Trust Fund (NSITF). His contributions helped to reposition these institutions as leading labour market institutions in Nigeria. He had served on the tripartite Federal National Minimum Wage, in 2000 and 2010 and Petroleum Products Pricing Regulatory Committee in 2003 as well as tripartite committee on Revival of textile and Garment industry. He has led negotiations and signed hundreds of national collective agreements on salaries, allowances, gratuity and pensions of textile, garment and tailoring workers over the years.

A visible leading member of mass national actions on socio-political issues during the struggle for democracy and against military dictatorship in the 1980s and 1990s, Comrade Issa is a weekly columnist with Abuja-based, *Daily Trust* newspapers. His published works include; *The Social Relevance of Trade Unionism, The Crises of Pricing Petroleum Products in Nigeria, Collapse of Textile Industry in Nigeria: Implications for Employment and Poverty Eradication and Tears Not Enough.*

Comrade Issa Aremu, mni was one of the labour delegates to the 2014 National Conference. He was the Deputy Chairman of the National Conference Committee on Civil Society, Labour, Youth and Sports. He is a strong activist and advocate on, Redistribution of national wealth, improved Productivity and Re-Industrialisation of Nigerian economy. Recipient of many distinguished awards and recognitions, the President of Nigeria, Dr. Goodluck Ebele Jonathan, GCFR, on August 21, 2014 in recognition of his contribution to national productivity improvement and consciousness conferred on him the National Productivity Order of Merit (NPOM) Award. He is married with children.

Thatcher's Second Visit*

Every good turn, they say, certainly deserves another. Undoubtedly this popular saying must have made a deep impression on the British Prime Minister, Mrs. Margaret Thatcher, in considering a new round of shuttle diplomacy to Africa. It is just over a year, she concluded one tour of Africa. The tour was widely acknowledged as an unsuccessful one, given the anti-Apartheid protests and demonstrations (Western media reported 'noisy demonstrations') that welcomed Her Excellency to Lagos and Lusaka in particular.

True to character, the Iron Lady insisted her controversial tour was 'successful' and said not "in the least" is she "nervous" to once again have a glimpse of the wild continent and its swarthy population. "I never think you should judge a country by the comparatively few people who demonstrate" she told the BBC. "Saturday Only" programme (25/3/89), in the most extensive interview the British Prime Minister would ever grant on Africa. Disapproving of the view of political pundits and demonstrating that her previous tour was a "good turn that deserves another", the recent tour even includes more Commonwealth family members, namely; Zimbabwe, Malawi, Nigeria and a strange mix, Morocco, which we were told hosts a number of "Jews" and whose leader, according to Mrs. Thatcher, has an "interesting view". In any case, King Hassan of Morocco has reportedly assured UNITA mercenary leader, Savimbi, an asylum after the end of a life long but unjust adventure. It is not clear if the Prime Minister would register British protest against King Hassan's offer, given UNITA's alleged involvement in the murder of Samora Machel, the Mozambique patriot. Mrs. Thatcher described

---

* *National Concord*, February 1988

belatedly as "our great friend". But she would definitely repeat British view on Salman Rushdie affairs only "it is raised" in a country, which has remained indifferent to the publication of *"Satanic Verses"*. "Islam, this great religion will endeavour long after the names of the people who have written things about it will be forgotten." Mrs. Thatcher remarked, combining sobriety with demagogy, which is not apolitical.

Meanwhile Britain still provides sanctuary for the most wanted "slanderer" of "this great religion", thanks to freedom of expression without responsibilities, perhaps.

Talking about "Freedom and responsibilities", however, Mrs. Thatcher wants this bedrock of democracy realised in South Africa.

But first, would the Iron Lady dare cross the…in the affirmative. "I could not go until something quite positive happens and Mr. Mandela is released", she remarked. Misinterpreted tour, she would not have it "for worth". It was intriguing for listeners to hear Mrs. Thatcher addressing a political prisoner who had "professed violence" and who has refused to yield to a wretched piece of freedom for a quarter of century like a perfect English gentleman, "Mr. Mandela." Perhaps it was not only the Boers that are "changing" after all but their supporters too. Witness hypocrisy: "I don't talk to these people (read: ANC), until they have called a halt to violence" was Thatcher's answer to a plausible question about her sincerity of purpose; while, on one hand, she "advocates the release of 'Mr. Mandela' but would not talk to his followers who are outside the jail house.

Never love the British Prime Minister. Mrs. Thatcher mischievously invoked the authority of the Eminent Persons Group (EPG) to justify her reluctance to talk to the ANC… 'I thought the Eminent Persons Groups really had it right when they said yes, we believe in negotiations in return for "a suspension for violence." It should however be noted that Thatcher never accepted the EPG report much less its conclusion, which singled out the Boers as the promoters and originators of violence. That in itself was a scandal during the Bahamas Commonwealth Conference when the Iron-Lady put up a stiff-neck opposition to sanctions and stood a lame duck. Yet the reference to the phrase: "Suspension of violence" exposed the latest in Thatcher's trickery. The truth is that, in order of priorities, the EPG spelt out five urgent steps for negotiations in the enclave, namely, dismantling of the system of Apartheid, terminate the state of emergency, release immediately and unconditionally Nelson Mandela and all others imprisoned or detained for their opposition to Apartheid, lifting of the ban on ANC and other political parties and suspension of violence on all sides, as a condition for a political dialogue.

Mrs. Thatcher certainly has no better ways of making the anniversary of a previous 'worth' tour than being on the streets of Africa, to teach the peoples she loves "very much" about the virtues of no-sanctions. Contrary to the popular belief that both armed struggle and sanctions by international community would bring the racists to reason, the 'argument' she put forward "Commonwealth-after-Commonwealth" "has in fact prevailed". Hear her: "'Those who in fact believe in sanctions have not imposed them."

Africa without Thatcher*

Every good turn deserves another, the saying goes. But perhaps it is important here to reflect on a situation, whereby a 'good turn' gives a great sense of relief and people say: it is a good turn nonetheless, but it does not deserve another turn.

Undoubtedly, the sudden resignation of Mrs. Thatcher as British Prime Minister on November 22 last year was one big relief for Africa. Big relief because, long before the war in the Gulf, the policy of Mrs. Thatcher passed for political and economic equivalent of war(s) against a continent. Thanks to the scores of her doctrinaire policies (read: missiles) for which the continent lacked the capacity (read: patriots) to repel.

Among other things, Apartheid in South Africa thrives on Mrs. Thatcher's 'no-sanctions' policy. The popular belief was that both the liberation efforts and sanctions by the international community would bring the racist Boers to reason and therefore to negotiation table. For Mrs. Thatcher, sanctions campaign was 'absurd' and commonwealth-after-commonwealth, she could not conceal her annoyance about the fact that sanctions would not set out 'to relive the poverty and starvation' in South Africa. In recent times considering Mrs. Thatcher's leading role in the campaign for 'sanctions plus force' against Iraq, one may then understand why she is being accused of double standards and rightly so. Successfully, the 'no-no-woman' defied reasoned positions of the of the Commonwealth's Eminent Persons' Group (EPG) on Apartheid and by doing so, guaranteed British security for the most inhuman system on the globe (still very much so). Not surprising then that the two

---

* Journal No. 1, January 1991

official 'African' tours of the Prime Minister in office, were marked by significant demonstrations and condemnations too.

Still on freedom, it is on record that Thatcher's UK did not promote any decolonisation policy or initiative on Namibia. Cold war perspective beclouds the policy perception of the legitimate efforts of SWAPO to restore the usurped rights of black men and women. The struggle for independence was reduced to a 'regional ideological conflict' according to which a 'linkage' existed between the withdrawal of the Cuban troops in Angola and the independence of Namibia. Indeed, with the unscheduled visit of Mrs. Thatcher to Windhoek in September, 1989, the world nearly had a caricature of UN Resolution 435 on Namibian independence as she displayed colonial bias and wrongly accused SWAPO of 'disrupting' decolonisation process, she never believed in the first instance. It is therefore an irony that Thatcher will now be in the fore front of the problem-solving activities of the UN in the Gulf. For one, it can be said that Africa problem solving was never her specialisation in office.

However, it was on the economic front, the legacy of her tenure remains a naughty obstacle to development of the continent.

Not by design, but the Thatcher period coincided with the worst economic crisis in Africa: balance of payment crisis, collapse of primary goods' prices, poverty and unemployment. These crises are in themselves attributable to the debt crisis. There was no doubt that Mrs. Thatcher was committed to debt collection and the better if the structural 'adjustment' programme lacks a human face. Britain remains the home of the 'Club of private creditors'. The Prime Minister was committed to free enterprise at home and did not hesitate to export same abroad through the support for IMF and World Bank reforms. Thus the continent became a showcase of mutually exclusive policies of devaluation, liberalisation, privatisation and cuts in public spending. The results: unemployment, brain drain, decline in income, and 'perverse flow of resources' through debt repayment.

West Africa Weekly summed up Mrs. Thatcher's tenure thus: 'Mrs. Thatcher never developed a coherent policy that remotely took account of the genuine interests of African people...' Perhaps now that Africa is without Thatcher (in office), a policy which will appreciate the plight of a continent will come from London.

Not yet 'Perestorika'*

One thing, a keen and not so keen observer of South African scene tends to agree on is the fact that many changes are taking place. Also agreement does exist that these changes cut across the great divide in the racist enclave.

For one thing, the Boer regime set the ball (always in its court) rolling with the release of political prisoners, the most notable being, Nelson Mandela. It 'unbanned' the liberation movements. Also, the regime opened 'talks about talks' with the ANC from such broad issues as 'a unitary educational system' in the country. On February 1, (opening of Parliament) President de Klerk announced the repeal of two 'legal expressions of Apartheid', namely the Group Areas Act and the Land Act.

In addition to these token changes, there have been verbal and rhetorical expressions of 'change of hearts', among the erstwhile racist spokesmen and even organisations. For instance, the Nationalist Party now thinks of having a black as a Provincial Chairman, while it has been accepted that entrenched Apartheid amounted to a sin against the blacks.

On the other hand too, the black community has been favourably disposed to this 'wind of change', long desired and prayed for. ANC has agreed to talk with a regime hitherto seen as an 'outlaw'. As if not to repeat the pitfalls of most liberation movements, the ANC is seemingly tempering commitment with modesty and publicly saying its tasks are enormous. Thus it acknowledged the world disillusionment with 'black on black' violence. This may well explain its recent affirmative non-partisan

---

* Journal No. 2 April 1991

actions when Mandela signed a peace accord with Inkatha, and met with the Pan African Congress. He also called for a multi-party Conference. Furthermore ANC has called for an 'international understanding' in working out a 'sound economic policy' so that 'God helps we don't mess up the country'.

Yet, these no less important changes have not been significantly translated into improved conditions for the black people. Apartheid is still active in forms of Political and Security Acts in Statute books. An estimated 3,000 political prisoners are still being held in prisons and some are on death row. Amnesty has yet to be extended to exiles. Importantly too, the violent Apartheid establishment still presides over wanton crimes and killings of blacks showing the myth of 'black on black' violence. The trial of Winnie Mandela is not a civil trial in a civil court but a continuation of age-long political harassment of the weak. The so-called white extremists might well be 'mild mad men' engaging in another feverish 'experiment in racial segregation as they purchase lands to build a 'new white only Jerusalem'. But the seemingly helpless racist government watches this land grabbing (property rights) unchecked.

Thus it may well mean that 'Perestroika' is nothing but a mere fantasy of Pretoria which has little to do with the realities of the blacks still trapped in squatters' camps and living with daily violence. Not yet Gorbachev Perestroika's analogy in South Africa.

Paradox of Hong Kong*

Hong Kong wears an independent outlook as it ceases being a colony of the United Kingdom. As the world celebrates the historic 'return' of this territory to mainland China, the naughty subject of colonialism (increasingly out of fashion) equally returns to the centre stage of public discourse. In Africa, ideas about colonialism have undergone some dramatic changes since Walter Rodney, the Guyanese African historian wrote his classic work: *How Europe Under-developed Africa.* Rodney was decidedly categorical about the overwhelming negative effects of colonial order in Africa. To him, the balance sheet of colonialism carried no "credits". Thus we need not give a thought to any "credits" of colonial order. It is more in the "debits". "Colonialism had only one hand," wrote Rodney. "It was a one-armed bandit." This insight constitutes the main thesis of the great radical scholar. He remarkably chronicled the banditry that was colonial rule in Africa with indisputable evidences of how the metropolis deliberately destroyed local entrepreneurship, stultified infrastructural development, encouraged capital flight and de-industrialised the colonies.

These pieces of historic evidence explained his conclusion that the "only positive development in colonialism was when it ended." Most, if not all, Africans share the perspective of the late Rodney. Indeed, post-colonial policies in Africa were truly meant to decolonize; witness import-substitution, indigenisation, Africanisation and other pet ideas meant to undo colonial legacies. The extent to which these policies have transformed the economies of the continent is still debatable. For one, late Kwame Nkrumah of

---

* *The Guardian*, 6th July 1997

Ghana, (himself a foremost nationalist) subsequently identified the new African leaders as new colonisers. These new leaders, according to him, continued the pillage of the continent in the very and even more vicious tradition of the overthrown colonial order. This then brought about a new subject of neo-colonialism, a subject as controversial as colonialism. But what has all these got to do with Hong Kong?

The question is whether the Chinese people today share the radical perspective of Rodney and indeed Africans that colonial Hong Kong was a 'curse' or better still, a reclaimed loot of a 'one-armed bandit', namely, Britain? The international media is hardly of any help in finding an answer to this intriguing question. This is the paradox of Hong Kong. We read more about a 'return' than 'decolonization' of Hong Kong. We hear that Hon Kong's political sovereignty returns to China than China's repossession of its original territory. One can almost allude to media conspiracy on Hong Kong given that people are at a loss about whether it was a colony or not. Perhaps the ambiguity in media discourse of Hong Kong may very well reflect the ambiguous character of the territory as a colony.

The history of China is intractably linked with the history of aggressive colonialism. Hong Kong dating back to early 19th century served as the base for British trading activities with China. With the Communist revolution in China in 1949, Hong Kong with Taiwan became veritable outposts for anti-communism and western influence, with the former under the heels of Britain. The point is that Hong Kong as a colony grew under the acute conditions of cold war between the East and the West. With Singapore, Korea and Taiwan, the Chinese island was deliberately cultivated into a functioning export processing zone and investment haven in East Asia. Thanks to Euro-American capital, cheap and ill-treated labour (no minimum wage policy) a colony prided itself as a model of economic miracle and World Bank's showcase of "the triumph of the market."

Hong Kong, for as long as it lasted, was more known for its ever-active stock market than its dependent colonial status. The second paradox of Hong Kong therefore lies in this economic "balance sheet" which overwhelmingly was more in the "credits".

With lower inflation, relatively low unemployment, rapid growth rate, high percentage of total trade to GDP and increasing productivity, a colony for once, merited the title of economic tiger. Hong Kong is a case of *How Europe and America 'Developed' Asia.*

True to expectations, development has more admirers than adversaries. Never before have a colonized people been caught at a cross-roads than the six million people of Hong Kong. They are caught between continuing with dependence that has built prosperity and remaining independent with the mainland and slide into poverty. Thus, as they celebrate the obliteration of "over 150 years of shame" which the British occupation represents, Hong Kong people still scramble for citizenship of European countries and America if only to immune themselves against the unpredictability of Beijing after July 1st. Whatever then happens to Nkrumah's theory of neo-colonialism in an interdependent world?

This then brings us to the real paradox of Hong Kong. The late Chinese leader, Deng Xiaoping, coined the concept of "one country, two systems". According to his concept, Hong Kong becomes part of China as one country, but its free enterprise economy will not be submerged within the larger socialist economy of the mainland. Which means 'colonial legacy' in Hong Kong has an appeal to Beijing.

With Deng's ideological paradox embodied in the concept of "one country, two systems", Hong Kong underscores the fact that a colony can prove an asset than a liability, a direct antithesis of Rodney's thesis of colonialism as whole scale banditry. The fact is that Hong Kong is bound to open a window of opportunities for Chinese economy, which in itself is undergoing significant reforms. The lesson of history here is that between a rewarding pragmatism and ideal-type doctrine, people could disregard the latter, without jettisoning it altogether, which in itself is quite paradoxical.

Reflection on Asian Crisis*

Is the "Asian Miracle" Over? This is one intriguing question recently put to Mr. Huber Neiss, the director of Asia and Pacific Department of the International Monetary Fund (IMF). Mr. Neiss' answer, published in the Fund's newsletter (and reproduced in *The Guardian* of October 8, 1997) is, however, no less intriguing. According to him; "There was never anything miraculous – in the sense of development that defied rational explanation about Asia's success story."

The IMF and its twin sister, the World Bank, have hitherto presented the "roaring success story" of Asian economics as nothing but some "miracle". A World Bank policy research report in 1993 was aptly entitled: "The East Asian Miracle". Paradoxically, every page of this report attributes Asian economic break through to those familiar rational factors embodied in "market-friendly polices" rather than to any miracle. "Miracle" has been defined as "something which man is not normally capable of making happen". "Conservative monetary and fiscal policies", "high private savings", "deregulation of economic activities" and "investment in human capital" which, according to the IMF, are the factors, among others, responsible for Asian success are obviously within human comprehension. Why, then, the mystification of the Asian process even by those whose preference is for rationality in discourse and policy formulation? Why do the bureaucrats (or are they courtiers?) of international financial and business interests choose to see Asia beyond the ordinary? Whatever explains mystification of Asia, on

* *Guardian* 23rd February 1998

thing is self-evident; it shows an interesting dimension of the ever-changing Western image of the Asian drama.

In the beginning, Asian "dragons" and "tigers" alike defied rational explanation, contrary to Mr. Neiss' claim today. Indeed, Western social scientists were once used to simplistic cognitive framework of analysis: *growing West versus stagnant East.* But in the 1960s and up to early 1970s with the emergence of Japan and others in Asia as industrial powers, Western image-makers sought solace in "traditional factors" such as religion, previously ignored in development studies. This was due to the failure of neo-liberal and neo-Marxist theories of modernisation and dependency alike to explain the dramatic Asian take-off; hence, the search to establish the "cause effect" relationship between Asian religion and economic development. Confucian ethic hypothesis, in the spirit of Weber's Protestant Ethic, was invented to explain polycentric modernisation in Asia. Diligence, work ethic, thrift, reinvestment and other similar traits ostensibly responsible for Asia's growth were attributed to Confucianism. The policy implication was palpable for Africa: seek motivational resources for development in religions and preferably, Confucianism, the Asian magic.

But the Asian drama enacted series of scenes, which further put to test Western framework of analysis. What with astonishing East Asian growth figures and value-added results. Asia not only "out-performed" developed economies of Europe and America but reportedly grew three times as fast as Latin America and twenty five times faster than sub-Saharan Africa. Inverse relationship exists between entrenched Afro-pessimism of today and intimidating statistics from the Far East. East Asian economies from being some mystique became show-cases of market orthodoxy ideologically promoted by Thatcherism Reaganomics. It is a case of what we cannot explain, we can claim. The celebrations of Asia find expression in every line of World Bank/IMF reports; "newly industrialised economics" or "high-performing Asian economies" of Japan, Hong Kong, Korea, Singapore, Taiwan, Indonesia and Malaysia and Thailand. No resident representative of World Bank in Africa would be worth his calling without recommending Asian models during the 1980s up to early 1990s. This was fine enough until the recent currency-quakes.

But whether recent development in East Asia would throw up new and altered image of Asia is not clear. It is, however, interesting that the sudden "stock-market meltdown" has led to some "language-melt down" and moderation which discuss the Asia processes. Indeed, thanks to "currency turmoil", we now read what could not have been imagined. For instance, it is an open knowledge that East Asia, though fastest growing region, "is also the home to the poorest," and that five to seven million of them are infested with AIDS. Beyond celebrated growth literature, recent commentaries now reveal that "Asia miracle" rested on huge domestic bad debts, shoddy insiders' dealings that make Nigeria's a child's play, lack of transparency, child and cheap female labour in utter disregard of international labour standards. The question is whether in the light of this complex reality, local *sermons from Asia* we were recently served with will carry more doubts than top-down recommendations. The lesson here is that we should be wary of institutional imports feverishly being pushed by "development experts" who mechanically recommend "models" for Africa, disregarding institutional and historical factors.

Our reflection on Asia will be incomplete without considering the roles of the great *dramatis personae* in the on-going damage control process, namely, the IMF and World Bank. The role of the IMF is the most visible. The rumour is that if there was no currency turmoil in Asia, IMF could have invented one. Confronted with the crisis of relevance of late, the Asian crisis offers new jobs to the Fund's bureaucrats. Thanks to the "contagious effects" of the crisis, the challenge is now how to shuttle from one crisis spot to the other. It is, however, instructive that though offered new opportunities to make a difference, the IMF is still going the same old way that put its credibility to test in the first instance. For one, the IMF and the World Bank should be blamed for the Asian shut-down without prior indication. The tasks of the two institutions include monitoring fiscal and monetary policies of member states with a view to anticipating problems that can have damaging effects on growth and development. In Asia, just like in Africa, the Bretton Woods institutions failed their supervisory role tests.

What is, however, unexplainable is the "business-as-usual" approach to crisis by both the Fund and the World Bank. Asia is again being told to "put its house in order", adopt "appropriate policies of adjustment", accept "bail-out" (read: bribe) loans and reach "understanding" with the Fund. South Korea celebrated its dramatic transition from debtor to creditor nation not long ago. The drum-beat barely died down before it was again pushed to the debt trap. It will be an interesting subject of development study in the 21st century to understand how "high-performing Asian economics" suddenly became non-performing and even "newly indebted countries".

Paradoxes of September[*]

We are in December, but the events of September still dominate public discourse. What then was in a month, which pushed humanity to the brink of hope and hopelessness; almost simultaneously? Better put in the imageries of our time, what explains why New York's Twin buildings, with such as an unprecedented big bang before our very eyes, turned to ground zero? This question hunts the chroniclers of September events, which for 'better' and certainly for the worse, shape, the beginning of our millennium.

Yours sincerely was putting finishing touches to his reflections on ever-desirous historic UN conference against racism held in Durban between August and September, when the unthinkable disastrous events of New York and Washington hit the world like a plague. Never before has a conclusion proved so difficult. Commentators are prudent with the truth when they say the world would never be the same after September 11. Put bluntly, post September 11 means altered world and it is our altered thought-process about this altered world that is the issue perhaps more than anything else. September will ever be remembered as the month of paradoxes, in which traditional aggressor states became aggressed and grieved, for once deserving our sympathy, (captured vividly in CNN's breaking news; America Under Attack), enemies of enemies turned instant feverish friends, 'end of history' turns out to very well be another chapter of another history, hitherto unanimous individuals and false prophets such as the Bin Ladins were transformed into global 'heroes' and villains alike, isolationist policies gave way to unprecedented global involvement and coalitions, human tragedies

---

[*] *Guardian* 4th December, 2001

played out as 'TV reality', Africa suddenly matters in the battle against new enemy; terrorism, sympathisers (or are they sycophants?) loose more than the bereaved and in general, hope got transformed into hopelessness for our increasingly stressed planet.

Pre-September 11 had raised hope for humanity. UN Secretary-General Kofi Annan was among the first to hail the outcome of Durban conference, which in spite of its bagful of controversies, ended with some thin compromised resolutions on racism, offering a rare hope for victims of racism. The conference meant to frontally come to terms with racism, intolerable and xenophobia, we all can remember, was hunted (for as long as it lasted) by neo-racism and new related intolerance exhibited arrogantly by United States, Israel and to some significant (xenophobic) extent, UK, France and Canada. These countries strived to belittle Durban significance with a walk away over the twin issues of slavery and Zionism. The compromised resolution, signed by 168 countries was therefore on historic moral instrument in the battle against racism. It was the notorious racist mind-set that informed enslavement of 100 million Africans (according to UNESCO) during the 400 years of Atlantic slavery and it was this racist mind construct that until recently barred Nelson Mandela on account of his colour from 'white only toilet' (as if the genuine worry of any human being, white or black, lies in toilet sharing). Durban conference pointedly declared slavery a crime against humanity, encouraged nation-states to overcome racist hangovers and all forms of intolerance. So liberating was the Durban resolution, even as every observer knows that it falls short in substance (given that no resolution in forms of reparations for victims and few apologies sound hollow and half-hearted) such that some enthusiastic commentators nearly proclaimed the end of history (of official racist practices). All these were positive development until September 11 big bang.

The greatest paradox of September lies in how raised hope for humanity occasioned by Durban conference got shattered into the smithereens on the altar of exploded Twin Towers. Whoever was behind the New York attacks, the motivation could only be undiluted ingrained hatred, some variants of which humanity frontally strived to confront in Durban. Historians of our time must unravel how humanity had a free fall from the Olympian height of plausible tolerance promised by Durban confab to the rubbles of hate-outcomes leading to estimated 4000 deaths down two New York in the month of September. Historians must explain how the summer of seeming global understanding and almost consensual tolerance ushered in a winter of new hatred, war-phobia and war itself.

The Canadian philosopher, John Saul, once observed that the 'vision of the world is not so much false as falsely focused.' Who will ever believe that the real desirable global conference of the millennium (in terms of priority) ought to have been on terrorism and not necessarily on AIDS. AIDS kills (and is killing African continent) but certainly not 4000 in few minutes and some seconds of terrorism callously did before helpless world viewers. Who will think that hitherto uninspiring Bush-Powell administration, with its isolationist policy unpopularly tried out in Kyoto and Durban would soon become vanguard of historic global coalition with unprecedented broad participation. How 'pariah' nations like Pakistan and Sudan suddenly matter with anti-terrorism coalition dividends in forms of lifted sanctions remains the great contradistinction of September. Cold War adversaries namely Russian and US are now best of friends in the battle against terrorism as human issues (remember Chechnya) and arm-race are pushed to the margin. From our obsession with proliferation of nuclear weapons by 'rogue-states', the moral fear now is the acquisition of weapon of mass destruction by stateless rouges operating from the caves, questioning the intelligence of those who invented the weapon over which they would ultimately lack control.

It there was any doubt left whether globalisation is real or not, September removes such doubt. A single attack on New York building led to casualty list of world citizens of all persuasions exposing those who are jubilant at that singular millennium tragedy, silly at worst and at best inhuman. Terrorism turned asunder demand-supply side-economics as we saw how panic and fear in the wake of a suicidal mission could usher in global economic recession of unprecedented proportions and dimension. Economics may very well be about our objective (human) perception of what is safe and good for humanity rather than some blind impersonal objective laws of demand and supply we were hitherto made to believe by IMF and the World Bank. Even ever irrepressible Havana now realises that peaceful but ever bullying Washington is still preferred to an harassed and terrorised big brother up North as America tourists have deserted the island (for legitimate fear of flying) creating huge economic crisis in Cuba. Conversely, Bush administration has come to the realisation that only impartial and transparent dealing on Middle East crisis will restore American moral authority hence its commending renewed peace talk to both Israel and Palestinians. The question is; why would humanity wait to be so dastardly awaken to the reality of its interdependence and vulnerability? September underscores the falsity of the nation of multiple civilisations. It is either there is human civilisation (security and prosperity) or no civilisation (chaos and ruination). We have to avoid the pitfall of a slide into fifth century jingoism of 'good' and 'evil'.

We unconsciously play the cards of agents' provocateur, which Mr. Terrorist (no woman has instructively been named a terrorist) is, when we pitched Islam against Christianity, Crusade against Jihad, Judaism against Islam, 'Western' against 'other civilisations', Islam against Buddhism. Such clinical delineation is only possible in the ideal terror laboratory of terrorists either operating from the cave or presidential executive mansions and parliamentary chambers. Civilisation cannot be divisible among cultures, peoples and religions. Apartheid South Africa that shamelessly erected white and black lager with terror proved ultimately unsustainable in the wake of human protestation and courageous resistance and sacrifices exemplified by Nelson Mandela. Reality of daily human interactions and human concerns shows that all of us desire security of food, lives and property.

It was remarkable and commendable too that African leaders found unanimity in anti-terrorism coalition that climaxed in an instant conference in Dakar. This is consistent with Africans' willingness to offer solidarity to others as they did with Allied forces to check the menace of fascism during the Second World War and recently halting Saddam Hussein's aggression. How Africans offer solidarity to others and still prove nauseatingly clumsy and shamelessly display incoherence on issues that directly affect them such as reparation for century-long Trans-Atlantic slavery (read: terrorism), (given their discordant, slavish and mutually destructive voices in Durban) remains a naughty mystery of September. African leaders are rightly concerned about other people's grief but they are inexplicably unconcerned about their own seemingly unending grief. General Musharraf of Pakistan has been 'civilised', no thanks to the events of September and Pakistan was rewarded for that with lifted sanctions. Even Sudan counts its gain for enlisting in coalition against terrorism. China is contended that for now global searchlight escapes its worsening human rights violations in Tibet and the Muslim province of Xinijing. The question is; whence Africa's anti-terrorism coalition dividends?

The African contradiction played out in Nigeria more than anywhere in the continent. Nigeria's delegates to Durban conference on xenophobia were welcomed back home with the worst forms of intolerance that is referred to as "Jos crisis' that claimed hundreds of innocent lives. So much for domestic lessons from South Africa, we join global coalition against terrorism but we are hard put to curtail domestic terror, which in Kano recently claimed almost a thousand, and in Benue and Taraba states, some hundreds. When, for once, are we willing to stop aping others without learning from their methods? In Kano, we lost hundreds on account of 'solidarity' rallies with Afghanistan, making us to bereaved than the bereaved.

Liberia: haunted by its lowly origin*

Liberia's progressive chaos assumes frightening dimension every other day that passes. Carl Sagan, the late legendary American cosmologist and evolutionist once observed that mankind is ever hunted by its lowly origin. According to him, we are all descendants of apes which perhaps explain our ever restlessness (read: recklessness). The extent Liberia is hunted by its rather less than dignified origin is a mischievous philosophical question begging for an answer. Freed African American slaves on the order of President James Monroe, to whom the capital, Monrovia, was dedicated, founded it in 1822. The great expectation was that a free land for freed slaves in Africa would more than atone for the criminality and eternal sin of two-century long trade in African human resources, by American rubber-barons. Liberia was actually a product of the struggle of the likes of Marcus Garvey to return to African root. It is a sad commentary today that almost two hundred years after, Liberia seems hunted by its lowly origin, sliding deeper and deeper into mayhem and killings comparable to the hated method of the slave-masters.

When Walter Rodney, wrote his classic, *How Europe Underdeveloped Africa*, he singled out slavery in which as many as 60 million Africans were trans-shipped amidst torture to South America plantations. The recent spectacular picture of innocent women (and women mostly) refugees amidst corpses in front of American embassy in the capital following the incursions of the rebels shows that history repeats itself in an uncharitable way in African continent.

* *Daily Trust*, 28th July 2003

There is certainly no lesson to learn for the rest of the continent from the despicable happenings in Monrovia.

Paradoxically, Liberia had not always been like this' under its founding fathers, such as late Sir Tubman, though a bastion of anti-communism and American neo-colonialism, Liberia was once a home of liberalism, conservatism, knowledge and commerce *not* the addictive violence of the recent times. Violence came when little tyrant, of lowly origin (i.e. military), called Samuel Doe shot himself to power and callously slaughtered the then President Tolbert, burnt the constitution and instituted a protracted reign of mediocrity and brutality true to West African military rule type. Recent tragic development in Liberia is a regular trademark of military meddlesomeness in civil politics in the sub-region, a cancer we must all exorcise. Doe himself was consumed by the inferno he triggered, as he was more humiliated than he did to his predecessor again by another man of lowly origin called Johnson. Meanwhile another man of shady character called Charles Taylor was equally shooting himself to power through the bush not through the street canvassing for votes, after escaping from a jailhouse for theft in USA. He had since instituted a 'democratic rule' the outcomes of which included killing of journalists, support for terror and military campaign of accursed Sankoy in Sierra Leone (deservedly earning him a conviction as a war criminal by UN World Court) and other sundry criminalities that included selection of second wife for him by no less person than his first lady. Some wives do have this criminal-cum-head (tail) of state. Meanwhile some rag tag armed bandits not known for any articulated ideas are traversing same roads the likes of Doe and Charles Taylor had woefully traversed; road of violence as distinct from compromise and consensus building. Liberia shows how one rogue leader succeeds another rogue-leader through brutality and force leaving in their trails deaths of innocent citizens.

The debate over Liberia has wrongly centred on whether international peacekeepers should be sent to Monrovia or not. At another level, the issue is whether the outlaw President Charles Taylor would leave or not. This controversy comes to naught, as it is not informed by memory and history of Liberia itself. Memory is in great recession in the continent today, especially in West African sub-region in which we are making insurgency and civil war contagious given our stubbornness and sheer stupidity not to learn from history. Witness Ivory Coast and (until recently) Sierra Leone.

The challenge is for all to rise up and put an end to the orgy of violence that pushes us further and further into poverty and imperil a worthy region. President Obasanjo has no business in providing sanctuary for criminal Taylor no less than he must within ECOWAS offer *urgent* protection and defence for innocent millions of Liberians caught in the cross-fire of armies of (mis)fortunes of both Taylor and the rebels. Our policy should be people driven and not dictator-preferred. We must learn from the pitfall of belated intervention of the 1990s in which it was not clear whether we were for peace process or rescue mission for a doomed petty common tyrant Samuel Doe. Our commitment cannot and should not centre on what President Bush of America does or does not do in Liberia either more so that we all know already what President Bush is not doing, i.e. sending rapid forces to halt the carnage. President Bush has again and again demonstrated that in the final analysis, oil (read: Iraq) is thicker than blood (read: Liberia). It is all well and good that Defence Secretary Rumsfeld has reportedly ordered an amphibious 'group led by the USS Iwo Lima to head towards Liberia from the Red Sea' but we cannot afford to be as ambivalent in urgently coming to the rescue of our dying brothers and sisters. Liberia is an acid test for a new African Union (AU) and New Partnership for African Development (NEPAD).

Mugabe at 80*

"The Greater the Visible Order, the Greater the Hidden Disorder." - Ben Okri, *A Way of Being Free*

President Robert Mugabe of Zimbabwe recently marked his 80th birthday. According to him, he is still very much active in politics, even as he signifies willingness (sic) to retire in 2008. Mugabe, the man, Zimbabwean opposition media derides as '*Big-Mouth*' reportedly boasts to say that he still remains the key actor in Zimbabwe's political terrain for quite a long time to come. Discussing Mugabe puts objectivity on trial. No Head of State has further polarised a distressed continent in recent times as Mugabe. The road Libya's Gadhafi increasingly finds thorny is where Mugabe finds smooth. It is either you are '*for*' or '*against*' *a 'liberation fighter', 'a land grabber', 'a dictator'*, ad infinitum. Yet, as controversial as Mugabe will ever be, we must still come to terms with an African statesman at 80.

Mugabe's life (political life) seems inversely related with Zimbabwean progress. One-time Maoist guerrilla fighter, famous for his African print wear at pre-Independence Lancaster Summit, a man imprisoned for well over a decade, but emerged as post-colonial leader in 1980 now 24 years with three-piece suit (no more African print) has truly come of age. Mugabe has undoubtedly survived and put his imprint on the Zimbabwean map. But how has Zimbabwe fared under his two-decade rule? Zimbabwean dollar was 8 to 1 in 1995, today, it is 6000 to 1. Price riot is the norm with the inflation at 600 per cent. Unemployment is 70 per cent. The political class is far more bitterly divided than at independence. 'Treasonable trials' arrests, draconian laws, detention and persecution of opponents,

---

* *Daily Trust*, 1st March 2004

characteristics of colonial settlers' rule are now common features of Mugabe's Zimbabwe. We may engage in academic sophistry identifying reasons for the forces responsible for today's Zimbabwean decay no less than we may explain why colonial settlers, subdued the African people in the 1890s. Yours truly is not unaware of some of these 'reasons '. One reason is the alleged conspiracy of the gang of three, namely British's Tony Blair, Jack Straw and the American's George Bush to strangulate Zimbabwe following the land reform that disposed few white settlers and returned land back to the disposed blacks. We are reminded of the 'smart' sanctions, which include the suspension from Zimbabwe of the Common Wealth and denial of Zimbabwe's access to IMF/World Bank aid and credit on the prodding of Britain and USA. Another reason is the 'subversive' and 'disruptive' politics of opposition represented by Tsavangirai's MDC. As alluring as these reasons are, they only explain but do not in any way invalidate the truism that despair statistics is fastly regaining hope in the last ten years of Mugabe's long rule. The truth of the matter is that Mugabe is fatigued. He has run out of creative ideas to move Zimbabwe forward and must necessarily bow out now before Zimbabwe collapses under the weight and the rot of his dictatorial unaccountable rule. It is a sad commentary that a land blessed with notable leaders like Joshua Nkomo, Ndabaningi Sithole, James Chikerema, Josiah Tongogara, Herbert Chitepo, Abel Muzorewa as at independence is today begging for notable successors, no thanks to Mugabe's long-dated repression of opposition. It is a sad footnote on Mugabe's rule that colonialism threw up more qualitative leaders than Mugabe's rule tolerated. Twenty years after, opposition is as mediocre as his dictatorship.

Mugabe's celebrated land reform is belated and diversionary. It was actually Nkomo's ZAPU which first championed land reform by frontally questioning the 1979 Lancaster agreement's ambiguous principle of willing sellers/buyers. Mugabe ZANU's answer was war of attrition in Matabeleland, ZAPU's political strong hold with unforgetfully brutality of the notorious 5th brigade. Mugabe is one 'liberator' who deployed instruments meant for his enemies against the opposition, made up of his own people. Almost like Saddam Hussein. With all the reported current forceful land seizures, the alleged violence against the white settlers is still nothing compared to the criminal violence in Matabeleland in the wake of independence in 1980, apparently without opposition (certainly with the support) from UK and America. The latest Mugabe's new mask of a '*Commonwealth conqueror*' (sounds like Idi Amin) is also deceptive. Since when? The Harare declaration (Mugabe's acid-test) was made in Zimbabwe and not in London with his then enthusiastic support. In 1991, he hosted the Commonwealth dining with the Queen and playing rugby with Australian Prime Minister, Bob Hawke. When Nigeria was suspended from the Commonwealth on account of bad governance in 1995, Mugabe never staged a walk-out in solidarity with Nigeria. But today he expects same solidarity instead of enthroning good governance. There may be conspiracy against Zimbabwe, but conspiracy only germinates on a fertile soil, the type under the heel of Mugabe. The point cannot be overemphasised that the responsibility for food shortages, inflation, and human and trade union rights' violations as well as abysmal performance of Zimbabwe team during the Tunisia 2004 soccer campaign, in the final analysis, is Mugabe's at 80 and *not* with Britain Blair's, Jack Straw or America's Bush or Queen's Commonwealth. By the way, kindly compare Mugabe's 80th birthday with Mandela's 80th birthday and spot the difference between exclusion and narrow mindedness and inclusiveness and broadmindedness, between reaction and progress respectively.

Reagan: Lest We Forget*

The volume, no less than the quality of discourse on Reagan and Reagan years remain a thought for food. Since Clinton's Lewinsky scandal, America has never been served on a daily basis on Nigerian media menu through a massive uncritical overload (sorry; download) of received wisdoms. Lewinsky's affair was understandably about sex which psychoanalyst, Sigmund Freud, long showed to arouse curiosity of humanity. If we recall Ken Sarr and his legendary pages of phonographic report and partisan star wars, global murky pond of sexual quirks which trailed Clinton's sexual relations, sexual affairs and textual relationships (apology to Clinton who recently reportedly apologised for the 'terrible moral error') seemed logical. It however beats imagination how sobering subject matter of death and funeral of the 40th President of United States elicited so much enthusiastic eulogies in Nigeria press. One writer was eager to impress those who care that he shared a birthday with the 'great American hero'. Thank God we have since left the primitive age of Mongol leader, Mangu Khan (5th century A.D.) during which admirers of the deceased joined their masters permanently in the grave, sharing death days. One columnist was even more daring; recommended a Reagan for Nigeria on the ground of his casual leadership style, share laziness and incapacity for staying power during working days (Reagan reportedly got to office 9 a.m. took a sister and closed 5 p.m.) We are enjoined not to ever speak ill of the dead. But the post mortem exaggeration over Reagan was too exaggerated in some Nigerian media for good and measured feelings among the most discernable living observers. Paradoxically here corpses in thousands arising from communal mayhem or motor 'accidents' are just mere statistics

* *Daily Trust*, Monday 21st June 21 2004, pp. 6)

worthy not of our sympathy much less active prompt commentaries. As a matter of fact, while Reagan was being laid to rest, unrest in Adamawa claimed scores of citizens' lives who were in turn buried unacknowledged by the media and columnists of various hues. In the age of globalisation, Nigerian writers' charity flows from overseas. But what about Reagan and Reagan years, which elicited such servile ill-informed memorials?

Lest we forget, Reagan's heroic traits feverishly sold through the media posthumously cannot be substitute for true heroic deficits we witnessed during his tenure. The truth is that Reagan was only a hero as what John Paul Saul called in his Doubters' Companion an 'illusion of leadership' rather than actual desired leadership that touched on humanity for the better. He was produced by American democracy, but more than any democratic leader, he subverted rather than advance the democratic frontiers in USA and beyond. Jimmy Carter liberalism was dogmatically trampled underfoot by Reagan rabid anti-communism and market fundamentalism. In mid-eighties, he abolished the 'fairness doctrine' of the Federal communications Commission requiring airing times for dissenting views, replacing voice popular with voice establishment. This singular narrowing of expression space contributed to voters' apathy from which America is yet to recover. Jimmy Carter attempted to rescue disillusioned citizenry through promotion of human rights and affirmative actions to uplift the blacks. We then saw the emergence of the likes of Andrew Young as Ambassador to the United Nations and Patricia Harris as Secretary of Housing and Urban Development. Conversely Ronald Reagan reversed this humanistic process, turned Carter's doctrine that law should not be used to protect the rich upside-down. In fact the law was bastardised under Reagan to promote conservatism and the hated status quos. To this extent both Reagan and Bush Presidency appointed more than half of 837 federal judges who are well known right wing justices known for controversial positions on races and women. The worst distortion was the myth that Reagan ended the cold war. The President who once joked that he was 'bombing' Soviet Union could not be said to be cold war weary. Lest we forget Reagan initiated the failed star-wars, which almost put humanity on the precipice of nuclear disaster. His administration also recorded contra-gate and invasion of Grenada. About the much taunted Reaganomics, Lance Kirkland, had this to say; it '… is known as the carrot-and-stick policy: for the rich, the carrot; for the poor, the stick". The African Head of States who attended Reagan's funeral must have shared the spirit of South Africa's Ubuntu according to which we are all human only through the humanity of other human beings. Reagan was not only Africa blind but 'visited' the continent through the bombing of Tripoli. Above all, at a time Apartheid was declared as a crime against humanity by UN, Reagan and Thatcher were fuelling the despicable system through the notorious policy of constructive engagement. It takes the spirit of forgiveness (or is it forgetfulness?) for any African Head of State to attend Reagan's funeral just as it will be nice seeing George Bush attending Bin Ladin's funeral. For all they care, Ancient Egyptians knew what wealth they expended to accompany their Pharaohs to their tombs but what they least forget were the misdeeds of the Pharaohs.

Return of Libya*

The global media had created an impression of return of Libya's Muammar Gaddafi to global arena following the dropping of UN sanctions in the wake of the earlier reported deal over the Lockerbie airplane bombing. Yet what we are witnessing daily are the massive in flocks of Western leaders and businessmen alike to Tripoli. The traffic is in the direction of Tripoli and not the other way round. Western leaders of note now scramble for photo-shots with Libyan Arab Jamahiriya leader, Colonel Gaddafi. British Prime Minister, Tony Blair was in Tripoli in April. Ostensibly this trip was to reward Libya for peacefully renouncing weapons of mass destruction in December last year. But political observers knew that Tony Blair (politically) needed Gaddafi more than the latter needed him after huge creditability crisis at home as a result of wholesome "sexing-up" of intelligence report (read: lying about Weapon of Mass Destruction, WMD, in Iraq) in a desperate bid to justify an unjust war in Iraq. A golden handshake with Gaddafi may convince (or is it confuse?) the British electorate that the "war on terror" was yielding dividends. With the reopening of the American embassy in Tripoli, it will not be unthinkable that before November election President George Bush (Jr.) may seek for a golden handshake with Gaddafi. It is the greatest paradox of Western democracies that democratically elected leaders feverishly fete else while 'terrorist' leader to ensure democratic legitimacy at home.

While the pictures of visiting Western leaders capture imagination, the unreported flock of unanimous Western firms and investors elude observers. While Blair talked with Gaddafi, Shell,

---

* *Daily Trust*, 12th July 2004

Anglo Dutch oil giant company, signed a business deal worth 550 million pounds for gas exploration. Libya expects as much as $35 billion worth of investment between 2003 and 2005 alone. US oil majors as well as European firms are all scrambling for Libya market.

Development in Tripoli shows that sanction imposed on Libya hit the "international community" no less than it undermined Libyan dynamic growth. Indeed with the frenzy to have a bite of the new Libyan cake by Western governments and firms alike, it was the world that missed Libya not the other way round.

Lessons from Libya are in legion for Africa. For one, the only thing constant in global diplomacy was permanent interest and not permanent enemies. With millions of dollars in pay compensation for Lockerbie bombing and Libya's voluntary hand over of devices of its infant instruments of mass destruction, western hostility instantly turned to western hospitality. In market economies, there is price for everything including human lives.

Secondly, African leaders who blindly follow western dictates should know that they hardly matter when the game is over. Both USA and Britain brought considerable pressures to bear on OAU (AU) members to isolate Libya when the UN sanctions lasted. The question is that how many of these dependent African leaders were consulted when same Western leaders and businessmen are scrambling for new Libya? Indeed only Nelson Mandela then President of South Africa truly proved independent by bursting the so-called sanctions and travelled by road to Tripoli to register South African appreciation for the role of Libya in the struggle against Apartheid.

Lastly, Libya shows that the world will only accept us to what we are and *not* what we are made to look like. In spite of sanctions, Libya is top on the top on World development index with mass subsidized housing scheme, full literacy and mass free health scheme. Libya does not implement IMF or World Bank agenda, yet with developed social infrastructure, it is now an investment haven. At a time, we are giving up on domestic refinery, Libya's refineries are functioning and its petro-chemical industry is alive. Libya is set to move from a non-cultural oil economy to a diversified economy with independent foreign policy. Let Nigerian leaders also take a trip to Tripoli.

USA; Once Upon an Election*

Tomorrow the Yankees go to polls and understandably the world is apprehensive about its outcome. Will the election for once duly certifies the incumbent George W. Bush (who in 2004 reportedly stole the presidency) or throw up a 'choice' in Senator John Kerry, the democratic challenger? The global frenzy and apprehension which trail this singular American election once again unwittingly confirms the ideological triumph (not necessarily superiority) of America in a univocal world. The world would care less about whether a lunatic rules (as he does) Russia as it is worried about who occupies the White House.

Paradoxically, it is the exhibited gross weaknesses of American democracy under the heel of George Bush in the past 4 years that in turn rejuvenated a hitherto moribund American democracy. Bad governance under President Bush characterised by tax cut for the rich, huge deficit, mass job losses and jobs export as well as international impunity as exhibited in the war of attrition in Iraq constitute the basis of groundswell of domestic and international opposition which in turn is reawakening American democracy from its slumber.

With all its does (not) worth, Bush bad administration will be 'credited' with the legacy of laying the foundation for quest for good democratic governance in America. Voter turnout tomorrow reaches an all-time level. Every other hitherto alienated voter, (from mass of unemployed to African American and Arab-American) strives to undo an all-time bad President. President Bush has the dubious

* *Daily Trust* 1st November, 2004

distinction of not being welcomed by Nelson Mandela when he visited Africa.

In 1960, as many as 60 per cent voted. By 1976, voters turnout fell to 50 per cent. During the Regan years it fell as low as 45 %. It's being predicted that turnout at tomorrow votes raises the prospects of mass participation of the 1960s. Bad governance is the beginning of democratic renewal. This is the only legacy of Bush first term.

The bane of the American contest so far, is that we are faced more with who 'looks' or 'sounds' more Presidential between George Bush and John Kerry than the differentiated vision and mission of the contestants. It is as if it is all a matter of public relations not public policies.

Of course there have been 'debates'. The 'debates' are however tall in forms than substance. Indeed there are no substantial differences between Kerry and Bush. Kerry is certainly different from Bush, but those yearning for regime change in Washington should know that Kerry is not Bill Clinton nor is he Jimmy Carter. The greatest paradox is that this election is driven by foreign policies but the policies are as foreign as they only affect United States and United States alone; namely Iraq, Al-Qaeda, Iran, North Korea (almost in that order). Indeed the issues are insularly foreign; globally American as it were. In the narrowly defined foreign issues, the difference between Kerry and Bush is the difference between six and half a dozen.

While Bush is unapologetically committed to unilateral bombing of Iraq from civilization to Stone Age, Kerry is for multilateral (UN) support for the same goal. In fact Senator Kerry voted for the very war. This means there is a bipartisan commitment to militarism and war as instruments of international diplomacy, the differences being in the methods of execution.

While Bill Clinton presidency envisioned an international social plan which could eradicate global poverty, (the recruitment base of terror), Kerry and Bush preferred bombing and killings (yes Presidential language) out of existence. Of course on Middle East the two candidates are as united to business as usual with respect to Israeli impunity. In an election in which the world is as involved as the American voters, we are yet to hear about the contestants' commitment to reforming UN, to the realisation of Millennium development goals (MDGs), eradicating the scourge of HIVS/AIDS, unfair global world trade and third world debt. In fact Bin Laden assumes special importance than all the above issues. Indeed, (Bin Laden) is both a person and issue such that he remains the only privileged 'outsider' (or is he an insider?) to 'address' American voters where Kofi Annan is a non-person.

As for Africa, throughout the debates, the Dark Continent was not mentioned by the contestants. The interviewers never asked the contestants either any question about how to pay reparations for slavery or cancel debts that has been more than paid for. Certainly nothing was said on NEPAD after scores of all the impressive photo clips of African leaders with G-8 leaders. Sorry. Africa was actually mentioned in the passing during the VP debates between Dick Cheney and John Edwards. The former accused the latter of non-eventful parliamentarian carrier. Edwards in return revealed how Cheney's achievements as a senator included voting against the motion urging American senate to press for the release of Nelson Mandela in the 1980s.

The point can therefore not be overemphasised; Africans who are yearning for changes of policies following tomorrow's elections must be modest to settle for either revalidation (God forbids) of incumbent Bush or election of a new candidate but certainly not new policies as such.

Next Time America Sneezes*

The last time an American report alluded to some human rights' violations in the current democratic dispensation; Aso-Rock information mill was quick to express some disappointment and something akin to official rebuttal. Paradoxically, the controversial down-loaded US Human Rights survey was not fundamentally different from scores of similar conclusions and findings by a number of Nigeria's non-governmental organizations and to some extent the official Human Rights Commission. Increasingly Nigerian officialdom catches cold once Washington, (not its own citizenry or institution) sneezes such that observers now say that Washington's smear report (recurring smear reports indeed) is the beginning of wisdom in Abuja. In this age of globalization, Dependency theory is hard to sell. But when there is a persistent unilinear hyper-reaction in response to what is a routine smear pass time campaign from Washington D.C. then it will not be out of place to talk of an emerging affliction called Abuja dependency syndrome.

Yours sincerely is still at a loss as to what weight to assign US Intelligence Report Council report (or was it America's Nigeria Democracy day gift?) according to which there may be '*outright collapse*' of Nigeria in the next 15 years. Afro-pessimism contained in that singular report can weigh down the best optimist. The report is a bagful of despair for a country trying hard to make some difference in the past six years of democratic dispensation. Coming from US, the assumed partner-country of this administration, observers insist

* *Daily Trust*, 30th May 2005

that with such report from friends better to say farewell to adversaries.

The Canadian philosopher John Saul describes intelligence as '*the ruling elite's description of its own strengths.*' If this definition is valid, then one can ask; of what relevance has been America's strength in the field of intelligence? We all know that it was on account of US Intelligence according to which Saddam harboured Weapons of Mass Destruction (WMD) that America rained bombs on Baghdad. The British 'sexed-up' version was that Saddam was on the verge of making the bomb. The spectre of that mass hysteria packaged as Intelligence nearly altered Tony Blair for Tony Liar in eyes of the British voters. Two years after the war, we have witnessed mass destruction of an erstwhile developing country, but no single weapon of mass destruction has been found. Your guess is as good as mine about the Intelligence that replaced tyranny and brutality of Saddam with generalized chaos and violence of insurgents. Given therefore its recent unimpressive intelligence gathering record, observers insist that America has enough to say about its own failed intelligence than getting concerned with another plausible failed state in Africa.

In any case, assuming intelligence matters, US intelligence never predicted failed states like Somalia. Indeed intelligence deficit was all Somalian warlords needed before they willingly opted for collective madness that has produced twenty-first century stateless society. US did not predict either fifteen years ago that the Chinese 'dangerous' growth would overrun American market with textile products, ruin millions of domestic jobs, such that America, (the champion of free-trade) would slam China with feverish import restrictions contrary to WTO rules. Intelligence tries hard to explain but it hardly tames humanity. What then the fuse about some conjectures from US?

The Nigerian official reaction was no less interesting. Having gone through the original text with respect to Nigeria (apart from its racist poetic license and top-down doom-day scenario), every other thing in the report was far from being original. At best it passes for an abridged version) of many printed words about the dark-continent in general and Nigeria in particular.

When Professor Chinua Achebe, the author of the classic, *Things Fall Apart,* rejected national honour and warned of the consequences of slide into political anarchy, it was to prevent a failed state as we dastardly once witnessed in Anambra. True to our contempt for *made-in- Nigeria*, Achebe was casually dismissed for his *political incorrectness* and his refusal to be counted for sycophancy. In fact both chambers of the legislature never debated Achebe's concern as much as they were seemingly worried by a US report.

Today we are witnessing unprecedented executive sensitivity and legislative activism on the account of efforts of what the President himself describes as prophets of doom. Are we rudely awakened to the danger ahead of us through the abusive and insulting prodding of 'outsiders'/ 'prophets of doom' or made accountable through the genuine measured concerns of mass of Nigerian compatriots and electorate? It is a partial truth (and certainly *not* the whole truth) to say that US report forewarns us when are daily forewarned by mass-unemployment, worsening income poverty, destitution and mass derivation even as we play ostrich as if all is well. US report is one additional warning too many.

Senator Uche Chukwumerije Chairman, Senate Committee on Inter-Parliamentary relations, reportedly said US report '*was not a product of prophets of doom but from accomplished terror psychologists'. 'They are out to cause social self-dehydration,"* he added. As a one time official propagandist who administered, as it were, *much self-dehydration* of a nation after June 12 political disaster (witness the alarm that Abiola was plotting an invasion of Lagos), Uche's view might truly have a benefit of some hindsight. But Comrade Uche's was another unhelpful national alarm that cannot substitute for national thought and introspection. The author of *Wealth of Nations,* Adams Smith confronted once with mass hysteria that British "nation was ruined" replied thoughtfully; "*There is a great deal of ruins in a nation*". Who dares deny the truism that we have enough ruins in failed power and water supply, failed hospitals, failed schools, failed enterprises, etc.

Daily restiveness in Niger Delta and our politicisation of fiscal federalism, the damning UNDP report that rates us 151 in development index with one time failed society like Sierra-Leone and bloody elitist acrimony for power, vain glory (tittles upon tittles) and money without responsibility are clear signs of ruins in a country that fails to resolve naughty issue of wealth generation and income distribution which countries with similar resources have taken for granted. Prosperous states don't fail (witness China and South Africa) but the poorest of the poorest do (witness Somalia and Liberia). Nigeria must just overcome its ruins otherwise Africa is ruined and America does not have to sneeze next time before we appreciate this cold fact.

(No) Lesson from EU*

The recent French referendum over the European Union (EU) constitution led to an unprecedented Euro-quake majority 'No' vote. As a matter of fact some observers talk of second French Revolution the contagious effects of which are better imagined of EU (the Dutch improved on the French NO with deafening NO). Europe-optimists are already on the draw-board analysing the impact of mass rejection of the Union constitution for the growth and prosperity of Europe in the face of ever-rising super-power America, ever-growing China and of course ever-stagnant Africa. We cannot be more European than the Europeans. Yours truly is certainly not here this week to pontificate on whether EU is sustainable or not after the mass revolt against the "bureaucrats in Brussels". When the elephants (in this case, Europeans) fight (remember the scramble for Africa in the 1880s) the grass (in most cases, the Africans) bears the brunt. Conversely, when elephants make love (remember slavery and colonialism) the * is even worse off. The outcomes of the EU referendum might therefore not be of any profound positive relevance to Africa whose woe was in any case never a factor in whole referendum hype. In fact, the strong factor in French NO vote was the fear that the disputed Constitution encourages immigrants (read: Africans). In the Netherlands, it was the resurgence of the worst form of xenophobia against "foreigners" and Islam that shamelessly informed Euro-scepticism.

Nonetheless there are still lessons the on-going EU integration process as well as issues the EU constitution-legitimization process has raised for Africa. For one, the referendum was not rigged because

* *Daily Trust*, 20th June 2005

President Jacques Chirac preferred YES votes. In quick succession electorate humbled their resident and Prime Minister alike in the true spirit of democratic process. Worthy of note is the fact that Chirac accepted dignified defeat. The EU commission President, Jose Manuel Barroso was quoted that the challenge was for European politicians to "reconnect with the people". How many African Heads of States would dare referendum on some of their policies talk less of accepting an outcome that is at variance with their preferences? Secondly witness how every French voter was availed 200-page controversial EU-constitution. In fact, the British Economist reported that in France, "... in brassieres, over dinner tables, on campuses, everywhere, they have been arguing and agonizing about it" (i.e. the constitution). Household constitution-delivery enhanced intense debate and participation over the provisions of the controversial constitution. Yours sincerely can bet that three-quarter of our Federal legislators have not seen the African Union Act which have long been signed by the country. If the country's law-makers are as knowledge-challenged with respect to the provisions of the AU constitutive act, then your imagination is as good as mine, about how disabled are the Nigerian citizens with respect to the appreciation and understanding of the aims and objectives of Africa Union formed and financed in our names. Why, when and how OAU got transformed into an Africa Union is one question that must task any Ministerial nominee perhaps more scandalous than the damage the meaning of NEEDS did to one ministerial nominee recently? Yours sincerely discovers from interactions with average South Africans that they are more conversant with continental/integration issues than an average Nigerian politician.

Paradoxically, Nigeria currently holds the chairmanship of AU. Is arguable if many undergraduates appreciate what chairmanship of AU is all about. In any case when last must have committed financial and human resources of immense proportions and for which we have taken positions on behalf of the country? When last did the opposition parties offer alternatives to the existing unilateral/authoritarian AU politics that include seeking NATO support in Darfur? If the national assembly is disabled as it were about presidential feed-back on AU activities what do the legislature feed their constituents about Nigeria's commitment in AU?

The lesson from EU is that the twin issue of transparency and accountability is not divisible; it is an imperative for public funds as much as (if not even more) it is fundamental for national commitment. African leaders' top-down approach to continental integration must give way to mass involvement of the citizens in the integration process.

AU operates through a number of commissions that include Labour and Social Affairs Commission. What is "social" about the social policy options of this Social Commission for a continent in which UN Secretary General Kofi Annan recently observed to be 50 years behind in meeting the Millennium Development Goals (MDGs), no thanks to scourge of HIV/AIDS, worsening poverty, debt burden and renewed illiteracy? There is a consensus of opinion that the French NO votes (just like the Dutch votes) were informed more by worsening unemployment occasioned by jobless growth. When will our leaders give us an opportunity to have a referendum on the current neo-liberal policies that have promoted job losses through public sector – downsizing, factory closures and collapse of infrastructure, notable water and power?

President Weah, Please Banish the Thought*

Yours sincerely knows George Weah as *Africa's first ever FIFA Footballer of the Year*, a feat he recorded in 1995. He is also a proud ambassador of UNICEF. When the Liberian state abysmally collapsed, Weah is remembered as a patriot (though he proudly carried French passport) who singularly financed the *Lone Stars*, his country's senior team. But the prospect of a democratically elected President Weah is simply unthinkable. This is not to say he cannot be elected. He actually nearly got elected. But mine is to make a case against his election. It is not all democratic outcomes that make sense or even desirable for a Republic. Hitler we all know was democratically elected, humanity paid dearly for it. Weah is far from being a Hitler but they share one thing in common-lowly intellectual base. I agree with (not necessarily that I support) Ellen Johnson Sirleaf, Weah's challenger that the President of the Republic should not have less qualification than a Liberian police recruit. Weah was a school dropout who is scared of returning back despite his enormous wealth to pay school fees. We dare not reward conscious mediocre. If Weah emerges as a President it is a clear return to sergeant- major presidency of the infamous Doe with all- the attendant muddling through and disasters. The fact that we are even talking of Weah's candidacy underscores the tragedy of West African sub-region. The region of Nkrumah, Nnamdi Azikiwe, Amilcal Cabral, Sekou Toure, Aminu Kano, Obafemi Awolowo, and Sir Tolbert cannot be footnoted by a President whose only pedigree is running round with

---

* *Daily Trust*, 21st November, 2005

leather ball. We have enough of sergeant-major presidency, may Allah spare us of a footballer presidential mansion.

Sonia Gandhi's "Inner Conscience"*

In a unipolar (read: unilateral) world, we are eager to uncritically down load half-truths about Reagan's legacy or celebrate Madonna's transformation from a controversial pop star to new-born again artiste and 'politician'. But let us know that there are more relevant experiences, globalisation offers. Both history and contemporary reality task us to follow the events in India and possibly learn from a sub-continent that has the semblance of Africa.

India got liberated from British colonial despotism in 1948 after a successful non-violent resistance of Gandhi and Nehru against the reactionary British violent campaign, which led to the massacre of hundreds of protesters at Amritsar in 1919. Pandit Nehru addressing the "Independence meeting" of the India Constituent Assembly said '*we end today a period of ill fortune and India discovers herself again*'. This singular triumphant Nehru's remark gave inspiration to widespread struggles for independence in the British colonies, Nigeria inclusive. Since independence, India remains a democracy compared to Pakistan and Nigeria, which at varying times came under the heels of military dictatorship which in turned underdeveloped the two countries when compared to remarkable growth of democratic India. Of course, the point cannot be over emphasised that Mahatma Gandhi the father of modern India started his political career in South Africa, where together with African compatriots stood up to combat racism. Indeed Mahatma's particular kind of protest in form of non-violent, non-cooperation with oppressors known as 'Satyagraha' was developed in South Africa. Indira Gandhi's India sustained this bond with Africa by resolutely supporting anti-Apartheid struggle at a time it was fashionable for Europe and

* *Daily Trust*, 28th June 2004

America to shamelessly fuel the obnoxious Apartheid machine. The Gandhis studied in the best of schools offered by the colonial oppressors, but they never forgot that the knowledge was for the liberation of their homeland and to serve their people rather than serve the same oppressors.

India has just concluded another successful poll retaining its lead as the world largest democracy. India proves again that in a multicultural and diverse society, democracy is not a passing fad but a necessity for sustainable growth and development. Issues in the concluded India's polls are as significant as the country's enduring commitment to democracy itself.

India's election took place against the background of xenophobia, reform without human face and opportunistic assault on secularity (thousands of Muslims and Christians have been murdered through officially motivated violence by the discredited B.J.P. party). It is refreshing to note that notwithstanding the enormous political challenges before the election, Indians never indulged in self-doubt and lamentation. On the contrary, Indians sought solace in deepening democracy by throwing out a bad government through the ballot box, just as they freed themselves from colonial despotism through Ghandi's non-violence struggle of the 1940s. Not even former Prime Minister, Alal Behari Vajpayee, who had called for earlier elections, contemplated such historic defeat by Gandhi's Congress party formed as far back as 1895.

Against the background of feverish campaign for a national conference in Nigeria, the lesson from India is that interpreting the world through debates and conferences may be desirable but such debates and conferences are no substitutes for changing the world democratically. In fact, what the electorate wants is NOT a debating society but a functioning and performing society.

India polls show that politics will ever remain murky and dirty, but politicians have the responsibility to abide by democratic outcomes. 2004 polls re-enacted 1980 election in which issues centred on the person of late Mrs. Indira Gandhi. BJP ran the nastiest of smear campaign against the prospects of appointment of widow of Rajiv, Sonia Gandhi as the Prime Minister. Mrs. Sonia Gandhi is an Italian born who got married to her oxford mate, Rajiv, himself assassinated in 1991; 7 years after similar fate befell his mother. This singular election once again confirms the robust nature of Indian democracy with its rich traditions of coalition politics that is inclusive of communists. It is remarkable that Indian constitution permits the candidature of a foreign born. This is unthinkable as it is illegal in 'developed' democracies including America. Our *follow, follow* pundits who always assume that 'true' constitutions (or is it 'true' federalism?) and 'democratic practices' are only available in America and Europe are hereby encouraged to also look elsewhere.

But significant was the indifference of mass of millions of Indian voters to the antecedents of Sonia. They resoundingly ignored BJP's Hindu jingoism and voted en-mass for Congress' campaign to combat poverty and give India's reforms some human face. Many Congress' supporters actually preferred Sonia as Prime Minister compared to Mr. Singh who eventually emerged as the Prime Minister. One placard reportedly demanded for '*Sonia or Suicide*'.

India's experience is a lesson for Africa. From Ivory Coast to Zambia and now Nigeria, dysfunctional identity politics is being played up by politicians in place of issues and ideas. African electorate must follow in the leads of their Indian counterparts insisting that what matters is who delivers on promises of water, education and health.

However, the true heroine of Indian polls is Sonia Gandhi in the heroic traditions of Indira Gandhi. She took the campaign to homes, mostly of rural peasants of India while BJP and stock markets are celebrating 'reforms' in Delhi and Bombay. People are ultimately the kings in a democracy.

How many of our desperate politicians would get such deserved victory and still decline nomination to lead as Sonia gracefully did? Conscious of history and the dirty antics of BJP Hindu fundamentalists (they threatened to boycott her swearing in) Mrs. Sonia Gandhi followed her "*inner conscience*" and humbly refused the post of Prime Minister. As we are again positioning for 2007, (even as despair is not ebbing) how many of the 'aspirants' (or are they draftees?) truly have "*inner conscience*" and truly follow this "*inner conscience*"?

Lessons from Davos*

2006 World Economic Forum in Davos has come and gone, but the critical question remains; of what relevance is the annual gathering of global economic and social stakeholders for Africa? Conversely what value-addition does Africa bring to world economic forum? In the age of globalization, the easiest way to confer a universal legitimacy on a vested interest-driven project is to give it a global stamp. How global is world economic forum in its annual agenda-setting and execution? Yours sincerely saw some television coverage of one of the high points of Davos forum, namely, "The Big-Debate" anchored by BBC's ace-man, Nik Gowing.

With reported 600 persons the platform expectedly set the "Business-agenda". It is not clear what to make of the "Business-agenda" but the process certainly pushed to the background issues that are pertinent to Africa. For instance, the local media head-lines had raised the expectation that Nigeria's Charles Soludo, the CBN governor would address the forum. But what we saw was selective Q&A that was titled towards a line of reasoning and some favoured speakers from America and Europe. Professor Soludo raised a critical question about the downside of globalization which confers an advantage to capital in terms of mobility compared to labour that is often treated as a national issue. This perspective which touches on increasing restrictive and discriminatory immigration policies of most countries in Europe was not exhausted until the "debate" got lost in the miracle of American flexible labour market with US secretary of labour, Elaine. L. Chao intervening more than twice.

---

* *Daily Trust* 30th January, 2006

One critical lesson of Davos for Africa is that in the era of globalization it is what you bring to the table for discourse that matters and not what you assume others will allow to do or say. Globalization is all about contestation as much as "creative imperative", which paradoxically was the theme of this year's forum. What creative imperative Africa brought to this year's forum is not self-evident. On the contrary we saw the same beg-the-donor orientation that has been the rule rather than the exception from Africa. Thus, while India was particularly the "darling" of participants with respect to prosperity and wealth generation, true to expectation star-musicians chaired discourse about Africa with respect to poverty. China reportedly turned the forum to show case its booming enterprises such that the forum announced that China "would be the location for a Global industry Summit." Even Pakistani's President Pervez Musharraf turned weakness to strength when he gave leadership lecture on how to manage disaster. The hope is that African leaders are learning from the global processes and procedures as much they are impressed with the results of other countries. The critical question is; what makes India and China achieve such remarkable growth rates in recent years? Is it due to uncritical whole sale liberalization as favoured by IMF and World Bank or gradual guided process with remarkable partnership between the state and the private sector? Are India and China preoccupied with poverty alleviation programmes or direct state-led policies of wealth generation? 600 annual meeting of global political and economic actors with cross-cutting themes under the building network of partnerships shows that sustainable development is too important to be left to some select "economic team" and that the politics of development is as important as the economics of it.

The high point of Davos debate however was the global acceptance that employment occupies the two sides of development coin. Whether the preference is with flexi-jobs like United States or permanent jobs like Sweden, it is job nonetheless. The hope is that those at home here who are eager to downsize on employment without creating new jobs will realise that the road to prosperity cannot be through idle capacity unemployment promotes.

Hamas: Phobia or Democracy?*

What was in the electoral victory of a resistance movement in a Palestinian occupied territory that alarmed governments in Europe and America? The recent mass hysteria in the West which heralded the proclaimed victory of Islamic Resistance Movement (Hamas) in the Palestinian parliamentary election has once again exposed the Western countries' triple-standard with respect to global movement towards democracy. Democracy is not meant to necessarily be efficient which explains why the world tolerated the outcome of controversial elections that produced President George Bush jnr despite the loud global opposition to his permanent war agenda. Democracy is not necessarily to be *manned* either which explains the new wave of feminization of democratic presidency from Liberia to Chile and Germany! The only thing constant in a democracy is change and the elements of suspense and unwelcome surprises are its ingredients! World-wide, (Middle East inclusive!) we have seen that democracy is not necessarily to produce saints or virgins as winners. Democracy has actually enthroned terrorists as leaders. Menachem Begin (1913-1992) was an acknowledged Israelis statesman and Prime Minister who shared Nobel Prize with President Anwar Sadat of Egypt in 1978. He was once a commander in chief of the notorious militant terrorist Zionist group called Irgun Zvai Leumi which metamorphosed to the coalition party that won election in 1977. Ariel Sharon, the Prime Minister currently in coma following massive stroke in January, was once a crime minister of sort who proudly presided over the massacre of Palestinian refugees in Sabra and

* *Daily Trust*, 7th February 2006

Shatila camps in 1981. He even regretted not having liquidated Yasser Arafat who was held up in the siege in southern Lebanon.

In fact Sharon was the only prime minister who came to power through terror-provocation that included provocative visit to some holly sites in East Jerusalem! Until 1990 Nelson Mandela, (the living global moral force!), was declared a "terrorist" by Apartheid South Africa backed by the West while ANC his organization was so lionized. But Mandela who spent 10,000 days (27 years!) in prison overwhelmingly won the first ever democratic non-racial election in 1994 and eventually shared Nobel Prize with F.W. De Klerk.

If the world came to terms with the above cited democratic outcomes why the frenzy and mass hysteria about Hamas victory which every discernable observer knew to be inevitable? The official propaganda had it that Fatah dominated PLO lost election because of corruption and cronyism at Palestinian Authority. Nothing could be more misleading. The voice of moderation lost in Palestinian election precisely because it was rewarded by both Israel and USA with hard-line posturing that meant mass murder of the Palestinians and further occupation of their lands.

Historians of Palestinian/Israelis conflict will be right to conclude that the campaign manager of Hamas in this historic election Hamas was strangely Mr Arial Sharon who through serial murders of its leaders, notables like venerable wheel-chaired 80 year old Sheikh Yassin and Dr Ranlisi popularised their cause and generated sympathy for them. It is a case of one extremism begetting extremism! United States, which paradoxically has been taunting Iraqi "elections" in which minority Shiites "won" over the majority Sunnis as the evidence of new democracy in Middle East has threatened to cut off aid to plausible Hamas-led Palestinian government urging other nations to take similar stands. It is precisely this lack of disinterestedness and sheer meddlesomeness that has imperilled United States' role in Middle East peace process! The aid came too late and too token in the first instance and total withdrawal of it means America is inadvertently making Hamas' case that it (i.e. America) only pays lip-service to the Palestinian cause. It is right if the Israelis voters elected bulldozers to power but unacceptable if the Palestinians chose wind-breakers to resist hurricanes. The question is if the West rejects democratic outcomes do they prefer a return to stone-throwing *Intifada* days which seems the only alternative to democracy? Before the death of Yasser Arafat the propaganda was that he was the main obstacle to peace process. A year after, it is self-evident that as long as the perceived and real injustice against the Palestinians remain, leaders and those who choose them are not the problems but those who are in the position like Americans and Europeans to ensure equity and justice to all parties in the age-long conflict in the Middle East.

Liberation Struggle[*]

Interrogate many Nigerians what was the global significance of 16th of June and you would be stunned by the amazing indifference and deepening dignified ignorance about African affairs on parade! Last week, yours sincerely searched in vain for some informed media commentary on the 30th anniversary of Soweto massacre. On June 16th 1976, fifteen thousand school children in South Africa rose in protest against the obnoxious Bantustan Apartheid education which was bent on forcing African secondary school students to learn compulsorily in the language of the oppressors-Afrikaans. True to its brutal character, the Apartheid regime opened fire on the defenceless black students armed only with sticks and stones killing hundreds of them the most notable victim being thirteen-year old Hector Pieterson. The multiplier effects of Soweto brutality and resistance reverberated throughout the Apartheid enclave and beyond, with heightened mass protests against the hated regime.

Soweto was the turning point in the struggle against Apartheid. Nelson Mandela, then serving life sentence on the notorious Robin Island recollected in his historic memoirs how Soweto students' uprising of the 70s uplifted inmates' morale which had been dampened followed the massive onslaught of Apartheid state in the 60s. According to him, "*There is nothing so encouraging in prison as learning that the people outside are supporting the cause for which you are inside*"! In Nigeria there was official denunciation of Pretoria brutality while Nigeria's anti-Apartheid students' movement enlisted in global protest. The most celebrated classic lyric on Soweto came from Nigeria's legend Sonny Okosun: *Fire in Soweto*! In fact BBC network

[*] *Daily Trust* 26th June 2006

woke listeners up on the anniversary day with Okosun's. There were manifestations world-wide in honour of the dead of 16th of June. There were also reaffirmations to the cause of justice and democracy. It is therefore a sad commentary that Soweto anniversary passed unmarked in a country (Nigeria) once classified as *a front line state* in the ranks of Zambia, Tanzania and Angola. There are different theories as to why increasingly Nigeria and Nigerians are becoming insular, more and more parochial, less pan African in orientation and deeds. One with special appeal holds that Nigeria and Nigerians of 70s were less preoccupied with survival issues such that they could be concerned with the liberation of others in bondage, South Africans inclusive. But today, the theory continues, Nigerians themselves need liberation from wants that range from power outages, water, job and job-losses, armed robberies, communal mayhem. Memory of massacre in distant South Africa of three decades ago is meaningless in a country in which mass funerals either from Okada riders or Onitsha murderers are becoming the order of the day. As Nigeria *Jaga-Jaga* hits the waves to the rude attention of even the Presidency, Sunny Okosun's *Fire in Soweto* sounds hollow and empty. In any case, if hundreds were murdered by Apartheid, how many lives have MOSSOP, NARTO and other similar acronyms for bloodletting wasted in Onitsha within the last two weeks? How many "Sowetos" have we replicated in our endless "communal"/ "religious" but senseless mayhem? A society that respects less the lives of its citizens can possibly not extend solidarity to others whose lives were endangered as it was during Apartheid. In any case liberated South Africa has also followed the trail of Nigerian leaders in wasting the lives of Nigerians either by omission or commission. Three weeks ago, a Nigerian street trader was reportedly shot dead in Johannesburg. Yours sincerely is yet to read an editorial decrying South African police brutality reminiscent of Apartheid days while we are yet to know the outcome of "Nigeria's embassy protestation".

Talking about liberation, have you read the news that all Obasanjo administration has been doing is nothing but "*leading a liberation struggle*". Presidential reform rhetoric has metamorphosed into liberation demagoguery that could make Fidel Castro sounds less militant! Hear comrade President Obasanjo:

> "With determination we have to continue to wage the liberation struggle. Liberation from those things that have not worked in the past. Liberation struggle from those things that have not helped the country before. Liberation, from the cabal that has held this country to ransom in the past. It is a liberation struggle and victory which is close, will be achieved."

The great metamorphosis of the president from a reconciliatory reformer of post third term debacle to a new liberation fighter will be a subject of interesting analysis for some time to come! But Bakassi people will wonder whether this great liberation struggle includes their accession to Cameroon while those of us in Nigeria eager to win American lotteries will be liberated from ever unending power outages of Power Holding company. *Victoria Acerta*! Forward the liberation struggle!!

Sullivan Summit: Dollars and Senses*

The 7th Leon Sullivan Summit has come and gone but the issues and ideas generated at this historic summit remain engaging subjects for students and activists of development of Africa. Yours sincerely was privileged to attend the Washington edition of the summit in November 2004. Michael Imoudu National Labour Institute, Ilorin and Washington based George Meany –National Labour College had entered into an Industrial Relations Partnership Initiative (IRPI) that involved exchange programmes and capacity building for industrial relations practitioners. Under this initiative a number of stakeholders in Nigeria visited US in 2004, during which Sullivan summit held and we were enlisted by the organizers as the privileged participants at the Summit ably addressed also by President Olusegun Obasanjo, then in his capacity as the President of Africa Union. I therefore bear testimony that the biennial summit truly connects Africa to the world in a mutually rewarding way. Put in another context, with its emphasis on opportunities, exchange of ideas, partnership, democracy and development, Sullivan Summit makes Africa comes to terms with globalization in a more pro-active and rewarding manner than scores of multilateral agencies that set unhelpful agenda for the continent.

True to expectation, the Summit recorded some harvest of financial support for Nigeria which included $1million worth of medical equipment and another $1million worth of books for the continent. There was also a promissory note of some $4 billion remittances by Nigerians in Diaspora. While dollar sums certainly matter for a continent with huge financial gap, the 7th Summit was

* *Daily Trust*, 24th July 2006

better appreciated for development senses and ideas it threw up than the financial support it generously offers. With the prospects of 3 million barrels per day at all time high prices of 85 dollars, the attendant wind-falls, $30 billion dollars external reserves and incessant acrimony over "excess" crude, Sullivan summit's dollar-tokenism either for health or for books for Nigeria, were mere public relations exercise. Paradoxically the great *dramatis personae* at the Summit were salesmen and women of international repute, including Andrew Young of the USA. This is not to say that Nigeria cannot make do with additional dollar but every cent matters more for Tanzania (the next host of the Summit) than a country in which Economic and Financial Crime Commission (EFCC) announced $5 billion recovery from few economic criminals and an Abacha loot once featured in a national budget estimates.

The relevance of the summit to Nigeria lies in some of its developmental common senses than the token-dollar baits taunted. Worthy of mention were the shared thoughts of the former President of United States of America (USA), Mr Bill Clinton. Clinton lived up to expectation as the greatest living inspiration-problem solving speaker of our times, when he took an exception to the corruption smear and graft stereotyping of the continent. According to him Africa is underdeveloped not due to corruption as such but the absence of "systemic capacity" that in turn creates a vacuum for "little bad things" to happen, corruption inclusive. Clinton noted:

> "I am convinced that the number one challenge today in Africa is building the systematic capacity that would enable people who live here to make their own future. One thing I have learnt in all the places I have been all over the world is that intelligence, ability and efforts are evenly distributed. But investment, opportunity, effective system are not."

Demystifying the so-called Asian Miracle, former President Clinton observed that beyond hard work and human capital (intelligence), it is the system that appropriately rewards people's efforts and intelligence that develops Asia and the absence of it that is impoverishing African continent. It is doubtful if this great insight of Bill Clinton made much impression on the concluded summit beyond. Judging from the remarkable thunderous applause that rightly heralded Clinton's insight, one can answer in the affirmative that he hits the right chord in an ordinarily plastic audience. Many fundamental senses flow Clinton's remarks for those who are sill concerned with growth and development. The first one is; stop bemoaning bad behaviours, namely corruption, lack of patriotism, low productivity, low skill, incompetence, etc., but critically examine the system (or lack of it!) that generates these dysfunctional traits. Anti-Corruption Commission yes! But of what importance is the relevance of the commission in a system in which according to EFCC chairman, Nuhu Ribadu, all leaders at all levels are corruption-prone? What makes all leaders potential criminals is the critical question begging for answer? This question tasks the imagination of policy makers, the type Bill Clinton exhibited. Since when have we made robbers rather than builders out of leaders? The Nigeria's leadership landscape in immediate post-Independence era exhibited greater integrity, commitment and competence. What was the system of rewards for efforts and intelligence which Clinton talked about compared to today? Are we even willing to identify efforts and intelligence when the most connected with heavy pockets get to public office? Clinton's challenge to African leaders is to evolve an "organized system" which is only achievable through "*...a thoughtful planning by the government.*" Is somebody listening and willing to make sense out of Clinton's observation and work out policy options that will make us frontally challenge underdevelopment rather than chasing the shadow. By all means we should keep on identifying criminals in government and get them punish. Yours sincerely is even in bold support for greater powers for anti-graft agencies such as EFCC to fish out economic and financial robbers in governance, even more so ahead of 2007 elections! After all, in China which we daily celebrate for its stunning growth rates, there and then economic criminals in public offices are summarily executed precisely because by their criminal actions they perpetrate more mass-deaths, given that what is stolen will not be made available for the common good of the majority. But beyond this there must be "*...a thoughtful planning by the government*" to create system in which the rule should be high turnover of integrity as distinct from the current turnover of disrepute and common thievery. It all comes to governance issues. And we can start with simple things like evolving a system in which public appointment is a call to service and not patronage as it is the case today. The system of public appointment that is accompanied by "civic/community" reception with president's representatives in attendance promotes the notion of governance as a prebendalism Lastly Clinton made the point that the challenge of fighting underdevelopment lies in creating investment and opportunities here in Nigeria and Africa and not in Diaspora (even as complimentary as the latter can be!). So why remittance of Africans in abroad are useful, what should border us is the system or lack of it that makes us send away doctors and nurses who should be adding value to halt infant mortality at home and who should be well paid and motivated. If America can reward efforts and intelligence, why not Africa?

Iraq: Study Group as a Metaphor*

The report of the Study Group on dire situation in Iraq was made public last week in America. The executive summary of the report of the ten members group co-chaired by James Baker III, former secretary of state and Lee H. Hamilton opened with the acknowledgement of global open sore: that the "*situation in Iraq is grave and deteriorating*". The group's singular admittance of the grim reality of the atrocities and mass human misery caused by senseless and criminal invasion of Iraq contrasts sharply with false grandstanding and whitewashing of a failed adventure by Bush-Blair war-cabinets. Many certainly loathed the despicable regime of Saddam Hussein and his litany of governance crimes but there is global consensus today that the American-British occupation has virtually brought total ruination to Iraq. In fact, the out-going secretary General of the United Nations, Mr Kofi Annan accepted as much that Iraq fared better relatively under Saddam Hussein. According to the report the score card of 2 years of occupation shows that: "…government is not adequately advancing national reconciliation, providing basic security, or delivering essential services. The level of violence is high and growing. There is great suffering and daily lives of many Iraqis show little or no improvement. Pessimism is pervasive." The point cannot be overstated that before the criminal invasion under a false search for weapons of mass destruction, Iraq was classified as an industrialized country of 22 proud million people. Indeed Iraq rated at the top of medium level countries in Human development index. The damning Iraq group report also shows that invasion and occupation have

* *Daily Trust*, 11th December 2006

atomised hitherto cohesive and united country. Iraq "*runs along the sectarian fault lines of Shia and Sunni Islam and of Kurdish and Arab populations.*" What then happened to the promised strong, prosperous and "democratic" Iraq by George Bush in the wake of serial bombing of defenceless independent country that Iraq was? Significant in this report is the admission that it's time for American troops to get out of Iraq. In fact the report accepts as much without saying so that American troops were the source of insecurity that has endangered sustained resistance among the Iraqis. "*Attacks against US, Coalition and Iraqi security forces are persistent and growing*", the reports notes. It adds "*that October 2006 was the deadliest month for US forces since Jan 2005, with 102 Americans killed.*" The critical point here is that just as it was from the beginning, the US and coalition forces are far from being forces of liberation for the Iraqis as the official propaganda in the wake of the invasion wanted the world to believe. On the contrary, the Coalition forces remain the hated forces of oppression and ruination that must be resisted and booted out. Indeed the study Group was candid enough to set agenda for the withdrawal of American troops starting from the first quarter of 2008. The major strength of this report is its bold acceptance of interdependence and multilateralism as solutions for Iraqi crisis as distinct from the dismal unilateralism and dictatorship of Bush and Blair. The group vindicates Kofi Annan's UN, (again without saying so), that the war on Iraq was illegal and by implication criminal. As a matter of priority, its recommendation stresses external approach that must involve all countries in the region. The linkage between the Iraqi crisis and Palestinian-Israeli conflict by this report shows that after costly and deadly drifting from hard reality of Middle-East crisis, America has come to accept that *"there is no magic formula to solve the problems of Iraq*". The limitation of the group report lies paradoxically in its strength: a desperate bipartisan way out of the huge mess America plunges itself in Iraq! Precisely because the group's goal was to rescue America from the self-imposed quagmire, the language of the report remains parochial and unhelpful. The group actually still sees the "Suni/Shite Muslims" as sources of violence. The report also lacks sense of history such that answers to critical question such as since when has Iraqis preferred "sectarian" crises cannot be found in the report. By and large, the Iraq group report remains a metaphor for failed global governance/leadership of UK's Blair and American Bush. Were it not for the balance of global power that confer them undeserved immunity, the two should be tried for war crimes on the account of the damning findings of the Iraqi group report. The idea of a study after much damage and carnage had been rained on Iraq underscores the incompetence of Bush administration in particular with grim global impact for humanity. Iraqi group report has indeed conclusively proved Nelson Mandela's acid test-message in the wake of the senseless and criminal war that US President George W. Bush jnr "*has no foresight*" *and* "*cannot think properly*"

The Other Singapore*

The eventual sad ending of Nigerian, Iwuchukwu Amara Tochi, convicted of drug trafficking downtown Singapura, capital of the Republic of Singapore, South-East Asia, occupies another chapter in the unending story of Nigeria's serial wastage of human capital. However what would not be easily obliterated with the cremated body of Tochi were the naughty developmental (read: underdevelopment) issues around 727.3 grammes of heroin, estimated by authorities to be worth 1.5 million Singapore dollars (US$970,000) allegedly found on him, the attendant belated response of Nigerian authorities and the dashed mass expectations that Tochi could have been saved. Once again Nigeria joins the globalization train from the last wretched coach of drug pushing and death by hanging under the Misuse of Drugs Act, 1973, of Singapore. It is a sad commentary that Singapore captures popular imagination in 2007 Nigeria via the hangmen of Singapura on Friday, January 26. Conversely notwithstanding the quality of his trail adjudged to be anything but fair and globally perceived as "phoney" and "racist", it remains a global scandal that a 21-year old Tochi discovered Singapore in search of a football carrier which was bad enough that ended in drug trade which was the worse enterprise. Singapore for those who care is a City state of just 4 million people compared to 140-million Nigerian federation. For good measure, in the 50s when Nigeria's multi-ethnic population was 80 million, Singapore had just over a million triple-ethnic population with majority being Chinese followed by some significant Malay and Indian. Singapore's per capital income of slightly above $600 dollars in the 50s and 60s was

* *Daily Trust*, 5th February 2007

miserably behind Nigeria's $1500 during this period. Singapore was a minor in international community at a time Nigeria was a proud and independent big player. As a matter of fact, Singapore joined the Commonwealth with cap in hand in 1965 while Commonwealth membership was a natural heritage of anti-colonial struggle for Nigeria. In his book, *From Third World to First: The Singapore Story:1965-2000* Lee Kuan Yew the founding father of modern Singapore accepted as much that while Nigeria could dare Britain and independently assert itself in pursuit of Africans' interest, Singapore was lackey of imperialism desperately seeking for relevance including justifying colonialism in Africa to appease Britain. In 1966, Sir Abubakar Tafawa Balewa the Nigeria's Prime Minister summoned the conference of Commonwealth Prime Ministers attended by British Harold Wilson. Lee Kuan Yew accepted as much that Prime Minister Tafawa Balewa who he described as a "dignified figure" talked straight to imperial Britain demanding direct actions against Ian Smith's declaration of Unilateral Declaration of Independence while he Lee on behalf of Singapore was being academic with colonialism by making a purely political issue a dubious "philosophical" issue just seek relevance with Britain. Memory is in short supply in present day's Nigeria governance infrastructure. But the critical question today is that could Lee Kuan Yew have imagined that independent promising Nigeria of the 60s would be cap in hand playing a reverse role seeking for clemency for its citizen on hangman's list on account of drug trafficking three decades after? How does President Obasanjo feel that he could not even delay Tochi's execution a day longer whereas South African President, Mr. Thambo Mbeki and his government promptly rose up against the death sentence passed on a South African citizen and reversed the sentence along with the Nigeria's Tochi? Conversely, how does President Obasanjo feel that Nigeria of 1960s and 1970s as a frontline state with remarkable global authority getting reprieve for other citizens from hangman noose couldn't even safe his own citizen amidst world-wide global campaign for stay of execution? What happens then to our much taunted new found global importance? Yours sincerely is strongly opposed to drug and drug trafficking. In fact, I have no disagreement with Singaporean choice of capital punishment against merchants of article of death which drug trafficking is. With population of 4 million 727.3 grammes of heroin, is an equivalent of atomic bomb without a declaration of overt war. The real issue is what has made Nigeria to slide miserably from independence and prosperity of the 1960s to the misery, poverty and drug trafficking in the new millennium and on the street of Singapura for that matter? Answers to these questions lie in the continuous growth and development of Singapore on the one hand and stagnation and muddling -through of Nigeria especially since mid-1980s on the other hand.

Judged by any standard today Singapore has escaped the clutch of underdevelopment. With nearly $30,000 annual per capital compared to Nigeria's miserable $500 it is clear that Singapore has said farewell to poverty. This is the other Singapore that has escaped popular imagination expressed in the information overload, (largely sentimental) after Tochi's execution. Paradoxically Nigerian government officials are quick to refer to Singapore as their model, a preference that shamelessly betray history and appreciation of the fact that between a city state and a Federal state the latter should be a source of envy. China which should be comparable to Nigeria and not Singapore! No miracle about Singapore's progress but commitment to development which Lee long noticed in Nigeria and Ghana as far back as 1960s. In this same book he accepted as much that: *"They (read: Nigeria and Ghana) were then the brightest hopes of Africa."* Singapore possesses a diversified economy with worldwide markets, which was what Nigeria was building in the 1950s and 1960s. Agriculture and industry until the discovery of oil and gas with its attendant non-value adding activities were the pillars of Nigeria's economy that recorded more than 10 per cent growth rate. In fact before 1960 Singaporeans had no identity of their own. Today it is the reverse with Nigeria which once had profound identity dating back to colonial era now in identity crisis occasioned by poverty and governance crisis. The critical success factor for Singapore is its people, which it jealously nurtures through Education and draconian laws against drug trafficking. Precisely because Singapore is a small society it insists that people have to be good and competitive in business and disciplined for productivity. The likes of Tochis that we allowed to waste in Nigeria first for football and eventually drug trafficking are the engines of growth of Singapore. This is the other and the real Singapore!

CNN or Dependency Syndrome*

The official hyper reaction to *CNN*'s damning insidious footage on Niger Delta of February 8th once again confirms the psychological and mental dependency of the country's official information managers. For all its "patriotic" icing on the cake, Minster Frank Nweke's response passed for nothing but a sickening and shameless exhibition of national weakness in place of a sovereign and original strength. The country's economic and political dependency is an open global sore that manifests daily in mixed bag of dumped second hand clothes, dumped fuel and dumped "intelligence" reports (one dumped 2005 US "Intelligence" actually predicted Nigeria's "*outright collapse*" in less than two decades!). CNN's dumped report of February 8th and subsequent feverish uninformed and inefficient official reaction shows the country's slide from political economic dependency to cultural symbolic annihilation. CNN's report was certainly detestable and unacceptable for its twisted and distorted account of Niger Delta reality as much as it was the only thing that could ever captured official imagination on Niger Delta in recent times after hostage taking. CNN is a private multinational media television based in Atlanta. It commenced continuous uninterrupted broadcast in 1985. The Atlanta-based tube is a private version of Nigeria's AIT. The only difference is that while American government cultivates its CNN to have such remarkable global outreach and impact even if dubious, Nigerian government undermines its own version through restrictive coverage and vindictive subterfuges that include suspensions and closures. How an Atlanta based tube would hold the Ministry of Information in the

* *Daily Trust*, 19th February 2007

heart of Africa spell bound is the critical question begging for answer. For all you care, CNN's Jeff Koinange could have invented the February 8th dubious problem compounding footage on Niger Delta from his hotel bedroom in Lagos or Abuja. And that would surprise nobody given that the reporter had a record of notoriety of "*black on black*" violence-reportage that once included alleged coup scare in Nigeria and Rwandan genocide. The issue is that there have been scores of similar reports of facts and fictions about Niger Delta that have not elicited the reaction of Federal Ministry of Information. Is it because the facts were distorted or that the art of distortion was done by CNN?

Talking about facts, yours sincerely was a witness to the launching and formal presentation of a 218-page United Nations Development Report (UNDP) report on Niger Delta Human Development in Port Harcourt last year. As a participant at the event I bear testimony to UNDP's damning observation about vicious tripod of poverty, backwardness and neglect plus mutually destructive violence between the region's militants and the Nigerian army. Worthy of note is that there has not been any official reaction to UNDP report which not only painted a grim reality but offered 7-point agenda for the transformation of the depressed region. The fact that Minister Nweke was seemingly depressed with CNN few minutes smear flash report and displayed abysmal indifference and even ignorance about 218 eternal Human development report shows that this administration is more concerned about its look via global media grandstanding rather than the impact of its policies (often lack of them) on its own citizenry. Assuming CNN had reported that Niger Delta was an emerging Dubai filled with honey and milk, there is no doubt that the Federal Ministry of Information would be contended with such distortionist propaganda and would even insult us with its repetition in its local NTA. It was this preferred white-washing of an increasingly Nigerian's damning reality in relations to our wealth that could only explain why this administration contracted the service of CNN for the so-called "*Heart of Africa*" advertisement. How *Heart of Africa* could be contrived in faraway Atlanta when we all see the decaying *body of the continent* in manifest poverty amidst wealth of Niger Delta points in the direction of slave mentality.

Thank God that what falsehood and propaganda (Heart of Africa project) brought together has been shattered into smithereens by similar propaganda not unusually done by CNN's Jeff Koinange. For President Chirac of France CNN is a pure and pure US government propaganda machine that was put into distasteful use at the height of UN debate on resolutions on Iraq. Chirac did not however spend precious presidential terms in office tasking his information mill to endlessly agonize on CNN distortion of global reality. On the contrary he set up the French version of CNN i.e. reportage of the world events as preferred by the French. Let the Ministry of Information first account for what went into failed *Heart of Africa* project. It could very well be channelled into intervention fund to alter the reality of Niger Delta for better and thus make CNN redirect its camera in the direction of Afghanistan. Better still, since the concern of the administration is about its image, let it channel such resources to do its own white-washing on Niger Delta via "*its largest network in Africa*".

In Praise of Paul Wolfowitz*

What about the global hysteria that heralded the piece of sensual news according to which the 10th President of the World Bank abused his office by generously awarding his mistress, Shaha Ali pay rise and promotion? That singular corporeal, not necessarily corporate, activity of Mr. Wolfowitz has elicited immense reaction of global revulsion and distaste. It was as if the World Bank was just rediscovered through Mr. Wolfowitz singular nepotistic indiscretion. But reflect over it. It was bad enough that a married global corporate boss would keep office mistress or be so insular in his indulgence. However, it would be clearly uncharitable and even hypocritical to expect less than unfair treatment for a bank staff turned mistress. Let whoever disagree cast the first stone. If you don't promote your girlfriend, (who by so-privileged, deemed promoted anyway!) who then in the establishment do you promote-a girl staff enemy? The lady has been unfairly prompted from a staff to you-name-it other steward. It is one unfairness assuming varying dimensions including the scandal that the World Bank President seconded the lady friend who is actually a British citizen to the US State Department with pay offer more than that of US Secretary of State. It was a case of proving the obvious; that corporate lust and love are thicker than tons of corporate rules and regulations. Thanks to global regulator Wolfowitz who should know it all and yet landed himself at the centre of messy conflict of interest.

Wolfowitz indiscretion has appropriately brought to the fore the triple standard of international managerial class who on the one hand dishes out hand-outs of ethics to Africa (and Africa in

---

* *Daily Trust* 14th May 2007

particular) but observe in the breach the same rules. The appointment of Paul as the President of the Bank was in the first place a product of conspiratorial corruption. He was the deputy secretary to discredited Don Rumsfeld US Secretary of State. They both started a war of aggression against Iraq based on sexed up/ dubious intelligence report that claimed Iraq harboured WMDs. His appointment was a reward by Bush administration for obstinacy and sheer rascality in the face of UN resolutions that showed that Iraq had no such weapons of mass destructions. Iraq had since been callously bombed and reduced from a promising developing country to a Stone Age of serial endless violence and multiple corruptions. The terror regime of Saddam Hussein is gone but terrorism and violence has been institutionalized in Iraq, thanks to the embattled Bank's boss legacy. My friend, Nuhu Ribadu, the EFCC Chairman put up a spirited defence for Wolfowitz on the ground that his current predicament was a function of his previous war misconduct and not the current kiss-for-promotion allegation for which he had apologized. So much for solidarity with Wolfowitz! A friend in need is a friend indeed! But should corruption and the battle against it be so divisible? Ever critical Ribadu who has commendably taken on corrupt Mongols at home despite their false claim of persecution should not put his brand stamp of credibility at the service of proven failed public servant like Wolfowitz . The argument that the Bank President was a friend of Africa who had generously put resources and energies at the service of the continent in the fight against corruption and poverty is simply untenable and point-blank; patronizing. Could he have been an enemy of the continent? What is the mandate of the World Bank? The charter of the post-WWII organization says the Bank should promote reconstruction and development of member states. Thus it is self-evident that Wolfowitz and indeed any Bank President had no choice than to promote development through among other options fighting corruption as its reportedly the case in Nigeria. Africans cannot be more grateful for what we statutorily deserve no less than we should praise sing others for doing the work they elected to do and for which they are handsomely paid. Africans should move out of slavish box of being helped or being empathized with to the plain arena of critical players in global arena. In doing so, we cannot but also be critical of worst practices of even "our friends". In any case it is one thing for the World Bank to help in fighting corruption, it is another story altogether that the World Bank policy trust of cooperate globalization and neo-liberalism entrenches worst forms of grafts and poverty in Africa. We are yet to read that Wolf leadership is altering the impoverishing policies of privatization and commoditization of public services in which the poor are increasingly losing out even in Nigeria.

Significantly too, the Bank President's travails have also exposed the informal corruption of governance structures of international institutions. Thanks to Wolfowitz impunity European members are now laying claim to the presidency of the Bank. What kind of international organization is it that the Presidency is reserved to the exclusion of other member nations especially Africans and Asians?

Kenyans' Folly, African Tragedy*

> "Well, that's it. Kenya has finally become part of Africa". (Western diplomat on the coup attempt of 1982).

It is a sad commentary that African students of current Affairs would almost today define Kenya as a 'new Rwanda' in which fifty Kikuyus were massacred in a church and over a thousand of varying persuasions were brutally murdered due to electoral violence arising from the globally acknowledged flawed December polls. Paradoxically, for African students of history and development, Kenya yesterday, today and tomorrow was (and still is) certainly more than senseless mayhem and politically motivated murders we have witnessed in recent weeks.

With a population of 28.2 million, Kenya is called *'Cradle of Humanity'*, precisely and legitimately because of archaeological finds in its historic Rift Valley:

> "Beginning about 200 B.C.E., Kenya became a major crossroads for peoples from all over Africa and the Middle East. Known for its game reserves, Kenya is today a major East African tourist site. Under the presidency of Jomo Kenyatta, newly independent Kenya became one of the most stable and prosperous nations in Africa, though political troubles have arising since the late 1970s."

Kenya is also rich in heritage of Resistance and struggles against colonial domination and British imperialism. The *'Mau-Mau War'* against British colonial rule was a classic African Peasants' Revolt comparable to similar resistance against imperialism in Vietnam, in

---

* *Daily Trust* (Monday, January 21, 2008)

China and Ireland among others. As far back as 1955 an American writer, John Gunther once describe Kenya as "---*the most marvellous game country in the world ---, Nairobi is the Safari capital of the World"*. Conversely as recent as 1999 a Nigerian musician Tunde Kuboye pointed out the difference Nairobi and Lagos by describing the former thus:

> "I call Lagos a city without pity. It's like a stunningly beautiful woman who is also very dangerous – you're attracted to it, but it's cunning, a combination of good and bad."

How Kenya, Nairobi so much celebrated transfigured into a subject of analysis in violence, murder and even genocide on account of avoidable political crisis is a subject of intense inquiry for students of African studies. It's a peculiar Kenyans' folly that needs not to be replicated anywhere in the continent.

Talking about replication, there are political observers who have argued that Kenyans are actually bad copy cats of the Big Brother Nigerians through attempted electoral reading that detonated as time-bombs. Again if this observation is true, then it further points to Kenyan folly to shamelessly copy the bad habits of Nigerians (i.e. April massively rigged election) from which Nigerians have not even recover and possibly may never recover given the serial madness that characterized the on-going local government elections.

In terms of integrity and sobriety, it has been globally established, that the difference is clear between Kenya's Electoral Chieftain, Samuel Kivuitu and his Nigerian counterpart, Professor Maurice Iwu. How the two Electoral Commissions' drivers turned electoral hope in the two countries into electoral despair in quick succession is a lesson not just in Kenyans' folly but indeed in African Tragedy! The likes of little and despicable tyrants like Liberia former President, Charles Taylor have been commendably arraigned before the International Court of Justice at Hague for their crimes against humanity, that included mayhem and murders arising from their actions and inactions while in office. The question is: Why would African electoral officers, who are paid to make the vote counts but end up criminally living in their trails devils' alternative of counting dead voters, not be charged with crimes against humanity? What is good for failed African irresponsible leaders is possibly better for Africa's criminal Electoral Officers! Certainly Electoral Commissions are under developing Africa!

Still on Kenyans' folly, how do the descendants of Jomo Kenyatta, Denda Kibati, Odinga Odinga, Bildad Kaggia and Tom Mboya, (great African democratic actors in their own rights) feel to be talked at by later day/sunshine democrats like J.J. Rawlings and Kufor of Ghana? The point cannot be overstated that when Ghana was bleeding under military dictatorship in the late 70s up to the late 80s, Kenya and Cote' de Voire (which is now another by-word for general disaster, save football) were oases of Liberal Democracy. How does it feel for the new coverts to democracy like Ghana to be more Holier than the Pope? Kenyans should NOT "*...finally become part of Africa...*", as a Western diplomat once cynically observed after the attempted coup in 1982. Kenyans should hold on to the banner of Constitutionalism, Civility and Democracy, the great heritage of Jomo Kenyatta, even with all his limitations, by making sure that the December votes truly count and by quickly making sure that the new emergency "international peace makers" are out work. Professor Wangari Maathai is a Kenyan Professor, Social Activist, founder of the Greenbelt Movement and 2004 Nobel Prize Winner. She once remarked that:

> "Kenya looks peaceful only in comparison to countries where there is fighting on the street. There is very little commitment by the political leadership to stop our country from going down the road of Rwanda or Somalia. Without that commitment, anything could happen".

May Kenyans *not* conclusively prove right Maathai's observation.

All said, the Kenyans' folly shows the inherent limitations of Liberal Democratic Project in Africa. What manner of Democracy is it that votes are increasingly proving difficult to count? What manner of Democracy is it in which donor Agencies and even World Bank are hidden 'voters' and even 'Retuning Officers'? What Democracy snowballs into Genocide and Disunity? If Kenya was at war it could not have lost a thousand within two weeks without a voluntary resignation of the Commander in Chief for gross incompetence and ineffectiveness? But after over a thousand counted dead, 'democratically elected' President Mwai Kibaki still had the *Audacity of Hope* (apology to Barack Obama who paradoxically is of Kenyan origin and whose legitimate campaign for American Presidency has been foolishly dented by blood clips from his home origin) to inaugurate a dubious cabinet rather than resigning in the face of self-afflicted pains and sorrows against his own people. From Abuja to Abidjan to Nairobi what kind of Democracy raises the spectres of civil Wars as distinct from prosperity? The rich actually cry and indeed the rich do fight. But only the poorest of the poor could be willing tools for self-destructions after elections as we have witnessed in Nairobi in recent weeks. What manner of democracy in which every election results produce more poor people swelling the ranks of ready-made army for new round of violence as we have seen in Kenya's new round of mini-genocide?

Kenya - What about African Peer Review Mechanism (APRM)?*

The avoidable, sickening and deepening political haemorrhage in Kenya with well over 1000 dead, spectre of ethnic cleansing and slide into economic meltdown amidst worsening poverty constitute a new acid test for the celebrated new Africa's development paradigm, NEPAD. From inception, the New Economic Partnership for African Development (NEPAD) was caught between great optimism and deep-rooted pessimism. Sadly events in Kenya have inadvertently proclaimed the triumph of the latter. Since its inception in July 2001 as a fruition of Millennium Partnership for Africa's Recovery Programme (MAP) and Omega Plan, NEPAD was afflicted with the notorious malaise of African policy shouting match of 'yes' or 'no'.

First is the 'yes' group. The optimists and promoters of NEPAD are familiar as their arguments. Enthusiastically promoted by President Obasanjo, South Africa's Mbeki, Senegal's Abdoulaye Wade and Algeria's Bouteflika, NEPAD was seen as a new African initiative that raises the prospects of an African Renaissance. The goals were alluring; good governance, growth and sustainable development, eradicate widespread and severe poverty as well as halt marginalization of the continent in the globalization process. NEPAD's advocates insist that it is not a Fund raising project but in their words 'a holistic, comprehensive integrated strategic framework for the socio-economic development of Africa.'

It rests on three pillars for Africa's development to laying the conditions for development (with emphasis on conflict resolution,

* *Daily Trust* (Monday, February 4, 2008)

peace and democracy), sectoral priorities (bridging infrastructural gap, with emphasis on energy, transport, agriculture, environmental initiative, public investment and human resource) and resource mobilization (through direct foreign and domestic investment, debt relief, overseas direct resource flows and market access initiative for agricultural and manufactured products from Africa).

The 'no' group underscored the dependency orientation of NEPAD by questioning a taunted notion of partnership, in which (as captured by a news agency picture) an obviously weather-beaten Obasanjo and Mbeki were once seen standing in front of a rather relaxed Tony Blair during one of their NEPAD's salesmanship trips to UK. NEPAD nurtures an ambitious expectation of as much as 60 billion dollars NEPAD annually as investment flows to the continent from abroad. It is seen as uncritical celebration of foreign investment as distinct from domestic entrepreneurship.

The 'no' group was reinforced by a number of African scholars and civil society organizations that subjected NEPAD to remarkable scrutiny. They argue that NEPAD couldn't fashion out new partnership since it remains uncritical and even apologetic of the existing world economic and trade arrangement with all its inequities. It is seen as another attempt to once again resell the continent to the same neo-liberal economic agenda that for long brought it to ruination and underdevelopment. Significantly, the pessimists hold that by being uncritical of the existing world multilateral agencies and even seeking engagement with them, NEPAD further locks African economies to the disadvantaged globalization process it atheistically strives to correct.

Whatever its merits or demerits, the recent events in Kenya constitute a practical case study on the relevance or otherwise of the new 7-year old paradigm. To the extent that NEPAD brought back the endangered concept of "development" at the turn of the Millennium, many observers hailed the initiative. There has almost been a conspiracy of silence about development since mid-1980s as countries of Africa were made to grapple with survivalist strategy to cope with balance of payment crises, through currency devaluation, removal of subsidy, retrenchment and stripping of states assets via privatisation. It was therefore refreshingly new to see Africa talking about a vision for development and a programme of realising this vision with clear targets for growth rates human resource development, education and health among others.

The strong point of NEPAD is its political component. NEPAD underscores that economic development is impossible without addressing the political question. African governments concede that democracy is not just fashionable but indispensable for development. To achieve this goal NEPAD puts in place a Peer Review Mechanism according to which member-states voluntarily subject themselves to development and governance tests. Today, the question: to what extent have African leaders kept to the promises of Development and Democracy? The events in Kenya have done more visible violence to the principles of development and good governance which these member-states pledged to uphold. The Chairman of the African Peer Review Mechanism, APRM, and Nigeria's Professor Adebayo Adedeji recently announced that as many as 28 countries have voluntarily subscribed to the principles of Peer Review. Top on the list of the six countries with "finalised" peer Review paradoxically is Kenya. Others are reportedly Ghana, Rwanda, South Africa and Algeria. Either something is fundamentally flawed with the on-going review process which makes a reviewed country slides into chaos as we are witnessing in Kenya or the entire NEPAD process is a fraudulent legitimization process to conceal African developmental and political rot. What manner of development paradigm is it that its proponents could not match its enunciated principles with their deeds? Where are the commitments of the likes of former President Obasanjo, South Africa's Mbeki, Senegal's Abdoulaye Wade and Algeria's Bouteflika when they could not pronounce talk less of halting the disaster in Kenya? What manner of Peer Review cleared Kenya of politicians and "democrats" like Kibaki and Odinga who betrayed no emotion as they quarrel while Kenyans slaughter each other? What about an economic paradigm, under which a promising developing nation like Kenya simply slides into self-inflicted underdevelopment on account of vote counting? African leaders have proved once again that NEPAD is another passing "development" fad imposed from abroad, not internalized by them.

NEPAD's document for instance, underscores accountability, freedom of association, and assembly, free and fair elections, and existence of several parties among others. In Nigeria, it will be very interesting to see how we interpret this provision in the light of accountability deficit and pure political brigandage under Obasanjo government, in which 8 months after "elections" Tribunal panels' judges are still counting votes and politicians are yet to deliver water and light as promised? How does the NEPAD's provision relate to the existing silly, obscene and clearly ineptitude of AU in the face of the madness at the Rift Valley of Kenya of Jomo Kenyatta? Whence the promise of investment flow to Africa under NEPAD, when we are confronted with investment collapse, no thanks to mutually assured madness of the Kenyan type?

Copy, Beg Not China*

President Umaru Musa Yar'Adua has just concluded a four-day state visit to China. This visit has once again brought into sharp focus SINO/Nigeria relations with more eyes on Nigeria's balance sheet, (ever in the red!) than China's accounts (ever in surplus). Development observers agree (and they now say so openly) that there are three global development challenges in the new millennium. The number one development challenge is *China.* The second development challenge is *China.* And the third development challenge is *China.* If China intrigues and confounds global development observers, it is certainly understandable why Nigeria has been striving to come to terms with China. No country has recorded remarkable rapid economic ascendancy in the past 25 years like China. With 1.5 billion population and consistent 12% growth rate in the past 3 decades, China has shown that huge quality human resource is indeed an asset and not a liability. China shows that development process is NOT a zero-sum game in which growth is traded off for jobs and in which few *are well-having* and many lack *basic well-being.* China shows that the issue is not extractive resources (China not an OPEC member) but value additions and manufacturing (China has more functioning oil refineries than Nigeria!). China shows that growing the GDP does not mean pushing mass of people into the margin of mass poverty. On the contrary, China is perhaps the only country since the great Industrial Revolution that has combined consistent aggressive industrialisation drive with high growth rate side by side with full employment. China makes nonsense of neo-liberal/ textbook received wisdom about jobless growth. We can indeed have

* *Daily Trust* (Monday, March 3, 2008)

job-led growth, China proves that. China has shown that addressing production issues is not mutually exclusive from confronting poverty and coming to terms with distributional issues. While many sub-Saharan African countries, including Nigeria have pushed millions into poverty due to IMF inspired "reform" process, (SAP) China is the only country that has recorded the largest reduction in poverty in history in recent time. Indeed it has lifted as many as 250 million people (twice the population of Nigeria!) out of poverty. In international trade, China's goods and services rule the world such that the new America's Cold War with China is about articles of trade rather than weapons of mass destruction.

Precisely because the challenge of China is about growth and development, no serious Head of government of a developing nation goes to Beijing without talking development. It is therefore not surprising that President Yar'Adua made major development pronouncements in Beijing (even though many observers would prefer such pronouncements on the floor of national assembly at Abuja if only to keep our legislators busy beyond "overseeing" oil revenue sharing, sorry, (budget debate)) .

Once again President Umaru Musa Yar' Adua has shown that energy is central to his 7-point agenda. In far away China, he disclosed that his administration plans to increase the country power generation by March next year. The government, the President stated, would make outages a thing of the past by the year 2011 to "successfully fast-track our economic growth". To this extent he welcomes the Chinese investors who want to partner "*on the use of coal, as we explore all possible sources for additional power generation"*. By the way, it is instructive that Yar'Adua's engagement with Hu Jintao was on development compared with his engagement with George Bush which was pointedly and one-sidedly about American strategic calculation on oil wells protection in Africa (remember Africom!). Also when compared to his predecessor's (President Obasanjo's) engagement with Switzerland on Abacha loot, it is self-evident that the difference is clear with China which is not yet notorious for looted Africa's fund.

The critical question however, is how do we translate speech making about development in Beijing to practical developmentalist steps in Abuja? What should be the content of Sino-Nigeria relations such that Nigeria will be one of the leading 20 economies of the world, which in any case China is?

Yours sincerely is excited that President Yar' Adua called for the setting up of *"a mutually-beneficial strategic partnership with China"*. This is a radical departure from the slavish/unequal relationship with China during Abacha and Obasanjo's era and the attendant scam (remember fake Railways deals!) and rot (ask NAFDAC about Made-in-China fake drugs). Beg Not China but copy China! Notwithstanding development gap, Nigeria has a lot in common with China and indeed could be another China, just as China used to be like Nigeria. Nigeria is the most populated country in Africa just as China is most populous country in Asia as well as in the world. In development parlance we are talking of two largest markets in the world. But while China is one huge working and productive house, Nigeria is yet to be unbundled to realise its potentials as it is weighed down by consumption and idle capacity.

Paradoxically the two countries are undergoing reforms. But while China's reforms are delivering on promise, Nigeria's reforms are far from the expectations. This is where Nigeria can creatively copy China. Yours sincerely recommends for President Yar' Adua Joseph Stiglitz book, *Globalization and Its Discontents*, (in particular chapter seven). President Yar'Adua should appreciate how China's reform has delivered prosperity compared to how Russia's reform (read: Nigeria) has promoted despair. Stiglitz, the Nobel Prize Winner in Economics shows that the strength of China lies in its home grown policy initiatives. China just like Poland ignored the so-called Washington Consensus (devaluation, uncritical privatization, trade liberalization, removal of subsidy, etc.) as promoted by IMF and the World Bank and went for creative alternative local policies that reflect national priorities. China employs *"gradualist approach"* to reforms compared to *"shock therapy approach"* of Russia which uncritically privatised public enterprises without addressing fundamental issues of goods and service delivery. China built democratic mass support for reform agenda not through election riggings, political thuggery and mass unemployment as in Nigeria OBJ's era. On the contrary China shows that stability, political unity of purpose and common wealth (as distinct from private aggrandisement and corruption) are indispensable to reform agenda. China also has negative (not just zero) tolerance to corruption (it engenders capital punishment in many instances). Lastly the point cannot be overstated that China appreciates the imperatives of labour-intensive industries for a populous nation. Nigeria is boastful with enclave sectors like Telecoms, banks and oil and gas but the labour absorption is therein insignificant. On the contrary China holds on to textile and agricultures where millions are employed. What is good for China is good for Nigeria; macroeconomic stability and protection of domestic market. The issue is not to be romantic with China but to use the President's word, be "strategic" with China just as China has been strategic in its dealings with Africa. President Yar'Adua seems on top of the challenges of China when he reportedly said:

> "Given their unique respective geo-political statures, Nigeria and China have a duty to mutually reinforce each other's' growth and development. Our administration is greatly encouraged by the fast-tracked economy development that China has achieved, which has made her the world's fastest growing economy and greatly enhanced her influence and stature in the world."

Good luck Nigeria.

Israel According to the Israelis*

As an age-long critic of Zionist Israeli state (not necessarily its people), in the absence of new evidences to the contrary, a reflection on the state of Israel at 60 must predictably be true to type: unapologetically critical. However, to do sufficient justice to an objective complex but peculiar mess (read: Israel) at anniversary and therefore avoid the pitfall of accusation of "*Israel bashing*", yours truly searched for what some Israelis could have said about themselves since 1948. I found quite handy a "*timely and well argued*" (witness *The Nation*) 248-page book by an Israeli patriot, Baruch Kimmerling. The book is entitled, *Politicide; The Real Legacy Of Ariel Sharon.* It was first published in 2003 but was "fully updated" in 2006. The book could have been entitled *Israel At 60* judging by rare historic and contemporary chapters that make up this rich text competently written by a sociologist who is "*highly committed to the fate and well-being of Israel*" his "*only country*". Paradoxically as a patriot, the author of this critical lucid prose of *sorrow, tears and blood* (apology to Fela!) is still hard put to underscore his objectivity in assessing his own country. He puts a caveat according to which the book is not "*Israel bashing*" by a *"self-hating Jew … but to make an additional attempt to open the eyes of a benevolent and humanistic people who do not yet see the real dangers besetting Israel."* Pray what manner of state is Israel in which after 60 years, its dedicated compatriots would be on defensive in subjecting it to critical analysis? Posing this question alone says volume about the state of Israel. No country has imposed on humanity (not even Stalinist USSR!) *dictatorship of political correctness* has Israel done even to its subjects.

---

* *Daily Trust* (Monday, May 12, 2008)

No state has painfully polarized humanity vertically and horizontally like Israel. It is either *for or against, Left or Right, Zionist or anti-Zionist, doves or hawks, terrorist or anti-terrorist, Muslim or Christian* (when we all know that theologically the Jewish state is not a Christian state). Kimmerling points out that explanation for controversy on Israeli discourse lies in the state's controversial origin which in turn tasks our sense of history.

"*The tragedy of Zionism was in its anachronism*" he wrote. Following the pogroms of 1880-1881 in Eastern Europe, some Jews moved towards the Holy Land of Jerusalem in nostalgia for their messianic homeland. To the local Arabs, the "return" of Jews after 2000 years of abandonment equalled colonial invasion. In 1917, the British occupiers confirmed the Arab suspicion when they forcefully took over the Holy Land from Ottoman Empire and gave it out to the Jews to form their homeland under the controversial Balfour Declaration. One forceful land acquisition and land grabbing begets another: from Golan Heights to West bank and Gaza Strip. The seed of endless cycles of violence was planted in 1948 during which the Jews had upper hand in an inter-ethnic war with the Palestinian Arabs. Even at that, Kimmerling points out following United Nations' resolution of the conflict, the Zionist founders of Israel state took more lands than the UN allocated them. UN granted the Jews 14,000 square kilometres of territory, but the Jewish military forces actually conquered 20,000 square kilometres, sacked as many as 750,000 Palestinian Arabs and put as many as 100,000 Arabs under their internal colonial control. It is self-evident that Israel is today hunted by its lowly unjust origin of forceful occupation and unfair land acquisitions that is comparable in history only to the discredited Apartheid South Africa's despicable litany of forceful eviction of Africans from their land. (Indeed Zionist Israel collaborated in acts of unjust deeds with Apartheid South Africa for as long as the latter was allowed to last by humanity!). The point here is that while countries like Nigeria at independence, allowed Cameroon to assume independent status, Israel Jewish state flourished on aggression, colonialism and addictive denial of Palestinian autonomy from day one.

The author shows that the bane of Israel is as much in its acquisitive origin as much as in the ideological orientation of its founding militarists. While nations-state historically took off with reaffirmation of existing territorial integrity, Zionist perspective of its founders aspires "*a maximal Jewish territorial continuum, cleansed from an Arab presence, as a necessary condition for establishing an exclusive Jewish nation-state.*" Israel state introduced *ethnic cleansing* into global lexicon well before Hitler madly accorded it genocidal /holocaust bent, before racist whites in South Africa "dignified" it into Apartheid and the Rwandans stupidly applied the notorious concept in its dastardly form as late as 1990s as home videos.

Israel's "Present Past" (the richest chapter in terms of memory and Part 1 of this book) shows that a state founded on sword might permanent live on the sword, unless there is a sincere renegotiation of contracts with its own people as well as with the Arabs. So far so worse: It has been a nation of tragi-paradoxes of unimaginable proportions in history. 60 years of state of Israel, means statelessness of the Palestinians, peace with wars, internal democracy/ creeping fascism, civility/militarization of public affirms, Jewish fundamentalism versus Arab fundamentalism (witness Sharon's Kadima/Hamas government), prosperity/emergence of the *new Israeli poor*, freedom/erection of New Berlin Walls, Roadmaps/ Roadblocks, state reaffirmation versus state non-recognition, ad infinitum!. The state of Israel at 60 is summed up by Kimmerling as *Politicide,* defined as a

> "process that covers a wide range of social, political and military activities whose goal is to destroy the political and national viability of a whole community of people and thus deny it the possibility of genuine self-determination. Murders, localized massacres, the elimination of leadership and elite groups, the physical destruction of public institutions and infrastructure, land colonization, starvation, social and political isolation are the major tools to achieve this goal."

By the way, what about Ariel Sharon? Is he *clinically dead* like Yasser Arafat was once enthusiastically so proclaimed by global Zionist media or are we to expect another 60 years of *Sharonism* without Ariel Sharon in Israel?

Zimbabwe for Beginners*

Willy-nilly, despite the abundant knowledge and information overload, we all turn out to be another set of students when it comes to the ever unending subject of Zimbabwe's political economy. Indeed we are all beginner-witnesses to Zimbabwe's story which daily and hourly alternates between some trilling comedy and scaring tragedy or both, tragi-comedy. Yours sincerely thought I had gotten it right when I proclaimed *Mugabe as history* following 29th March polls in which the opposition won as many as 105 seats in the 210-seat parliament, leaving ZANU-PF with 93 seats. Watching the 84-year old President casting his votes at weekend in an apparent no- contest election (opposition had withdrawn), it was clear that as far as Mugabe was concerned, it was not yet the end of history as we knew it with great statesmen of honour such as Nelson Mandela, President Sam Nujoma of Namibia and President Kenneth Kaunda who knew when to bow out when the political ovation was loud. As a matter of fact, as far as Robert Mugabe is concerned, it is the beginning of history of sheer profanity and brigandage for which he's fully prepared. While casting his votes in Harare, the 84 year old contestant was reported as feeling "*very fit, very optimistic*"!

Until recently Mugabe polarized the Africa continent and indeed the world either for (in support of the land reform) or against Zimbabwe (for free and fair elections). No thanks to the combined forces of Tony Blair/George Bush who concealed their racist uncritical support for few white land owners opposing land reform while remaining hard on politics of free and fair elections. But today it is Zimbabwe versus the whole world as Mugabe digs in into

* *Daily Trust*, 30th June 2008

political isolation against the background of global pressures and Euro-American blackmail in particular. Mugabe once declared that Zimbabwean crisis was African crisis arguing that the success of Zimbabwe is the success of Africa. Yet at the weekend he effortlessly dammed the Africa Union (AU) following the latter's suggestion for election postponement when opposition MDC alleged insecurity. Mugabe pointedly said the continental body has "*no right to dictate to us what we should do with our constitution, and how we should govern the country*."

Former President of South Africa, Nelson Mandela, the global surviving moral force, at the weekend in London aptly described the unfolding events in Harare as manifestation of tragic leadership failure. Nothing could be more perceptive. Mandela did not elaborate on this but we can imagine that with respect to Zimbabwe, failure of leadership is not peculiar to Robert Mugabe which is crystal clear anyway. The ambiguity and duplicity of Africa Union to Zimbabwe underscores failed leadership at continental level. Lacking independent criteria to assess Zimbabwe (notwithstanding much taunted pair review machinery of NEPAD), AU has become willing stick of the Gordon Brown and George Bush with which the duo whip the entire continent into line to condemn already condemned Mugabe. When Washington and London sneeze from Cairo to Cape Town, there is instant climate change! But think about it. The ambiguity of most African nations is clearly understandable. With all its imperfections, Zimbabwe elections are certainly better than Kenya's and Nigeria's elections. Kenya's elections for instance, featured near ethnic cleansing in which as many as 1000 were slaughtered before the ruling party and the opposition had deal (typical of dealers, not leaders!) of a government of national unity. Violence certainly features in Zimbabwe's elections more than any known election in recent times. However Zimbabwean violence as despicable was not certainly along mutually destructive ethnic line but vested issues that unite the likes of opposition Tshangirai with the Dutch embassy. Zimbabwe has happily not brought back the painful memory of Rwanda as much as Kenya painfully and shamelessly did. In Nigeria, one year after "elections", we are still counting the "votes" which made both the controversial March and June polls of Zimbabwe far more preferred. It is true that opposition sought refuge in foreign embassy (instructive not in Nigeria's or Kenya's embassies!) but many opposition leaders in Nigeria such as Harry Marshal, Bola Ige were not as privileged in "democratic" Obasanjo regime. In any case how can Nigeria demand for equity in Zimbabwe when 15 years after it annulled a free and fair election, it is yet to organize any election so described as free and fair? With all his criminalities, Mugabe is yet to annul elections as Nigeria shamelessly did.

This then raises the failure of leadership at international levels. It is a scandal that United Nations (UN) which adopted a constructive approach to Kenya despite the hard lines posturing of both the government and opposition now apply destructive (at least non-constructive) approach to Zimbabwe. By its ultimatum to Mugabe to postpone the weekend elections and attempted move at sanctions, UN has proved to be willing tool of EU and America, completely lacking independent creative and helpful thinking. Pray where was UN when we are assaulted with "free" election in Pakistan where opposition Bhutto was murdered well before elections? The feverish activism of UN on Zimbabwe underscores the crisis of global leadership that Mandela talked about. The point here is that Zimbabwe story is certainly a bad one but it is not the worse of stories. The worse story is failed global leadership in which the Zimbabwean masses are made to queue for bread no less they are forced to queue for 84 year old "fit and very optimistic" President.

South Africa after the Xenophobia*

"I had fallen into the Apartheid mind-set, thinking Africans were inferior and that flying was a white man's job," Nelson Mandel in 1962 expressing shock at the sight of an African pilot flying him and other ANC comrades from Sudan to Ethiopian during the campaign for armed struggle against Apartheid.

Every visit to the great land of eminent and remarkable rainbow of historic global citizens like Nelson Mandela, Walter Sisulu, Chief Albert Luthuli, Oliver Thambo, Ruth First, Mariam Makeba, Chris Hani, Winnie Mandela, Desmond Tutu, Steve Biko, Hugh Masekela, among others is often filled with some political excitement and nostalgia of immeasurable proportions. My political excitement flows from the personal challenge of coming to terms with the historic paradox of a country which via sheer persistent commitment and enormous human sacrifices throws up robust human capital which shines more than diamonds, glitters more than gold. South Africa (SA) is definitely endowed in prolific deposits of diamond and gold (which spurred British imperialism between 1870 and 1910!). But SA which captures global imagination in the 21st century is not a land of celebrated resource endowments (which nonetheless are creatively being applied for consistent economic growth) but a country of great peoples who stood against Apartheid tyranny and internal colonialism. Every visitor of note is eager to visit Robben Island (not necessarily SA's mines) where courageous men for years were confined into solitary existence to ensure liberty for the multitude. My excitement fills a cup when it is realised that almost 50 years after independence, Nigeria has almost been uncharitably defined in

* *Daily Trust*, 25th August 2008

relations to discovery of its rich deposits, (Oloibiri) no less than the wastage and squander of the very hydro-carbon (Niger Delta!).There were certainly imperial deposits barons that included the likes of Barney Branato, Cecil Rhodes, but Robben Island inmates and struggle heroes like Ahmed Kathirada, Billy Nair, Mac Maharaj, Eddie Daniels and of course Nelson Mandela and Walter Sisulu among other political prisoners are the acknowledged makers of modern SA. Of course Nigeria in equal, (if not even in greater measure) paraded great patriots and independence struggle heroes even well before the emergence of the Mandelas in South Africa. They included great patriots like Raji Abdallah, Michael Imoudu, Tanko Yakazai, Mokwugo Okoye, Nnamdi Azikiwe, Chief Obafemi Awolowo, Ahmadu Bello (who in spite of his acknowledged conservative bent gave Mandela as much as £100,000 to his armed struggle campaign in early 1960s) and Aminu Kano who stood up to British imperialism and demanded for independence. Alas! Today, it is the notoriety of misapplication and corruption of billions of oil receipts that feature in modern day Nigeria discourse than celebration of leaders who are increasingly more in quantity than quality.

As a partisan of anti-Apartheid struggle in my undergraduate days, the nostalgia any South African trip invokes is crystal clear: the great campaign for the release of Nelson Mandela (of struggle is my life fame!), solidarity rallies and fund raising for victims of Apartheid, the inspiring revolutionary lyric of the late Sonny Okosun; "*Fire in Soweto*", commemorative days of solidarity with South Africans: (for instance, Sharpeville Massacre Day 21 March, "Soweto Day", 16th June, and the unprecedented foreign policy activism of Nigeria which made it a frontline state in the league of other vanguard nations in the struggle against Apartheid regime, namely Zambia, Tanzania, Mozambique, Angola and Namibia. I recall that Nigeria offered six times uninterrupted the chairperson of the prestigious UN special Committee Against Apartheid featuring highly respected ambassadors like Leslie O. Harriman (1976-1979, Alhaji Yussuf Maitama Sule (1981-1983), late Major General Joe Garba (184-1990) and Ibrahim Gambari (1990-1994) among others. There was a solidarity wage contribution by Nigerian working class paid into a solidarity Fund headed by Senator Olusola Abubakar Saraki.

My latest trip to South Africa, (the 6th since its liberation in 1994) was with a mix feeling. The theme of the conference was alluring and irresistible in the wake of globalization of production that has left in its trail collapse of industries and mass unemployment in many African countries including Nigeria. But my usual trip enthusiasm was for once undermined by the rude xenophobia of May and June this year that left scores of African immigrants massacred in broad-day light serial mayhems by marauding youths wielding weapons of mass assault against defenceless immigrants. Watching the gory pictures of helpless burnt immigrants on TV reminded one of the Apartheid state sponsored *black on black* violence of the dying days of the hated system. Are we back to the era of the notorious "third force"? What about the African Renaissance promised by President Thambo Mbeki when African immigrants are being slaughtered for whatever reason by a liberated South Africa? Of what value is NEPAD's peer review mechanism when basic values of tolerance and brotherliness are being trampled upon by member-states? South Africa prides itself with vibrant pan-African civil society, why then the resurgence of chauvinistic violence against immigrant workers who in the main have historic and linguistic affinity with SA's major tribes like the Zulus and Xhosa? SA once hosted UN international conference on Racism and Xenophobia parading its credential of a rainbow country. Why would the country soon after be identified with despicable terms like "pogroms" and "genocide"? These are some of the critical questions I was posed to confront my SA comrades with and I did.

Yours sincerely bear testimony that the great peoples of SA represented by their government and formidable progressive organizations like trade unions (COSATU) deeply regret the events of May. Often Presidents talk of prides of nations. But President Thabo Mbeki described the mayhem as "a national disgrace", the three words of profound and deep felt regrets repeated by all SA's activists. Significantly there has also been a robust debate on the causes and remedies to the tragedy. The most incisive is the one by a political commentator, Hein Marais who writes for the progressive journal: *Amandla.* According to him beyond the tendency towards "introversion and enclosure" as the new features of the dark side of globalization, there are material underpinnings summed up as crime, housing, women and jobs. With respect to crime, the media generally portray foreigners as being responsible for mounting crimes in the country a dubious stereotype that makes them subject of ridicule and cheap attack. Foreigners might be crime prone but no less than the South Africans themselves as witnessed recently by a school boy Eerie who certainly under Satanic spell killed a pupil with a sword and wounded three others. All said, what is clear is that the "Apartheid mind-set" Mandela decried as far back as 1962 still persists 14 years after liberation. South Africa has definitely made progress in that last decade. What about historic reconciliation, strong and vibrant economy, strong currency and remarkable export-led economy. But the human gap persists as the neo-liberal market policies fuel 40 per cent unemployment rate and worsening poverty of the many.

Barack Obama: A Content Analysis*

"I have a dream that my four little children will one day live in a nation where they will not be judged by the colour of their skin but by the content of their character. I have a dream today"- *Martin Luther King, Jnr*

"If John McCain wants to have a debate about who has the temperament, and judgement to serve as the next Commander in Chief, that's a debate I'm ready to have"- *Barack Obama*

The rise and rise of Obama phenomenon in American nay global politics assumed some anti-climax last Thursday night with his remarks entitled "*The American Promise*" in Denver, Colorado at the democratic National Convention. The remarks pass for acceptance speech as a nominee of the Democratic Party for the presidency of United States of America (USA). The global media outsmart each other to "privatize", (as it were), the dramatic emergence of the Senator from Illinois as the flag bearer of the Democratic Party. But a critical scrutiny of the 4,718 word/wisdom load betrays personalization on the part of Obama. On the contrary, the Thursday remarks pass for historic exercise in humility and collective enterprise very well in huge deficits in Washington, the heartland of individualism and self-accomplishments. While the tag of the "first" African American to climb the power ladder of America so far is put on his neck, Obama parades no such chest-beating colour-bar credentials. Acknowledged that he is truly an unconventional candidate, this historic speech (which tasks the staying power of yours sincerely all night Thursday), further adds impetus to the rewarding efforts of the candidate to avoid the pitfalls of race politics

* *Daily Trust,* 1st September 2008

which his adversaries would have used to an electoral advantage. Witness vintage Obama:

> "I realised that I am not the likeliest candidate for this office. I don't fit the typical pedigree, and I haven't spent my carrier in the halls of Washington. But I stand before you tonight because all across America something is stirring. What the nay-sayers don't understand is that this election has never been about me. It's been about you."

In effect, ever alert and conscious of his emergence in trajectory of American electoral process, nominee Obama attributes the historic glory more to the American electors and indeed America that makes this a possibility. Obama's speech was made exactly 40 years Martin Luther King Jr made the prophetic 1,651 words/speech at the Lincoln Memorial Washington D.C. dramatizing "*a shameful condition*" of the blacks and spelling out a dream of redemption. It is to the eternal elegance and consensus-building orientation of Obama that he discusses King not in relations to the historic injustices of the past but in relations to King's definition of politics as hope and art of possibility and reconciliation. Without mentioning King's name he recalls the "preacher's (his word) admonition that realization of America's dream lies in unity regardless of colour adding that it should be forward ever, backward never:

> "We cannot walk alone", the preacher cried. "And as we walk, we must make the pledge that we shall always march ahead. We cannot turn back."

Simon Montefiore, the great chronicler of the world's speeches which "changed the world" writes that as "a rule, simplicity of language marks superb speechmaking, as with Mohammed, Jesus or Martin Luther King, and it helps when the orator has written the words himself." Yours sincerely bears witness that Obama's are printed words in simplicity and his ownership radically departs from the cold detached written speeches of Nigeria's "leaders". Again witness this verbal simplicity:

> "Our government should work for us, not against us. It should help us not hurt us. It should ensure opportunity not just for those with the

> most money and influence, but every America who is willing to work. That's the promise of America-the idea that we are responsible for ourselves but we also rise and fall as one."

Obama's speech is truly presidential in authority and content. He not only frontally takes head on John McCain and tasks him to a debate on his presidential resolve but he demonstrates that with best of efforts and intention on the part of his republican challenger, he simply "*does not know*" and even when he cares he "*does not get it*". This speech is remarkably issue-loaded and person-shy. It is full of details about energy independence, jobs, jobs, and jobs for Americans, investment retention, education and widening opportunities for all Americans, as well as tax equity. He celebrates his opponents both within and outside the party even while spelling out his policy disagreement. He singles out the two Clintons for recognitions even after the bitter contest of the recent weeks. The unparalleled appeal of Obama to bipartisanships of Republicans, Democrats and even Independents alike makes his patriotism and character virtues unassailable as a politician. It is intrusive that Iraq, Iran, Afghanistan and Europe (Georgia and Russia) feature in Obama's speech. May be acceptance speech does not say it all. Africa certainly does not feature in the 4000 plus word count. Middle East also features in relations to energy independence for the empire. Of course this is an American president (note American!) in waiting and not necessarily global president. He actually ends with *God Bless the United States of America* (note not necessarily the world) just like any American Presidents and America presidential hopefuls would end great speeches. Obama's is a recommended read for those who *can* and working for change.

Libya; Who Is Fooling Who?*

Last week visit of Miss Condoleezza Rice, US Secretary of States to Tripoli has once again renewed global media focus on Libya under the leadership of Muammar Al Gaddafi, (the author of the Green Book which spells out original alternative to the old West/East development paradigms). Which again brings us to a well-known open knowledge, according to which, the difference between the Western *sphere of influence* and the Western *media area of coverage* might not be as clear. Apparently the Big-Brother ubiquitous camera beams its search light to every corner of the globe, feverishly visited by high profile Western diplomats in search for you-know-it all, (*oil-nuclear weapons-terrorists-investment outlets, human rights, almost in that order*). Undoubtedly Miss Rice is the first Secretary of State to visit Tripoli since 1957 when Vice President Richard Nixon visited. But so what? What is the big deal about the Big Brother (is it "darling African sister" as Libyan leader flattered Rice) visiting the desert 50 years after *(even though President Ronald Reagan visited Tripoli with tornado of bombs in a 1989 mad cow raid of a "mad dog")?* For whatever Rice visit amounts to, it cannot be disputed that Libya has always been there in these past 50 years recording dramatic progress amidst sanctions, the most notable being the construction of the multi-million dollars Great Man Made River (GMR) water engineering project on earth!

In recent years, the global media had created an impression of return of Libya's Muammar Gaddafi to global arena following the dropping of UN sanctions in the wake of the earlier reported deal over the Lockerbie airplane bombing. Yet what we are witnessing daily are the massive in flocks of Western leaders and businessmen

---

* *Daily Trust*, 8th September 2008

alike to Tripoli. The traffic is in the direction of Tripoli and not the other way round. Who then is fooling who? Western leaders of note now scramble for photo-shots with Libyan Arab Jamahiriya leader. British Prime Minister, Tony Blair was in Tripoli in April 2004. Ostensibly this trip was to reward Libya for peacefully renouncing weapons of mass destruction in December last year. But political observers knew that Tony Blair (politically) that time needed Gaddafi more than the latter needed him after huge creditability crisis at home as a result of wholesome "sexing-up" of intelligence report (read: lying about Weapons of Mass Destruction, WMD, in Iraq) in a desperate bid to justify an unjust war in Iraq. A golden handshake with Gaddafi may convince (or is it confuse?) the British electorate that the "war on terror" was yielding some dividends. With the reopening of the American embassy in Tripoli the same year, it was self-evident that it was a matter of time before Washington chieftains would seek for a golden handshake with Gaddafi. Rice's visit to Tripoli must be seen in this perspective. It is the greatest paradox of Western democracies that democratically elected leaders feverishly fete else while 'terrorist' leader to ensure some democratic legitimacy at home.

The most far reaching of the harvest of visits was that of the Italian Prime Minister, Berlusconi. On 1st of September, as part of the 39th anniversary of Libyan revolution, Italy announced a deal of $5 billion compensation for Libyan occupation during Italian colonial rule. The deal in Benghazi was signed in the presence of over 1000 descendants of victims of Italian colonialism. While the speeches of Western leaders in Tripoli have dramatically altered from dictatorship and dominion to business and diplomacy, Gaddafi's rhetoric of independence and respect for African nations' sovereignty remain strident. He was not too eager to be "grateful" to Italy for paying so much as reparation for the pre-World War 1 colonial campaign of violence and brutality. On the contrary, Gaddafi recommended similar deal as precedent for other oppressed nations which were under colonialism. Similarly while Condoleezza Rice said US rapprochement with Libya underscores the principle that America cultivates no permanent enemies, Gaddafi insisted that Libya was not courting friendship at all costs but demanding to be "left alone".

While the pictures of visiting Western leaders capture imagination, the unreported flock of unanimous Western firms and investors elude observers. While for instance, Blair talked with Gaddafi Shell, Anglo Dutch oil giant company signed a business deal worth 550 million pounds for gas exploration. Libya expects as much as $35 billion worth of investment between 2003 to 2005 alone. US oil majors as well as European firms are all scrambling for Libya market.

Indeed Berlusconi's reply to the criticisms of the seemingly expensive pay-back deal with Libya is that the deal confers advantage for Italian firms to access Libyan gas which is in huge reserves.

Development in Tripoli shows that sanction imposed on Libya tended to have hit the "international community" no less than it undermined Libyan dynamic growth. Indeed with the frenzy to have a bite of the new Libyan cake by Western governments and firms alike, it was the world that missed Libya not the other way round.

Lessons from Libya are in legion for Africa. For one, the only thing constant in global diplomacy was permanent interest and not necessarily permanent friends or enemies. With millions of dollars in pay compensation for Lockerbie bombing and Libya's voluntary hand over of devices of its infant instruments of mass destruction, western hostility instantly turned to western hospitality. In market economies, there is price for everything including human lives.

Secondly, African leaders who blindly follow Western dictates should know that they hardly matter when the game is over. Both USA and Britain brought considerable pressures to bear on OAU (AU) members to isolate Libya when the UN sanctions lasted. The question is that how many of these dependent African leaders were again neither footnoted nor consulted when same Western leaders and businessmen are scrambling for new Libya? Indeed only Nelson Mandela then President of South Africa truly proved independent by bursting the so-called sanctions and travelled by road to Tripoli to register South African appreciation for the role of Libya in the struggle against Apartheid.

Lastly, Libya and Gaddafi have shown that the world will only accept us, Africans for what we insist we are and NOT necessarily what we are made to look like by others. Gaddafi the "terrorist" so defined by others has shown that he's simply a Libyan and African patriot wadding off expansionist policies of Europe and America at the risk of isolation and sanctions. In spite of the sanctions, Libya is top on the top on World development index with mass subsidized housing scheme, full literacy and mass free health scheme. Libya does not implement IMF or World Bank agenda, yet with developed social infrastructure, it is now an investment haven. At a time, Nigerian leaders globe trot the world ostensibly seeking for foreign investment, Libya shows that with good infrastructure, any country is an investment destination. At a time OBJ gave up on domestic refinery, Libya's refineries were functioning and its petro-chemical industry is alive. Libya is set to move from a non-cultural oil economy to a diversified economy with independent foreign policy. When will Nigerian leaders also take a trip to Tripoli now that those who once discouraged then from going are hitting the headlines with photo news in Tripoli?

USA, Once Upon an Election*

Tomorrow the Yankees go to polls and understandably the world is apprehensive about its outcome. Will the election for once duly certifies the incumbent George W. Bush (who in 2004 reportedly stole the presidency) or throw up a 'choice' in Senator John Kerry, the democratic challenger?

The bane of the American contest so far, is that we are faced more with who 'looks' or 'sounds' more Presidential between Gorge Bush and John Kerry than the differentiated vision and mission of the contestants. It is as if it is all a matter of public relations not public policies.

Of course there have been 'debates'. The 'debates' are however tall in forms than substance. Indeed there are no substantial differences between Kerry and Bush. Kerry is certainly different from Bush, but those yearning for regime change in Washington should know that Kerry is not Bill Clinton nor is he Jimmy Carter. The greatest paradox is that this election is driven by foreign policies but the policies are as foreign as they only affect United States and United States alone; namely Iraq, Al-Qaeda, Iran, North Korea (almost in that order). Indeed the issues are insularly foreign; globally American as it were. In the narrowly defined foreign issues, the difference between Kerry and Bush is the difference between six and half a dozen.

While Bush is unapologetically committed to unilateral bombing of Iraq from civilization to Stone Age, Kerry is for multilateral (UN) support for the same goal. In fact Senator Kerry voted for the very war. This means there is a bipartisan commitment to militarism and

---

* *Daily Trust*, 3rd November 2008

war as instruments of international diplomacy, the differences being in the methods of execution.

While Bill Clinton presidency envisioned an international social plan which could eradicate global poverty, (the recruitment base of terror), Kerry and Bush preferred bombing and killings (yes Presidential language) out of existence. Of course on Middle East the two candidates are as united to business as usual with respect to Israeli impunity. In an election in which the world is as involved as the American voters, we are yet to hear about the contestants' commitment to reforming UN, to the realisation of Millennium development goals (MDGs), eradicating the scourge of HIVS/AIDS, unfair global world trade and third world debt. In fact Bin Laden assumes special importance than all the above issues. Indeed, (Bin Laden) is both a person and issue such that he remains the only privileged 'outsider' (or is he an insider?) to 'address' American voters where Kofi Annan is a non-person.

As for Africa, throughout the debates, the *Dark Continent* was not mentioned by the contestants. The interviewers never asked the contestants either any question about how to pay reparations for slavery or cancel debts that has been more than paid for. Certainly nothing was said on NEPAD after scores of all the impressive photo clips of African leaders with G-8 leaders. Sorry. Africa was actually mentioned in the passing during the VP debates between Dick Cheney and John Edwards. The former accused the latter of non-eventful parliamentarian carrier. Edwards in return revealed how Cheney's achievements as a senator included voting against the motion urging American senate to press for the release of Nelson Mandela in the 1980s.

The point can therefore not be overemphasised; Africans who are yearning for changes of policies following tomorrow's elections must be modest to settle for either revalidation (God forbids) of incumbent Bush or election of a new candidate but certainly not new policies as such.

Ghana Election: Too Close To Matter?*

Kofis (next door Ghana) go to poll next Sunday, 7th of December. Yet we carry on in Nigeria as if the historic political event in this great country of our sub-region does not matter at all. Of course a country that is enmeshed in Mutually Assured Self-Destruction (MAD) as we sadly again witnessed during the weekend Jos political violence might possibly not be endowed with the luxury of some reflection about a distant election in Accra. And that's precisely the issue! Just because 2008 Nigeria, (decades after colonial Nigeria conducted free local polls in which Herbert Macauley won!) is incapable of conducting simple local government election or worse still, that under our very nose, political stalemate degenerated into burning of churches and mosques and mass burials, the more reason we must be concerned about how Ghanaians conduct polls without mass burials, our very shameless regular electoral trade mark.

Even at this eleventh hour in which candidates are rounding up their campaigns, yours truly searches in vain in Nigeria's print and electronic media for a discernable perspective on Ghana's electoral process. It is a scandal that a continent in which media coverage of unhelpful details about America's presidential primaries and presidential election could fill tons of some *Ghana-must-go bags*, there is very little space for elections next door that have more impact and direct relevance to us. Ghana's black out (as it were) compares with African media under-reportage of the recent Zambia's presidential election in which the acting President Rupian Banda won, an election that took place almost same time American election held and at a

---

* *Daily Trust*, 1st December 2008

time we were inundated with petty details about Obama and McCain but less about President Rupian and his formidable challenger, Michael Sata. It further underscores media imperialism in which it is what is news to Uncle Sam that is the news to Africans.

The point cannot be overstated! The political events in Ghana have more relevance to Africa and Africans than the events in Washington. Our political charity turns into political hypocrisy or worse still, political folly, if it does not start at home. Yours sincerely is scandalized to hear and read that "*Obama victory in America gives hope that black people can make it.*" "*Obama raises hope that our continent can be fixed.*" *Haba* Africans! For one, the half white-man president-elect of the United States of America who was abandoned by an African father has never said he was a Black Presidential candidate. He possibly paraded his maternal lineage more. Nor has his campaign centred on fixing Africa's problems either no less than he has unapologetically declared to reinvent America (not Africa) under the spell of economic stagnation and moral abyss. Indeed Barak Obama won the historic election in spite of race chain we uncharitable put on his neck. Secondly to say that free and fair election which produces Obama is the singular thing to happen to Africans is to assume rather hopelessly that Africans have never merited in fair process. Nothing could be more ahistorical and certainly misleading.

Indeed Ghana (past and present) and not necessarily Obama's America (with all its current sexual appeal) gives more hope to Africa and Africans. Indeed Ghana's history and present reality prove that Africa can be fixed. The late Julius Nyerere of Tanzania once observed that: "Ghana was the beginning, our first liberated zone. Thirty –seven years later-in 1994-we celebrated our final triumph when Apartheid was crushed and Nelson Mandela was installed as the president of South Africa." Ghana won Independence in 1957, (a decade before Martin Luther King made the prophetic speech about the "Dream"). But that was after series of struggles and pressures led by late Dr Nkrumah, a "prophet" imprisoned several times by the British. Mandela noted that the events of 1957 in Accra which led to the historic pulling down of the Union Jack and its replacement with Ghana flag were sources of inspiration against Apartheid. Many have rightly venerated pastor King's dream speech, but the first dream speech was that of Nkrumah who prophetically declared that: "Our independence is meaningless unless it is linked up to the total liberation of the African continent." Since that historic speech colonialism has been defeated from Cairo to Cape Town. It is an open knowledge how the combined destructive forces of corrupt Generals (Ankrah, Afrifa, Akuffo, Acheampong - in that order decadence) ruined Nkrumah's enterprise. But the dramatic resurgence of Ghana from the ashes of deafening collapse of the 1980s to amazing recovery in the 1990s to 2000 shows that indeed Africa and Africans had made it well before current Obama's consolidation in faraway America.

The issue at stake here is that a presidential election will be held in Ghana on 7 December 2008, at the same time as a parliamentary election. This singular election holds promise for West African democratic renaissance and regional stability than Obama's election in America. This is 16th year of robust uninterrupted democratic. This is the 5th of the unfettered election since multi-party democracy. While Nigeria marks a controversial one time power transfer from one elected leader to another, Ghana is set to have a second run. *Eight candidates have been registered formally by the Electoral Commission of Ghana for the December 7 elections.* They emerged in robust inrenal democratic processes compared to Nigeria's *carry-go* regimentation. Witness this: former Vice-President John Atta-Mills, who unsuccessfully ran as the National Democratic Congress (NDC) presidential candidate in 2000 and 2004 was overwhelmingly elected by NDC as its candidate for the 2008 presidential election with a majority of 81.4%, or 1,362 votes. Ekwow Spio-Garbrah was second with 8.7% (146 votes), Alhaji Mahama Iddrisu was third with 8.2% (137 votes), and Eddie Annan was fourth with 1.7% (28 votes). Former Foreign Minister Nana Addo Dankwa Akufo-Addo was elected as the 2008 presidential candidate of the governing New Patriotic Party (NPP) at a party congress on December 23, 2007, receiving 47.96% of valid votes (1,096 votes). Although he fell short of the required 50%, the second-place candidate, John Alan Kyeremanten, conceded defeat and backed Akufo-Addo. Others are Paa Kwesi Nduom of the CPP and Edward Mahama of the People's National Convention (PNC), Emmanuel Ansah-Antwi of the

Democratic Freedom Party (DFP), Thomas Ward-Brew of the Democratic People's Party (DPP) and Kwamena Adjei of the Reformed Patriotic Democrats (RPD) and an independent candidate, Kwesi Amoafo-Yeboah. The strength of Ghana's process is that the three leading candidates in robust debates focus on issues which include diversification of Ghana's economy and on how to avoid the pitfall of Nigeria's oil tragedy. The leading candidates parade intimidating credentials, being the hallmark Ghana's human capital, a country that occupies medium rug of United Nations Human Development Index. But the real threat to next week election is the increasing crisis of confidence with the Electoral Commission by the politicians especially the opposition. Our prayer is that the Ghanaians will not tread the discredited paths of Nigeria and Kenya in which flawed elections end in votes not being counted but innocent bodies being buried after which dubious power deals are worked out among politicians. The notorious images of burnt bodies and mayhems in Governor Jonah Jang's Plateau state after last week local government election are not worthy of emulation by the Ghanaians. Happy polls Accra!

Again Ghana Proves That Africans Can*

"Freedom and Justice"-Ghana's national motto

"Ghana was the beginning, our first liberated zone. Thirty –seven years later-in 1994-we celebrated our final triumph when Apartheid was crushed and Nelson Mandela was installed as the president of South Africa"- *Late Julius Nyerere, President of Tanzania*

"I assure Ghanaians that I will be President for all"- *John Atta-Mills-Ghana President elect and Opposition Candidate*

As stories of political despair from West Africa (from the military meddlesomeness in Mauritania and Guinea Conakry to complete degeneration of simple local government election into "religious" crisis in Nigeria's Jos), hit the headlines, it is gratifying that serial news of hope of democratic consolidation and sustainability keep coming from Accra, Ghana. The weekend successful conclusion of Presidential election in Ghana which recorded a narrow win of opposition candidate, Attah Mills (50.23%) over the ruling party candidate, Nana Akuffo Ado (49.77%) in a run-off election points to the fact that Africa and Africans are rich and tested in democratic traditions.

The point cannot point cannot be overstated! The political events in Ghana are of profound relevance to Africa and Africans than the events in Washington which remarkably too on January 20th mark the historic inauguration of the 44th President of United States of America (USA) and indeed the first African-American to be in a White House. Our political charity turns into political hypocrisy or worse still, political folly, if it does not start at our regional backyard. Yours sincerely has always been scandalized to hear and read that

* *Daily Trust* (Monday, January 5, 2009)

"Obama victory in America gives hope that black people can make it." "Obama raises hope that our continent can be fixed." For one, the half white-man president-elect of the United States of America has never said he was a Black Presidential candidate. He possibly paraded his maternal lineage more. Nor has his campaign centred on fixing Africa's problems either no less than he has unapologetically declared to reinvent America (not Africa) under the spell of economic stagnation and melt down. Indeed Barak Obama won the historic election in spite of race chain we uncharitable put on his neck. Secondly to say that free and fair election which produces Obama is the singular thing to happen to Africans is to assume rather hopelessly that Africans have never merited in fair and open process. Nothing could be more ahistorical and certainly misleading.

As far as Africans are concerned the *Man (and Woman) of the Year* is the anonymous Ghanaian voter who resisted temptations of least resistance of dysfunctional violence, persevered to cast votes more than twice (December 7th, December 28th and Friday 2nd of January 2009 in-that-order). He or she is the *Person of the year* who insisted that votes should count at polling centres (compared to Nigeria's law courts or Zimbabwe's ruining party headquarters!) and came out with remarkable democratic outcomes that indicate that there is a real democratic contest in Africa's election (50.23% / 49.77%!) compared to the celebrated Obama's landslide in America. Ghana's electoral outcome raises the nostalgia of the historic role of Ghana 52 years ago when Nkrumah and his compatriots for the first time in the continent raised the banner of independence against British colonialism. This election has once again shattered into smithereens the myth of Afro-democratic pessimism. Will Ghana's weekend electoral victory once again set into motion series of democratic resistance in the continent that will put an end to budding and incipient discredited dictatorships in West Africa in particular and Africa as a whole?

Ghana (past and present) gives more hope to Africa and Africans. Ghana's history and present reality prove that Africa can be fixed. Ghana won Independence in 1957, (a decade before Martin Luther King made the prophetic speech about the "Dream"). But that was after series of struggles and pressures led by late Dr

Nkrumah, imprisoned several times by the British. Mandela noted that the events of 1957 in Accra which led to the historic pulling down of the Union Jack and its replacement with Ghana flag were sources of inspiration against Apartheid. Many have rightly venerated pastor King's dream speech, but the first dream speech was that of Nkrumah who prophetically declared that: "*Our independence is meaningless unless it is linked up to the total liberation of the African continent*". Since that historic speech colonialism has been defeated from Cairo to Cape Town. It is an open knowledge how the combined destructive forces of corrupt Generals (Ankrah, Afrifa, Akuffo, Acheampong-in that-order-decadence) ruined Nkrumah's enterprise. But the dramatic resurgence of Ghana from the ashes of deafening collapse of the 80s to amazing recovery in the 1990s to 2000 shows that indeed Africa and Africans could.

The outcomes of this singular election hold promise for West African democratic renaissance and regional stability. For one this is 17th year of robust uninterrupted democratic dispensation. This is the 5th of the unfettered elections since multi-party democracy. While Nigeria marks a controversial one time power transfer from one "elected" leader to another, Ghana had successfully had a second run. *Eight candidates contested the elections.* They emerged in robust internal democratic processes compared to Nigeria's *carry-go* regimentation. Witness this: former Vice-President John Atta-Mills, who unsuccessfully ran as the National Democratic Congress (NDC) presidential candidate in 2000 and 2004 was overwhelmingly elected by NDC as its candidate for the 2008 presidential election with a majority of 81.4%, or 1,362 votes. Ekwow Spio-Garbrah was second with 8.7% (146 votes), Alhaji Mahama Iddrisu was third with 8.2% (137 votes), and Eddie Annan was fourth with 1.7% (28 votes). Former Foreign Minister Nana Addo Dankwa Akufo-Addo was elected as the 2008 presidential candidate of the governing New Patriotic Party (NPP) at a party congress on December 23, 2007, receiving 47.96% of valid votes (1,096 votes). Although he fell short of the required 50%, the second-place candidate, John Alan Kyeremanten, conceded defeat and backed Akufo-Addo. Others are Paa Kwesi Nduom of the CPP and Edward Mahama of the People's National Convention (PNC), Emmanuel Ansah-Antwi of the

Democratic Freedom Party (DFP), Thomas Ward-Brew of the Democratic People's Party (DPP) and Kwamena Adjei of the Reformed Patriotic Democrats (RPD) and an independent candidate, Kwesi Amoafo-Yeboah. The strength of Ghana's process is that the leading candidates in robust debates focused on issues and issues alone such as diversification of Ghana's economy and measures to avoid the pitfall of Nigeria's oil tragedy. Ghana just discovered oil! The leading candidates also paraded intimidating credentials, being the hallmark Ghana's human capital, a country that occupies medium rug of United Nations Human Development Index. It was a mark of enhanced human political capital that the defeated candidate congratulated the winner while the winner sounded less triumphant but measured and inclusive; Attah Mills says he's "a President for All"! Ghana has passed the acid test that the run-off will engender crisis of confidence in the Electoral Commission. It is to the eternal glory of the Ghanaians that they did not tread the discredited paths of Nigeria and Kenya of flawed elections, the notorious metaphors included "annulment", "rigging", "ballot snatching", endless litigations, "power sharing" and the recent notorious images of burnt bodies and mayhems in Governor Jonah Jang's Plateau state after a local government "election". Long Live Ghanaian democracy!

Obama: Once Upon an Inauguration*

"I am comfortable in my own skin"-*Barack Obama*

True to global excitement, President-elect Barack Obama would be sworn in as the 44th President of United States of America (USA) tomorrow. Never before has a singular inauguration captured popular imagination as that of Barack Obama who becomes the first African American CEO of the most powerful corporate country on earth! Not even the cynical, criminal and clearly diversionary Israeli's campaign of attrition and annihilation in Gaza undermines the significance of tomorrow's historic earth shaking events in Washington. No Presidential hopeful has been so much debated in relations to his forms and appearances than his substance. He was certainly born black but not few African Americans think he was not "black" enough (read: not having root in slavery ancestry and the attendant misery). Conversely the conservative racist Americans doubt his "whiteness" (read: business as usual) and question his patriotism altogether. In his book, *Audacity of Hope,* Obama recalls the "cruder broadsides" of the smear campaign according to which his names were twisted to read "Osama Obama". In all this, elegant Barack replied "*let them have their fun*" adding that name-calling "is not such a bad deal". Even the intellectual capital that ought to be a political asset was nearly made a liability for the President elect. Though a tested community organizer, not a few still interrogate his Harvard pedigree and intellectual eloquence to doubt whether he can truly connect with ordinary folks and initiate do-able pragmatic policy proposals.

---

* *Daily Trust* (Monday, January 19, 2009)

Tomorrow's inauguration will certainly put paid to appearances and will make us face up to the real substance of Obama's presidency. Sadly Africans and indeed Nigerians are more romantic rather than being realistic with the historic Presidency. Even those who shamelessly deny Africans the benefits of change (free and free elections, electricity, water, roads, ad infinitum) that democracy promises in abundance hypocritically celebrate Obama ascendancy as symbol of change. Just witness Mousier Olusegun Obasanjo on *"Obama's Election and the Needed Change*" (his cheeky words!) ; according to him: "The feeling of change that Senator Obama engender through his campaign for the White House represents a significant theme of change we have all aspired and fought for in different cultures, areas, culture and historic times." *Haba!* Only Maurice Iwu and other "do" or "die" foot soldiers/ co collaborators of Chief Obasanjo can edit that above printed words of mischievous ownership of Obama's theme of change by well-known apostle of status quo (read: third term) and entrenched vested interests!

It is remarkable therefore seeing Nigerians of varying hues (high and low) eagerly preparing for tomorrow's inauguration (not the way they were loudly indifferent to next door Ghana's in January this year!). Understandably Obama proves a handy therapy given that some of our votes in 2007 polls are still being counted in courts, a tribute to Obasanjo's cheeky celebration of Obama's theme of change. Nigerians and Africans must realise that with the best of expressions of interest and passion our votes did not produce tomorrow's outcome. Not even the dubious feverish /bullish activism of Ndi Okereke-Onyiuke- led Nigeria Stock Exchange (NSE) desperately raising unsolicited funds (long disowned) for the campaign mattered in the final election of Senator Obama as the President of United States. This truism must task our imagination on how we must engage Obama presidency.

What policy initiatives are we bringing to the table to make sure that Africa matters for the better in global affairs? Or what value will Africa add to make Obama's presidency truly historic and does not engender another Afro-pessimism?

May be the inaugural speech tomorrow will feature Africa but his nomination acceptance was Africa-shy. Iraq, Iran, Afghanistan and Europe (Georgia and Russia) feature in Obama's nomination acceptance speech, a speech that was truly Presidential in content and delivery. May be acceptance speech does not say it all. Africa certainly does not feature in the 4000 plus word count. Middle East also features in relations to energy independence for the empire. Of course tomorrow's inauguration is for an American president (note: American, not African-American!) not even necessarily global president. He actually will end his speech with *God Bless the United States of America* (note not necessarily the world) just like any American Presidents in the past. All hail the 44th President of USA!

Obama: New Washington Consensus*

Professor Bolaji Akinyemi's serial thoughts and reflections on Barack Obama's candidature and eventual presidency are worthy printed words to keep. The essays add up to some timely quality control of the quantitative global media items on President Obama. The latest: *"Obama: What next for the world and Africa* (*Guardian* 23rd January 2009) however has more heuristic value. "The Obama In Us And The Us In Obama" (*Guardian* 1st November 2008) with all its usefulness and inclusive interpretation of "US", comes out as an abridged version of the very same unhelpful race/ identity/tribal political discourse which Obama courageously and rightly puts into dustbin of history thanks to inclusive campaigns and triumphant presidency:

> "A victory for Obama will be the ultimate catharsis in purging the African race (Arabs are not really regarded as Africans) of the stigma of slavery". "The election of Obama rather than what he does in office is the ultimate victory". "An Obama victory will be the ultimate reparation (compensation").

Haba Prof! Despite these outlandish alluring lines, a day after Obama's historic inauguration, global Monuments dedicated to the eternal memory of the despicable trade in Africans, are still standing. And the struggle for reparation continues even if African patriots, like Moshood Abiola are endangered species. Nothing would ever obliterate Walter Rodney's thesis on how *Europe underdeveloped Africa* through hundreds of years of Trans-Atlantic Slave trade and colonialism (*in-that-order-of- devastation*!). UNESCO estimates that Africa lost as many as 20millions human resource to slavery by

* *The Guardian* (Monday, February 9, 2009)

"*Peddlers of human flesh*". Obama's ascendancy as the first "African American" President (he has rightly not described himself as such) heightens the noise level of slavery, does not diminish its historic significance. We are reminded of the endurance of the "*lash of the whip*" and those who "*ploughed the hard earth*", making the point that his victory was far from being some *catharsis.* Obama happily puts on hold the tele-humiliation of Guatanama Bay and saves humanity from the daily spectacle of humans in chains on legs and hands in the 21st century (not necessarily necks like dogs when Africans journeyed with terror in the 15th century). America once again *truly leads.* It instantly transforms the notorious image of a Rogue nation under George W. Bush to a refurbished moral power.

Please let's not rig the issues, a la Nigeria! US presidential election is neither about slavery nor reparation, nor African/ Arab races! Obama is the first statesman in recent times to uplift the spirit in a bitterly divisive world: "… *old hatreds shall someday pass;… lines of tribe shall soon dissolve;"*! For the American voters that singular election was about American *economy, economy and economy*, war and peace, energy independence. And when you look at the depth of Bush's rot, we dare not talk of victory yet until Obama delivers on promise. Too much of writings about Obama from Africa are unduly passionately romantic about some "horse-race" stories which inadvertently step-down his singular political achievement to some affirmative actions by some American "good society". Nothing could be more unhelpful.

Often we ignore the substance of his political ideas articulated in his manifesto (*Audacity of Hope)*, 2004 DNC speech, 2008 nomination acceptance speeches and above all, January 20th inaugural speech! We judge a landmark political enterprise based on colour (*is he white or black enough*?), his "*small frame*" as distinct from "*the content of his character*". The race bandwagon is convenient in a continent of conveniences. "*US*" paradoxically is inclusive of those whose public times and lives are antitheses to Obama's political agenda: from scandalous feverish "Obama fund raisers" (or are they money launderers?) to those who deny genuine political changes while in public office.

Witness the political hypocrisy inherent in Mousier Olusegun Obasanjo's advertised word-overload: *"Obama's election and the needed change"* or the loud unspoken words of "*Basket mouth*" Robert Mugabe of Zimbabwe about Obama's presidency. "Change" on their feet! What have Obama's ideas and ideals had to do with this cabal multitude that sit tight and politically suffocate their peoples including an audacity to annul free and fair elections without apology?

Akinyemi recommends Obama's Economic stimulus plan for Nigeria. Good enough! Precisely because Obama's New Deal mirrors the worsening Africa's crisis it is definitely misleading to say: "*The election of Obama rather than what he does in office is the ultimate victory.*"

We compare *like* with *unlike* when we say that "*..America and Nigeria face similar problems*". It's another "*follow-follow/colonial mentality* (apology to Fela). We glamorise new slavery to say "*More than at anytime in recent history, an American President may in fact be the solution to economic problems in Nigeria*"! America is in crisis but Nigeria has always been in crisis of greater proportions. Indeed the military regime Akinyemi served as foreign Minister was no less a crisis regime than successive ones that improved on the crisis. And that was two and half decades ago! Our mix-bag heritage, (not necessarily Obama presidency), shows that Nigerian economy once delivered on promises. Check out the developmentalist/democratic regional governments and national development plans of the 60s, 70s and even up to early 1980s. Akinyemi openly accepts that unemployment and collapsed factories are symptomatic of deep seated crisis. Perhaps Obama's open acceptance of the depth of the crisis in USA and transparency is robbing on us to say the obvious. Nigeria's officialdom however is still in denials. After accepting that "*Homes have been lost; jobs shed; businesses shuttered*", Obama tasks Americans to rise to the "*challenges*" *that "are real, "serious" and "many" but will nonetheless be "be met"*. We await similar official star words of confessions and rededication from Abuja. In the face of mounting mass unemployment (45 per cent!) and gross underemployment (*okada* riders!), persistent power failure, low capacity utilization (about 25 per cent national average), mass smuggling (cargo/containers economy!), double digit inflation/interest rates, falling prices of crude oil, collapsed share prices, factory closures, run-down external reserves (by 10 billion in a month!) and Naira devaluation (50 per cent in two months!), CBN still acts the legendary ostrich. Washington's televised constructive engagement is about Economic Stimulus plan. The wars of attrition from Abuja are about revenue sharing (2009 budget!), *co-chairmanship* (endless constitution-reviews) and *business as usual* official indulgences (*serial advertised state weddings).* Granted we elect to join Obama train, please lets know that it is another paradigm shift altogether.

The old Washington Consensus/neo-liberal toolkit we uncritically swallowed via the notorious IMF/ World bank SAP pills, is too familiar. Devil is in its details: *privatiztion, downsizing, lean governance, glorification of capital market and assault on labour markets and unilateral/partisan politics that imposes terror and wars on a global scale.*

Obama's new Washington Consensus happily lashes out at "*worn out dogmas*". The " *question….is not whether our government is too big or too small, but whether it works*"

Not few of my compatriots (*Gani Fahemihins, Hassan Sunmonus, Professor Alukos, Ali Chiromas, Dr Ayagis, Femi Falanas, Dotun Philips, Adams Oshiomholes*) have long sounded familiar like Obama. Paradoxically, discredited regime of TINA (*There Is No Alternative*) Akinyemi faithfully served not only ignored our *Obamas* but had the audacity of meanness to hound them. The new Washington Consensus acknowledges that we might very well forgive but we dare not forget.

Obama: 100 Days That Reshape the World*

True to global excitement, on January 20th President-elect Barack Obama was sworn in as the 44th President of United States of America (USA). On Wednesday this week, it will be 100 days of eventful governance that daily reshapes our world. Never before has a singular inauguration captured popular imagination as that of Barack Obama who became the first African American CEO of the most powerful corporate country on earth! Not even the cynical, criminal and clearly diversionary Israeli's campaign of attrition and annihilation in Gaza on the eve of inauguration undermined the significance of the historic earth shaking January events in Washington. No Presidential hopeful had been so much debated in relations to his forms and appearances than his substance. He was certainly born black but not few African Americans thought he was not "black" enough (read: not having root in slavery ancestry and the attendant misery). Conversely the conservative racist Americans doubt his "whiteness" and questioned his patriotism altogether.

Even the intellectual capital, a political asset was nearly made a liability for the President-elect. Though a tested community organizer, not a few still interrogated his Harvard pedigree and intellectual eloquence to doubt whether he can truly connect with ordinary folks and initiate do-able pragmatic policy proposals.

100 days after, yours sincerely bears witness that Obama is rich in substance than the forms ascribed to him by the global media. Indeed true to Martin Luther King's dream, we can now judge

---

* *Daily Trust*, 27th April 2009

Obama based on the rich "content of his character" rather than the colour of his skin.

Obama presidency has definitely brought about an unprecedented paradigm shift in governance world-wide. He has somewhat steered our globe from the brink of catastrophe of Bush terror-tenure to a much more sensitive, war-shy, less-trigger excited world. Of course human wastages continue in Afghanistan no less than in Sri-Lankan. Darfur still remains a metaphor for genocide no less than Somalia is a failed state. There is even renewed deadly insurgency in Iraq. The beauty of Obama presidency as a global power, however is that these flash spots of bullets and sorrows are not to be celebrated. There is a programme of withdrawal from Iraq. Obama's hailed triumphant entry to Iraq contrasts sharply with shoe-slammed miserable Bush! Obama envisions a world free of nuclear weapons of Mutually Assured Destruction (MAD) in his historic speech in Prague, notwithstanding the weapon proliferations. If there is the will, there will be the ways.

In his augural speech, he reminded the world about the torture and human humiliation that characterized Trans-Atlantic: the endurance of the "*lash of the whip*" and those who "*plowed the hard earth*". True to his commitment to human values, Obama happily orders the termination of the tele-humiliation of Guantanamo Bay and saves humanity from the daily spectacle of humans in chains on legs and hands in the 21st century (not necessarily necks like dogs when Africans journeyed with terror in the 15th century). America for once again *truly leads*. Obama instantly transforms the notorious image of a Rogue nation under George W. Bush to a refurbished moral power. The recently ordered published memos of authorised serial tortures of suspects on the Island shows that by naming it, America might shame torture and its promoters, the notorious chieftain of which is shameless former Vice President Dick Cheney.

The America's election that produced Obama was about the *economy, economy and economy*. Indeed coming on the heel of global economic crisis, the apprehension was how Obama would lead the world and not just USA out of global recession. The world is certainly not out of the wood, but it's not getting worse either as Obama brings to bear activist state governance to rescue the global market from itself. The Obama administration definitely faces a crisis in the housing bubble, securitization, bank failures and the leveraging and borrowing previously done by banks. But it's no more business as usual as he rolls out unprecedented trillion dollars Stimulus plans reminiscent of Roosevelt New Deal of the 1930s. He restores confidence in America's presidency terribly diminished by Bush.

Obama's financial, monetary and fiscal stimulation to alleviate the recession has proved handy and contagious in Europe and Asia. Indeed the Obama's stimulus package provides the conceptual framework for G-20 meeting in London recently.

The strong point of Obama is his remarkable engagement with the world as an informed no bar liberated free global partner rather than notorious ill-informed global bully. Witness his historic speech in Turkey. The global media dubbed this speech "a conversion with Islam" as if Islam or Christianity is geography bound. That singular speech, (rich in history) contains practical proposals for new-globalization. But if Obama's America reshapes the world, is the world really changing?

In Africa, Obama paradoxically remains a brand (ala Nigeria) rather than euphemism for substantial changes. Even at this hour, we are still counting votes in Ekiti with tears and tension. Fuel scarcity, power failure, corruption, economic shut down, kidnappings convey the image of Changes for worse without changes for better, even when Obama shows that YES WE CAN for the best. Many thanks to Ghanaians (they actually had free and fair elections before Obama was sworn in) and South Africans, who have made the point that Africans are not just spectators in the last 100 days!

President Zuma: Once Upon an Inauguration*

"In my country we go to prison first and then become President."-
Nelson Mandela

Last Saturday, the fourth President of the democratic Republic of South Africa, Mr Jacob Zuma took the oath of office. President Umaru Musa Yar'Adua was there among other thirty plus Heads of government. What bagful of lessons does President Yar'Adua bring from Pretoria? Posing this question alone raises further questions about the persistent political underdevelopment of Nigeria. History shows that indeed it is South Africa that has a lot to learn from Nigeria and not the other way round. As far back as 1960, at independence, Nigeria was democratically governed with vibrant political parties and notable political leaders in their own right. As at then, the likes of icon Nelson Mandela were groaning under Apartheid dictatorship, the most inhuman contraption that brutalized and exploited for decades on account of colour. Nigeria was among the notable front line states that included Tanzania, Zambia, Zimbabwe, and Mozambique which fought for the liberation of South Africa from the clutches of Apartheid, understandably, Abuja was the first point of call in Mandela's historic global appreciation tours in the 1990s. South Africa's Çonstitution has been repeatedly singled out as the most progressive governance documents in recent times. But the point cannot be overstated: SA's constitution draws heavily on Nigeria's 1977 constitution especially with reference to

---

* *Daily Trust* (Monday, May 11, 2009)

how to manage a diversity and multi racialism via Federalism. However all the above add up to history.

Today 15 years, South Africa has dramatically advanced politically with four successful globally acclaimed democratic transition elections and four Presidents in smooth, quick, consensual and acceptable ways, namely Nelson Mandela, Thabo Mbeki, Kgalema Motlanthe and now Jacob Zuma. South Africa proves right the dated observation of Arch Bishop Desmond Tutu according to which "*South Africa, so utterly improbable, is a beacon of hope in a dark and troubled world.*"

Will Zuma's ascendancy wake Nigeria up from its intolerable and clearly unacceptable political slumber? Zuma's presidency assumes a special importance. It puts to test all the democratic institutions of the country, from the judiciary to the Independent Electoral Commission. But it is to the eternal glory of SA's democratic process that it overcomes all the critical challenges. Run up to the election, Zuma was slammed with corruption/rape charges clearly timed to undermine his political credentials. Unceremoniously he resigned on the 14th of June 2005 as the Deputy President of the Republic. SA's judiciary lived to popular expectation by dismissing the corruption charges as politically motivated. The robust contestation within the ANC pressured Mbeki to untimely resignation as the President leading to the emergence of Motlanthe. For as long as the partisan bickering lasted, the Independent Electoral Commission of SA remains truly independent. The Commission not only conducted the elections but counted the votes which saw the retrenchment of incumbent break away COPE of Mbeki and recorded the success of ANC's flag bearer Zuma. It is a sad commentary that while SA navigates successfully though the political land mines Nigeria is weighed down with inconclusive state election re-run in Ekiti which reveals conquest rather than contest. The lessons of SA are remarkable. First is the triumph of civility in SA as distinct from entrenchment of Nigeria's militarism. The serial resignations of Zuma and Mbeki in the wake of the controversial corruption charges indicate that political actors subject themselves to political institutions in SA. Also worthy of note is that political contestation in SA is issue-based notwithstanding the visibility of individuals. Mbeki was accused of excessive neo-liberal economics that has undoubtedly recorded growth for South African economy but left many South Africans in poverty and deprivations. Zuma rose to power on the crest of popular agitation to reconcile South Africans in the tradition of Nelson Mandela as well as focus on education, health, land reform, combat crimes and ensure decent work. Pray with all the bloodletting in Ekiti re-rerun, what are the issues electorate were called upon to choose from? Certainly none! In place of issues in Ekiti state, we were inundated with intimidating actors that include non-electoral agents like police and the army! Nigeria must urgently reinvent its democracy that must start with free and fair elections. This calls for patriotic (Not partisan) leaders who must look at the global picture of strengthening democracy rather than narrow interest of their parties and their persons in power. Notwithstanding the bitterness that characterize SA's campaign it is remarkable seeing at inauguration Zuma, Mbeki his bitter rival. Zuma's inaugural speech is a compulsory read for our leaders in the art of statesmanship and patriotism.

After celebrating Madiba, for "showing us the way" in national reconciliation, he dutifully acknowledged the former second Deputy President of the democratic republic, the Hon FW de Klerk, who according to him "worked with Madiba in the resolution of the Apartheid conflict, and participated in shaping a new South Africa".

He then went to salute former President Mbeki: "as a true statesman" (his words) who made "a remarkable contribution towards strengthening our democracy, and laid a firm foundation for economic growth and development."

According to Zuma, in his last address to the nation Mbeki "demonstrated his patriotism, and put the interests of the country above his personal interests." Pray when will Nigeria's politicians have the audacity to acknowledge the strengths of their opponents in the great task of nation building?

Obama's Speech in Cairo*

"...the interests we share as human beings are far more powerful than the forces that drive us apart..."

"...moral leadership is more powerful than any weapon."

- President Obama

June 4, 2009 commemorative speech of President Barack Obama at Cairo University (co-hosted by Al-Azhar University), continues to capture global imagination than the state functions he undertook during his equally historic June 3 trip to Riyadh, Saudi Arabia. It would be recalled that the Obama had consultations with King Abdullah on issues including the Middle East peace process, energy and terrorism. But score of thematic issues contained in Obama's speech in Cairo dominate global discourse than bilateral deals in the region. Never in recent times are global agenda ably set by thought provoking word counts of the President of United States of America! In April in a major speech in Prague before a 20,000 multitude he envisions a world free of nuclear weapons. That singular speech certainly did not stop Pyongyang's nuclear test which was audaciously done same morning Obama delivered the very speech. One thing is however clear: recent U.N. Security Council's unanimous loud condemnation of North Korea's latest nuclear test flows in the main from Obama's persuasive speech in Prague about the danger of globalization of weapons of mass annihilation. In his first trip "overseas as President of the United States" it was again Obama's speech rather than his state activities in Turkey that dominated the global discourse. What then therein in Obama's speeches which hunt the world like a spectre? A Moroccan proverb has it that: "The

* *Daily Trust* (Monday, June 15, 2009)

speech of a man which is beautiful and understood is better than the speech of a thousand mouths that is not." Obama's speech in Cairo is undoubtedly beautiful and understood and worthies reading again and again. Which explains why it elicited unprecedented rounds and rounds of spontaneous applauses, in sharp contrasts to President Bush's Iraqis speech, which provoked historic spontaneous indignation, via historic shoe-throwing. True to character, President Barack Obama audaciously pushes on with the agenda for global renaissance anchored on mutual respect and global partnership as distinct from hitherto patronage and dependency that characterized relations between USA and others. Again this singular speech brings to the fore the character virtues of the 44th President of United States. Almost instantly, (thanks to Obama's wisdom!) the world is being rescued from the unhelpful dogmas of "Clash of fundamentalisms" which assume notoriety in "crusade" and "Jihadist" or even "modernity" binary discourse to something refreshingly new: harmony of civilizations and unity of human purpose. The global media dubbed Obama's speech as "dialogue with Islamic world". That is clearly misleading. Obama's speech in Cairo is aptly seen as *Dialogue with humanity* given the all- inclusive messages contained therein. At the last count, yours truly identifies the following subjects in Obama's 6000 plus word count: Development, freedom and democracy, interfaith dialogue, education, science and development, history and Development, youth and women, Palestine Israeli conflict, nuclear proliferation, war and peace, Afghanistan and terrorism. All the above subjects are not Arab or Islam specific as the global media caption them but of profound interest to contemporary humanity.

One recurring theme in Obama's speeches whether in Prague, Ankara or Cairo is that what eventual binds humanity together is weightier than what divides us. One binding factor is history! For instance, we are reminded that Morocco, an Islamic developing country was "the first nation" to recognise USA after its war of independence from Britain. Since one historic good turn deserves another, Obama as a proud student of history shows that in signing the Treaty of Tripoli in 1796, America's second President, John Adams, wrote,

> "The United States has in itself no character of enmity against the laws, religion or tranquillity of Muslims."

Some food for thought for those who permanently erect Berlin Wall between Islam and the world! For the demagogues who profit from hatred and divide Obama reminded his audience that Islam is also part of American heritage .Witness this: "American Muslims have enriched the United States. They have fought in our wars; they have served in our government."

Obama is not only comfortable in his skin but his multiple identities and indeed in the two holy books. Again witness this:

> "I'm a Christian, but my father came from a Kenyan family that includes generations of Muslims.
> As a boy, I spent several years in Indonesia and heard the call of the azaan at the break of dawn and at the fall of dusk. As a young man, I worked in Chicago communities where many found dignity and peace in their Muslim faith."

For the medieval Taliban (and if you like) modern day Maitasines, who want to return to the despicable mediocrity, masquerading as Islamic, we are reminded of "civilization's debt to Islam" which "paved the way for Europe's Renaissance and Enlightenment".

> "It was innovation in Muslim communities that developed the order of algebra; our magnetic compass and tools of navigation; our mastery of pens and printing; our understanding of how disease spreads and how it can be healed.
> Islamic culture has given us majestic arches and soaring spires; timeless poetry and cherished music; elegant calligraphy and places of peaceful contemplation. And throughout history, Islam has demonstrated through words and deeds the possibilities of religious tolerance and racial equality."

The question is if America through Obama is changing the world, is the world changing at all? It is amazing how Obama presidency has put the world on the defensive from Iran to Israel, North Korea to Europe, Sudan to Zimbabwe on governance issues in general. The danger is that in the absence of creative refreshing thinking elsewhere as are witnessing from Washington in recent times, we might be inadvertently promoting another global monologue albeit with applauses in place of robust dialogue which certainly Obama craves for. We await another word-wisdom count on Africa certainly with applause, when he deservedly (and rightly too!) visits Ghana next month.

Ghana Proves Governor Sule Lamido Wrong*

"We have a responsibility to support those who act responsibly and to isolate those who don't, and that is exactly what America will do"- *President Barack Obama*, Accra, 11th July 2009.

"We should not expect to help Africa if Africa ultimately proves unwilling to help itself. But there are positive trends in Africa often hidden in the news of despairs"- *Obama, Audacity of Hope* (2006)

At 2009 edition of Daily Trust Dialogue, in Abuja, Alhaji Sule Lamido, Governor of Jigawa arrogantly dismisses almost arrogantly, the success governance story of Ghana (which then just concluded a successful rerun presidential election that retrenched an incumbent New Patriotic Party (NPP)). The governor argues that because of its small size and population, Nigeria's and diversity are incomparable to Ghana in democratic performance. Will the Governor still hold on to this false consciousness of size (not democratic performance), after watching the historic remarks of President Barack Obama to the Ghanaian parliament at Accra International Conference Centre during his weekend African tour? Posing this question to Governor Lamido underscores the free fall political decline of Nigeria. Once upon a time, Lamido was on the progressive side of the Nigeria political divide. In the second Republic he and his great compatriots in PRP made the great political point that just democratic deeds and progressive political best practices (and not necessarily might and bigness) that matter. PRP, though controlling only two states (Kaduna and Kano) was a formidable credible alternative to the

* *Daily Trust* (Monday, July 13, 2009)

ruling "big" NPN which controlled seven (7) states than any of the opposition party. For instance, it was PRP which first as political party declared May Day a public holiday before ruling NPN made it a national public holiday. The massive industrialization of PRP in Kaduna dwarfs NPN's housing pet projects nationwide. Therefore, the point is that size is NOT the issue but performance either in governance or development. If the issue is size, Singapore, a city state of 2 million people would not be taunted by the likes of OBJ and in development studies in general as a case study of a nation that transformed from a Third World to a first world in less than three decades.

Beyond the legitimate choice of Ghana as his second point of call in Africa after Cairo (Egypt), by his words alone, President Obama confirms the popular position of participants at Trust Dialogue forum according to which Ghana records legitimate successes in democracy while Nigeria shamelessly muddles through. Obama mentions Nigeria, the "giant of Africa" once in his 4000 plus words. And even at that, not in relations to the best practice of the Nigeria's state and its officially acknowledged decaying institutions. On the contrary, it was the collaborative efforts of the churches and mosques in Nigeria he singles out, in facing up to the scourge of malaria. Witness him: "In Nigeria, an Inter-faith effort of Christians and Muslims has set an example of cooperation to confront malaria." Note: malaria not votes counting! Conversely, on good governance Obama celebrates South Africa, (which is certainly not "small" as Ghana) but in his words, "where over three-quarters of the country voted in the recent election -- the fourth since the end of Apartheid," Ghana and Botswana. Nigeria once legitimately prides itself as a frontline state in the struggle against Apartheid and match towards democratic rule (Nigeria announced a programme for civil rule at a time Ghana groaned under open ended military dictatorship).

It is a sad commentary that Nigeria is being talked down by the first African American President (who was not born when Nigeria started with democracy at Independence in 1960). Nigeria is being recognized after South Africa (we helped to liberate!) and Botswana, (whose Nigeria's seed money and human resources put on the path of sustainable double digit growth!).

But President Obama almost acts another 19th century British explorer, Mungo Park discovering River Niger. The point is that Ghana has always been there setting the pace in African renewal. Obama only raises the noise level of Ghana not that he discovers it. Only that to the eternal credit to Obama, he showcases Ghana's thriving democratic institutions unlike Nigeria's elite who turns Accra to retreat city of sharing unspent health budgets!

At the height of the historic feat recorded by Obama's electoral revolution in USA, yours sincerely pointed out that: "Indeed Ghana (past and present) and not necessarily Obama's America gives more hope to Africa and Africans. Indeed Ghana's history and present reality prove that Africa can be fixed." It is remarkable that Obama accepts as much in his historic Accra speech. The late Julius Nyerere of Tanzania once observed that: "Ghana was the beginning, our first liberated zone. Thirty –seven years later-in 1994-we celebrated our final triumph when Apartheid was crushed and Nelson Mandela was installed as the president of South Africa." Sule Lamido should know that the whole world cannot be wrong on Ghana's undisputable democratic heritage and contributions to Africa's renaissance. Ghana won independence in 1957, (a decade before Martin Luther King made the prophetic speech about the "Dream"). And that was after series of struggles and pressures led by late Dr Nkrumah, a "prophet" imprisoned several times by the British. Mandela noted that the events of 1957 in Accra which led to the historic pulling down of the Union Jack and its replacement with Ghana flag were sources of inspiration against Apartheid. Many have rightly venerated pastor King's dream speech, but the first dream speech was that of Nkrumah who prophetically declared that: "Our Independence is meaningless unless it is linked up to the total liberation of the African continent." It is refreshing that Obama, a competent student of history, reveals the obvious that Martin Luther King's: "I have a Dream" speech was inspired by Ghana's lowering of Union Jack and raising of Ghanaian flag. He rightly recalls that Dr. King when asked how he felt while watching the birth of a new Ghana said: "It renews my conviction in the ultimate triumph of justice." Obama's visit to Ghana is not only right but historically correct. No nation deserves it better in contemporary Africa. It is significant that the 44th American

President gives sermon about good governance. I agree with him that "Africa's future is up to Africans". But that "simple premise" has not been as simple as Obama presents it in Accra. The current tragedy of Congo has much to do with the activities of imperial powers including USA which supervised serial and criminal eliminations of African patriots from Patrick Lumumba, to Amilcal Cabral, Murtala Muhammed. America even fuels Apartheid South Africa for as long it lasted. Certainly we cannot be prisoners of the despicable past but we dare not forget! To this extent, the world hails Obama's visit with his wife and daughters to Elmina Cape coast castle, the notorious memory of the evil of slavery. His remarks that slavery equals holocaust is refreshingly new but will there be reparations which late Chief Moshood Abiola courageously fought for?

Nkrumah, a "prophet" imprisoned several times by the British. Mandela noted that the events of 1957 in Accra which led to the historic pulling down of the Union Jack and its replacement with Ghana flag were sources of inspiration against Apartheid. Many have rightly venerated pastor King's dream speech, but the first dream speech was that of Nkrumah who prophetically declared that "Our independence is meaningless unless it is linked up to the total liberation of the African continent". It is refreshing that Obama, a competent student of history, reveals the obvious that Martin Luther King's: "I have a Dream" speech was inspired by Ghana's lowering of Union Jack and raising of Ghanaian flag. He rightly recalls that Dr. King when asked how he felt while watching the birth of a new Ghana said: "It renews my conviction in the ultimate triumph of justice." Obama's visit to Ghana is not only right but historically correct. No nation deserves it better in contemporary Africa. It is significant that the 44th American President gives sermon about good governance. I agree with him that "Africa's future is up to Africans". But that "simple premise" has not been as simple as Obama presents it in Accra. The current tragedy of Congo has much to do with the activities of imperial powers including USA which supervised serial and criminal eliminations of African patriots from Patrick Lumumba, to Amilcal Cabral, Murtala Muhammed. America even fuels Apartheid South Africa for as long as it lasted.

Still on Obama's Cairo Speech*

President Barack Obama's words of change come in torrents. Not few are overwhelmed with multiple issues thrown up in Obama's spoken and written words: from a major speech in Prague before a 20,000 crowd where he envisions a world free of nuclear weapons to Turkey's speech during his first trip "overseas as President of the United States". Many are simply paralysed by analysis of sundry issue-motivated speeches of the 44th President of United States of America. Thanks therefore to the likes of Disu Kamur (*The Guardian*, June 18) for facing up to the challenge and opting for some informed analysis of Obama's Cairo Speech.

Fidel Castro Ruz (retired but intellectually activist Cuban leader) and the master communicator is his own right spanning decades of despicable American blockade accepts as much that Obama's outing in Cairo is exceptional. In Fidel's own words: "*Some time will go by before we see anything like it again*". As significant as Disu's review of Cairo speech is, it regrettably betrays deep appreciation of Obama's inclusive vision of the world. He exhibits same exclusivist premises for an assessment of an inclusive historic presidential speech. As men and women of faith it is legitimate that we see issues from our "religious" prism. The challenge however lies in our capacity not to trade our preferred partisan and political views for our religions views because they are hardly one and the same.

After drawing inspiration from Churchill (who is certainly not an American founding father as he claims) and warns against easy "Words" without "great deeds", Disu unhelpful slides into stupor of words and words and indeed religious rhetoric/labelling of little heuristic value. It is misleading to characterize Obama's as "6000

---

* *The Guardian* (Thursday, July 16, 2009)

words to Muslims everywhere". The speech is not so-called or so captioned. Yes the US President delivers a speech at the Muslim University of Al-Azhar of Cairo but his audience is global regardless of race, creed and ideology. His quotes are not limited to Holy Quran but other Holy books: The bible and Torah.

Just as he is "comfortable in his skin" to contest and win as President of USA, Obama refers to the books with ease neither as a Rabbi, or Pastor nor an Imam but as the 44th President of the United States. It is a misreading of his text to write that: "Obama put religion at the core of the peace-making process in issues involving Muslims and America". We dare not assign unhelpful religious dogmas to Obama who has significantly moved from the notoriety of "crusade" /"Jihadist" binary brigand ship of Bush era. The global media erroneously dubs Obama's speech as "dialogue with Islamic world".

At the last count, just like Disu, yours truly identifies the following all-inclusive subjects: development, freedom and democracy, interfaith dialogue, education science and development, history and development, youth and women, Palestine Israeli conflict, nuclear proliferation, War and Peace, Afghanistan and terrorism. All the above subjects are not Arab or Islam specific. They are of profound interest to contemporary humanity and global peace and justice. One recurring theme in Obama's speeches whether in Prague, Ankara or Cairo (and I bet certainly in Ghana too!) is that what eventual binds humanity together is weightier than what divides us. Relying on memory, he reminds us that Morocco, an Islamic developing country was "the first nation" to recognise USA after its war of independence from Britain. One historic good turn deserves another. Obama, a proud student of history shows that in signing the Treaty of Tripoli in 1796, American's second President, John Adams, wrote: "The United States has in itself no character of enmity against the laws, religion or tranquillity of Muslims."

For the demagogues who profit from hatred and unhelpful divide Obama reminds his audience that Islam is also part of American heritage. "American Muslims have enriched the United States. They have fought in our wars; they have served in our government." Obama tasks our imagination to bring to the fore similar historic examples of international solidarity which shatters into smithereens our artificial "religious" divide. It will be a good tune for once to complement Obama by also pointing out that Islam right from the times of the Prophets has been with peace with other faiths. As far back as 616, persecuted Muslims, sought sanctuary in the Abyssinia (present day Ethiopia!), "that ancient bastion of Christianity in Africa whose religious traditions could be traced to the time of genocide which leave in their trail hundreds of thousands killed are human (and not necessarily Muslim) tragedies.

Indeed the anti-war protests and solidarity with Iraqi peoples are as profound and loud in Europe and America. The sense of outrage against injustices anywhere is not religion or race determined but ethically driven by our political convictions and choices. Venezuela, Peru and Cuba initiated diplomatic actions against Zionist Israel in the wake of Gaza bombings than scores of "Muslim nations". The struggle against Apartheid (for as long as that inhuman madness lasted) shows that human solidarity heroic combatants in Cuito Cuanavale in South western border of Angola struck a decisive blow against Apartheid troops (aided by Israel and United States of America) in the late 70s. Cubans shed their blood so that Nelson Mandela among others can be free. Cuba just as Nigeria (which used to be part of the front line states!) offered solidarity to the liberation movement, motivated by UN'S lofty resolution which classified Apartheid as crime against humanity. Historically, the global train of justice contains remarkable mix of noble passengers of diverse faiths and conventions that include Mahatma Gandhi, Nelson Mandela, Fidel Castro, Murtala Muhammed, Desmond Tutu, Che Guevara, Mother Teresa, Patrick Wilmot, Oliver Tambo, Julius Nyerere, Kwame Nkrumah, Amilcal Cabral, Franz Fanon, Walter Rodney, etc.

Disu asks the critical "relevant question": will these nice words (of Obama) transform into real policies and actions in Washington? And that's the real problem. His question begets another question: if America through Obama is trying to change the world, are we also changing and moving out of straight jacket of dogmas to take another look at our methods and perspective? It is amazing how Obama's presidency has put the world on the defensive from Iran to Israel, North Korea to Europe and Sudan to Zimbabwe on governance issues in general.

The danger is that in the absence of creative, refreshing thinking elsewhere, we might be inadvertently promoting another global monologue punctuated with applauses in place of robust dialogue which certainly Obama craves for. Lastly, a Nigerian has no luxury of interrogating Obama's choice of Egypt. Whether Egypt is a "repressive" or "undemocratic" or not what should be of interest to Nigerians watching was that for as long as Obama's speech lasted in Al-Azhar University, (described as the greatest Islamic institution of learning in the world,) there was no power failure!

Iran: Once Upon an Election*

Iran and Nigeria share much in common. But the controversial elections of June 12th in 2009 and 1993 respectively are paradoxically two events that captured imagination. For one, both countries are regional powers. Iran proudly asserts that singular power with self-made rocket satellite lunch into the orbit and long drawn nuclear power plants officially meant for peaceful purpose. Conversely Nigeria did controversial commercial satellite launch with little or no local content and even at that still crawls in its potentiality with repeated power failure and systemic disorder. Nigeria and Iran are notable members of club of leading ten oil producers and critical key players in OPEC. Again Iran parades value adding chains of functioning refineries and petrochemicals compared to Nigeria which intolerably refines off shores, no thanks to failed refineries and insecurity in Niger Delta region. They are both founding members of Non-Aligned Movement, visible members of United Nations that subscribe to basic international best practices including good governance and democracy. Iran is the second largest country in the Middle East. Nigeria is the largest in Africa. Both are rich in fascinating civilizations that span thousands of years. In recent times, Iran was thrust into the worldwide spotlight with the 1979 revolution that deposed US backed Shah's vicious dictatorship. The spectacular Iranian students' occupation of the US Embassy in Tehran remains the brand of that great revolution. It is not yet Nigeria's revolution however defined. But Nigeria witnessed 7 years bloody civil war which left in its trail almost a million dead. The war ended on the great unprecedented reconciliation tone of *No Victor, No Vanquished*!

* *Daily Trust* (Monday, July 27, 2009)

Iran conversely under Ayatollah Khomeini muddled through a bloody and disastrous senseless (*no win*) eight-year-war with Iraq in the 1980s. Nigeria and Iran have rich heritage of mass passion for democracy and popular governance, notwithstanding repeated interruptions by external and internal anti-democratic forces.

Military ruled Nigeria well over two decades of 50 years of independence. But the popular aspiration has been in the direction of popular votes and democratic governance in Nigeria. Nigeria even parades richer democratic traditions that spanned over a century. Democratic forces represented in vibrant political parties fought for Nigeria's independence in 1960 with first political party established as far back as 1920s. Significantly too, Iranians also desired and struggled for democracy in the face of external interference. In 1953, for instance, the CIA backed coup toppled a popularly democratically elected socialist government of Mossadegh who courageously and patriotically dared to nationalize the oil sector to the utter chagrin of American imperialism. In the words of acceptance of American complicity in that coup, President Barack Obama in the Cairo, Egypt recently told his audience that: "In the middle of the Cold War, the United States played a role in the overthrow of a democratically elected Iranian government."

Iran prides itself as "Islamic Republic" following the great revolution of the late 70s. Regrettably recent electoral outcomes in Iran, (just like its acquisition of nuclear technology for officially proclaimed peaceful purpose) have degenerated into another "*clash of fundamentalisms*" of self-righteous *right or* others that are always seen to be *wrong*. Globally (and indeed here in Nigeria!), discourse of Iranian democracy has assumed the same unhelpful binary dogma. On the one hand are the shouting matches of enthusiastic uncritical sycophants of Iranian process parroting "Yes" to an election in which they were no observers anyway. On the other hand are adamant opponents rudely chorusing No (true to Western media reportage) to an outcome that runs in the face of their preferences? Either way, it has been heat on what the *votes should be* rather than light on what *the votes and the issues were.* As Nigerians, on the threshold of another electoral reform, beyond sentiments and unthinking dogma, what lessons can we learn from Iranian elections? The June

12th is the tenth presidential election. This indicates that 30 years after the revolution, Iran keeps faith with democratic process compared to many countries in the region that trample under feet peoples' democratic aspirations. Let's also keep faith in democracy regardless of its imperfections. As we mark ten years of "uninterrupted" democracy, look at Iran which has thrown up great conscientious democratic actors like former President Mohammed Khatami (one time Guest speaker at Yar'Adua Foundation while on a state visit). With Iran democracy is a process and not an event with all the attendant smooth and rough turns. Iranian process has been nurtured by fear of invasion and sheer aggression by USA and West in general. The external aggression was real. Former President George Bush's demonized Iran, (together with Cuba and North Korea) as axis of evil. The world has since outlived the evil administration that Bush regime indeed represented (from unilateral bombing of Iraq and Afghanistan to global melt down and climate disorder!). But as long as Bush regime lasted, it dubiously helped to undermine genuine democratic process in Iran. Legitimate alternative views and resistance to sundry anti-democratic methods of demagogue President Mahmud Ahmadinejad are perceived as kowtowing to imperial USA. Earlier many were brutally suppressed reminiscent of Shah Dictatorship. Only a brutal dictatorship (NOT democracy) could have waged the grim senseless 8 year conflict with Iraq with more than a million Muslims killed on both sides of Iraq and Iran. President Barack Obama refreshingly hopes to deal with Iran based on mutual respect as distinct from mutual hostility. This makes the Iranian election for once insular, domestic-issues driven. June 12th election shows that Iranians desperately desire reforms of a theocratic top down process which is increasingly hard put to count votes. My findings show that Iranians in Nigeria voted more for challenger Mir Hussein Mousavi, one time Prime Minister. The official results gave 63 per cent to the incumbent while Mousavi had 33 per cent. The bane of Iranian process is the unelectable ubiquitous Guardian Council of clerics who bring to bear their partisan preference on what is supposed to be a disinterested vote counting process anyway. Whatever the outcome of the recent Iranian debacle, what is clear is that just like Nigeria's process, reform is necessary and urgent.

Meanwhile democratic forces worldwide must demand for the immediate release of all political detainees in Iran.

What Then about Hillary's Visit?*

The impact assessment of the recent visit of Hillary Clinton, US secretary of State, on the political environment of the continent and that of Nigeria in particular will be subject of debate for some time to come. But one thing is clear: Nigeria's political climate witnessed some remarkable heat following Mrs Clinton's serial engagement with the broad spectrum of Nigeria's political landscape before she rounded up a continental tour which arguably had bigger impact than the celebrated Obama's visit to Accra. A day after her departure, we can indeed talk of some political climate change in Nigeria. For one, the instant big bang impact of Hilary's underscores a kind of a new dependency syndrome afflicting Nigeria. On the eve of 50th independence anniversary, it seems the basic components that influence the state of the Nigeria's political climatic system are predictably external or extra-terrestrial (to borrow from the climatologists). Well before her visit, the nation had witnessed internal ruptures such as Niger Delta carnage, the subsequent amnesty deal, *Boko Haram* with as many as 1000 officially proclaimed dead and of course ever cancerous closures of universities in the wake of ASUU strikes. But none of these internal factors (comparable in impact and devastations to some volcanic eruptions, or tsunami) rudely woke up the political class from their sheer indifference or slumber (or both) like a singular two-stop over visit of a lady and secretary of State of United States of America, with her few thousands word count on governance.

Senate President David Mark was smart by half by playing the patriotic card. Witness him:

---

* *Daily Trust* (Monday, August 17, 2009)

> "The country is ours; we will decide what form of democracy we want. And I think she was very clear on that - that every country will decide the form of democracy. We will decide for ourselves what we want as a democratic system."

He was reportedly angry over US Secretary of State Hillary Clinton's remarks on Nigeria. Fine enough. But regardless of his legitimate ravings, the reality is that Nigeria was indeed "dictated" to anyway, assuming Hilary's mass applauded word counts on good governance amounted to some dictation. Indeed the issue is not the alleged dictation from Washington but the fact that we helplessly could do nothing about it. The real scandal is that the national assembly (under Mark's co-leadership (?) made up of people "elected" and paid to speak for us) was on recess when the country was being "dictated" to. Put in another language, it would go down in history that when Nigeria was being "carpet bombed" by "dictator", sorry, Senator Hillary Clinton the national assembly was simply not on duty. For a retired General-turned-Senator who took a sabbatical abroad, for as long as Abacha regime lasted, few can certainly rival David Mark in sermons on absentee patriotism a la Nigeria. That is generously granted to him with voice vote. But future generation of Nigerians would still wonder why patriot Senator Mark would opt for some reactionary lamentation in place of proactive rebuff (say via a motion of non-invitation of US Secretary of State). Mark's belated reaction only further legitimizes dictation to Nigeria and smacks of some political hypocrisy. The South African satirist, Piete Uys once reminded us of an old diplomatic wisdom which seems to have escaped the Senate President altogether: *"Diplomacy is the art of getting on with those whom you cannot stand"* he said. By *not getting on* but pretending to engage Hilary, rather belatedly, the Senate President has actually increased the noise level of Hilary's star words on good governance in Nigeria. Hilary said nothing that Nigerians have not said umpteenth times. Why would political leaders show only sensitivity to what Hilary said in a flash and displayed indifference to what Nigerians say every other day? Hilary said Nigeria ought to be a legitimate member of G20 if and only if it puts its house in order. That sounded like Yar'Adua's 2020 vision of making Nigeria one of the leading 20 countries in 11 years to go. It was President Yar'Adua who first humbly accepted (even at a time it was not fashionable to do so even by America under President Bush), that 2007 election was flawed well before Hillary repeated the obvious with some advice for Nigeria to get the sums right by 2011. Hillary said that without Nigeria there would not have been Liberia and Sierra Leone. No American leader had objectively acknowledged our role in the sub region. No patriotic Nigerian leader either had been so much pointedly categorical. Not even Liberia's President Johnson Sirleaf who delivered Mandela Foundation lecture in 2007 without acknowledging Nigeria's sacrifices and without a motion of national importance from Mark-led Senate to interrogate her. David Mark's reaction to Hilary further points in the direction of crisis of governance in Nigeria. Just spot the difference between the methodology of Hillary Clinton and that of David Mark! Whatever it is worth (and she got applause all the way!) Hilary's word counts flow from eyeball to eye ball engagement with Nigerians including a Town hall meeting with the critical civil society community. Conversely David Mark addressed us through some reporters on arrival from Abuja at the presidential wing of the Murtala Muhammed Airport, Ikeja, Lagos. When will the Senate President do his own Town hall meeting with his own people? He does not need a Hilary bashing to address lingering ASUU strikes. He does not need a Hilary to tell us that Yar'Adua's electoral reform is jinxed (*What is the problem with the electoral system? I have read the Electoral Act. What is the problem with it?*). President Obama observed in Accra that what Africa needs are strong institutions and not strongmen. The responses of the likes of David Mark and the ruling PDP to an open engagement by Hilary show that Obama got it wrong after all. Africa does not need strong men or strong institutions. On the contrary, Africa needs a completely new relationship between the leaders and the mass of the people of the continent. There must be a connect between the people and the leaders in such a way that we don't need foreign visitors to get some arrogant belated answers from our leaders on persistent questions we pose every day without acknowledgement from our leaders from collapse of schools to power failure. Hillary Clinton's Town Hall meeting held in the University in war torn Congo. It held in university in Nairobi Kenya. Thirty years after the late Samora

Machel addressed Ahmadu Bello University convocation lecture, no university to hold Town hall meeting with local or foreign leaders in Nigeria. It's time for new relationship between the led and the leaders in Nigeria.

Obama and Ghaddafi at UN: Spotting the Differences*

Comparing like with unlike! An attempt at some content analysis of the speeches of the 44th President of United States of America (USA) Barack Obama and the umpteenth (?) Libyan leader Muammar Gadhafi at the 64th General Assembly of the United Nations (UN) in New York tasks imagination. Paradoxically the two leaders are heads of governments of countries which have assumed some notoriety either for better, for worse (depending on what you see). They are first timers at the General Assembly not necessarily by political design but some political accident.

President Obama was conscious of the historic significance of his address and said as much indicating how honoured he was "…*to address you (the assembly) for the first time as the forty-fourth President of the United States.*" The Libyan leader who has not visited the UN since he took power in 1969 in a coup betrayed no emotions about the historic import of his first address to the assembly. However observers noted that Gadhafi was as conscious of the impact assessment of his rhetoric after a long absence "and clearly wanted to make up for it by giving his views on the past four decades of history".

Obama's clear and audible word are some 5000-plus in the record allotted time of ...while Libyan leader's words-lorry (or is it camel?) load tasks listening capacity and certainly proved uncountable. Indeed you search in vain for Gadhafi full text. He reportedly talked through some hand written pages which in turn

* *Daily Trust* (Monday, September 28, 2009)

reportedly exhausted an Arabic translator who had to be relieved by a colleague.

The two speeches are test cases in a lesson on verbal communication, sense of purpose and mission. Why is it that some speakers hold their listeners spell bound command their attention and elicit spontaneous applause? Conversely why is it that some speakers induce yawns, reading of text messages, even sleep and indeed walkout on the part of their audience? You just have to read Obama's and Gaddafi's at the 64th General Assembly to respectively get some clue for some answers. I bear witness that Muammar Gaddafi's delivery was symbolism for arrogance, incoherence, hate, unbridled lust, mendacity, and it is simply unhelpful to (AU) Africa Union's cause. The token substance in his speech (reform of UN, interrogating history of imperialism, reparations, etc.) is eroded by his empty styles (witness his symbolic tearing of the UN charter. On the other hand, Obama ably combines rhetoric with substance, with clear cut powerful messages for listening global community with effective delivery that did more PR for Uncle Sam than his disastrous predecessor Gorge W. Bush.

Gaddafi is older both in age (he was even cheeky enough to rhetorically patronize Obama as his "son") and in power too (40 years in power). As many as nine American presidents have passed him by. From Lyndon Baines Johnson, 1963-1969, Richard Milhous Nixon, 1969-1974, Gerald Rudolph Ford, 1974-1977,James Earl Carter, Jr., 1977-1981, Ronald Wilson Reagan, 1981-1989, George Herbert Walker Bush, 1989-1993, William Jefferson Clinton, 1993-2001, George Walker Bush, 2001-2009, to Barack Hussein Obama, 2009-

Gadhafi came to power deposing a monarch in 1969 but is proudly being presented as "King of Kings" in 2009. The author of Green Book in which he scorns party system and monarchical rule has certainly run a full cycle.

But the difference between Barack Obama and Gaddafi is not so much in natural age progression but in the age of their ideas. Gaddafi belongs to what Obama in his speech rightly sees as "...a generation that chose to drag the arguments of the 20th century into the 21st; that put off hard choices, refused to look ahead, and failed to keep pace because we defined ourselves by what we were against instead of what we were for." He was against "terror council" (read: Security Council) but whence his practical pragmatic proposals to make for a reform of the Council?

We knew what he was up against but nobody is clear about what he stands. Inadvertently he shares a lot in common with Israelis' Netanyahu who criminally also blocks proposals for change on the Palestinian crisis without alternative proposals for change. The bane of Gaddafi's is that he demands so much for reforms but he is not reforming either and indeed he is only standing conservative statesman of his times. The strength of Obama's lies in his courage to critique America's recent past and make a difference. He not only demands for a terror free world, but he demonstrates leadership by examples by showing that it is no more business as usual in the USA. According to him, "On my first day in office, I prohibited - without exception or equivocation - the use of torture by the United States of America. I ordered the prison at Guantanamo Bay closed, and we are doing the hard work of forging a framework to combat extremism within the rule of law." We are yet to read such star words of reforms from the "King of Kings". Gadhafi castigated the UN "for failing to stop 65 wars since 1945". Well said. But how many of such wars in West Africa, from Liberia to Sierra Leone was at Libya's prodding? And what commitment is he giving that we have seen the last cut limbs and fingers in Africa under his chairmanship of AU? On the contrary even at this hour Gadhafi still holds war criminals like Charles Taylor in high esteem. When the history of UN is written Gadhafi's Libya comes out more as war promoter compared to peace keeper like Nigeria. All said yours sincerely is diminished that we are doing content analysis of foreign leaders at the 64th general Assembly. Whence the address of my President, Musa Yar' Adua at the UN on the eve of 49th Independence anniversary? For better worse, America and Libya are counted. Wither Nigeria.

President Tandja's Politicide*

Another avoidable coup d'état occurred in Niger Republic on 18 February 2010. This reactionary development has once again brought to the fore the imperatives of good governance in West Africa's sub region. For discernable political observers, Niger was actually a political disaster waiting to happen anyway. President Mamadou Tandja's rise and predictable fall confirms the old received wisdom that those who dare to live by the sword end up somehow consumed by the very sword. His entry into politics started with the 1974 coup d'état that brought Seyni Kountche to power. He held various high-level posts under that undemocratic regime before heading the National Movement for the Development of Society (MNSD) as an opposition leader during the 1990s. A 1999 coup paved the way for a free and fair election in which Mamadou Tandja was elected President. His reign has been characterized by messianic complex of indispensability which in turn made him to criminally alter the rules of political engagement to his favour as an incumbent. It is an open knowledge that the recent coup was preceded by a year-long political crisis in Niger related to President Tandja's efforts to extend his mandate beyond December 2009, when his second term was originally scheduled to end.

Arguing indispensability and claiming that the people wanted him to remain in office, Tandja dissolved the National Assembly in May 2009 and subsequently appointed a new Constitutional Court, enabling him to push forward with a constitutional referendum in August 2009 that extended his mandate for an additional three years. Tandja went further. He promoted addictive coups, as it were, against

* *Daily Trust*, 22nd February 2010

constitutional order by scrapping the semi-presidential system of government in favour of a presidential system.

Opposition legitimately reacted furiously to Tandja's efforts to remain in office and denounced him as a dictator. Tandja also faced strong international and regional criticism as a result of the events of 2009; Niger was suspended from the regional body ECOWAS.

Tandja said that he needed to remain in office to oversee various projects of tremendous economic value, as if one of the poorest nations in the world, could risk isolation.

With disastrous record of constitutional violations, it was self-evident that bad governance Tandja promoted would end up with worst case scenario as we sadly witnessed recently. Niger under Tandja had been what a democracy should not be.

In 2005, the country hit the global head line through a famine which the whole world acknowledged but falsely denied by the ousted dictator. According to Niger President, Mamadou Tandja, then there was no famine. '*The people of Niger look well-fed as you can see*' he reportedly told *BBC*. According to him, famine was no famine but something close to it, namely food shortages occasioned by usual endemic poor rains and locust invasions in Niger. He accused the media, aid agencies and opposition parties of exaggeration and smear campaign against his administration.

The controversial remark of President Mamadou Tandja about zero-hunger in Niger brought to the fore the poverty of his leadership in particular and leadership challenge in Africa.

According to the Human Development Report in that year, Niger was 176th i.e. second to the last (war-weary Sierra Leone) on the Human development index. The life expectancy at birth of President Tandja's "well-fed people" was 46 years, adult literacy was 17.1% and combined gross enrolment ratio for primary, secondary and tertiary schools was as miserable as 19 per cent, 85.3 % are bellow income poverty line while as many as 41 per cent of children are under weight for age. These sobering statistics are NOT manufactured by the opposition nor aid agencies as President Mamadou was quick to make cheap political capital then from the misery of his own people that time. Niger shows the linkage between poverty and lack of democracy. The challenge of governance is to deliver prosperity for the people. The world cannot resolve on end to poverty while some miserable politicians in the continent play politics of poverty and sit tight denying alternative to their mis-governance.

The event in Niamey has also called to question the relevance of NEPAD once enthusiastically promoted by President Obasanjo, South Africa's Mbeki, Senegal's Abdoulaye Wade and Algeria's Bouteflika in 2000. NEPAD was seen as a new African initiative that raises the prospects of an African Renaissance through sustainable development and good governance. NEPAD underscored the fact that economic development was impossible without addressing the political question. It called for pair review mechanism among member states to promote best democratic processes such as free and fair elections. The events in Niger show that pair review mechanism is not working. The ease with which Tandja defied the warnings of AU about the danger of subversion of constitutional order tasks leaders to rethink pair review methodology. The new military junta in Niger must quickly return the country to democracy and avoid further isolation of the country. The disgraced former President Tandja already brought ruination. The new military junta should not entrench dictatorship. It must immediately organize free and fair elections so that the people of that impoverished nation would determine who rules them according to the best global political practices.

Gaddafi: the Making of a False Hero*

With his last week's unprovoked verbal aggression against Nigeria, Libya's Muammar Gaddafi has run a full cycle. From a self-acclaimed champion of African unity (with his added insult to Nkrumah's genuine vision; United States of Africa) Gaddafi is a false living hero of the continent belatedly recommending balkanization of Nigeria and indeed Africa (because without 150 million Nigerians Africa is nominal). The infamous Berlin Conference held 125 years ago. In 1885 the European marauding nations, namely Germany, Britain, Italy, Belgium, France, Spain and Portugal crudely partitioned the continent without regards to affinity, bond ship, history and cultures of the peoples. Libya was partitioned to the Italians and only got independence in 1951. It is a scandal that Gadhafi, the immediate past chairman of Africa Union (AU) who until recently was parroting instant pan African United of African States would recommend a silly imperial "religious" carving of Nigeria. *It is in the nature of false heroes to transform into direct opposites of what they project outwardly.* The Libyan leader reportedly advocated:

> "the dismemberment of the Nigerian federation into two new countries. The boundaries of the new entities, he proposed, would be along the geographical lines of the north and south. This, he believes, is the antidote to the kind of crisis that has seized Plateau State in recent times, occasioning the mindless waste of hundreds of lives."

As a precedent, Gaddafi reportedly cited the creation of Pakistan, which was excised from India in 1947. Pakistan is predominantly Muslim, while India is majorly Hindu, and rampant

* *Daily Trust*, 22nd March 2010

religious strife had resulted in frequent bloodletting. The Libyan leader described the Plateau violence as "a deep conflict of religious nature" caused by the nature of the Nigerian federation, "which was made and imposed by the British, in spite of the people's resistance to it". Assessing Gaddafi's provocative thoughtlessness on Nigeria is as thoughtless if the assessment is not put in perspective of his age long false un-heroic deeds even to his country and to his continent, Africa. The author of the Green Book came to power without firing a shot in 1969. The then 27-year old captain had deposed King Idris who was absent on a visit to Turkey. Not a few had held Gaddafi and his notorious second-in-dictatorship, one Major Jaloud (where is he anyway?) in some orgasmic adoration. The junta had created for decades a myth of some triumphant revolutionaries. It is in the nature of false heroes to put up make-ups. Gaddafi has many women with make ups as bodyguards!

The make-ups saw Gaddafi transformed into commander in chief of the armed forces and chairman of the Revolutionary Command Council since governs Libya. From 1979 he proclaimed self as Leader of the Revolution. Today the man who overthrew a monarch and decried party and class system in his Green book is proudly parading a feudal medieval medal as the *King of Kings*. Libya has entrenched official nepotism with clear cut signals that Gaddafi would be replaced by his son just like his partners in false heroism, namely Hussein Mubarak of Egypt and George Bush Snr of United States of America did.

Gaddafi projects the image of a philosopher King. The various roots of his political philosophy include – Islam, Arab nationalism, and socialism. But pray what manner of Muslim would dare to exclude Christians in his kingdom for dubious political calculation? Gaddafi is the only Arab nationalist who expelled Palestinians (who are also Arabs and Muslims) from his kingdom even as he rhetorically decries Israelis Zionism which daily oppresses the Palestinians. Never judge a philosopher by the cover of his book. So much for a socialist who prides self as *King of Kings!* -

Gaddafi pretends to be an expert on how Nigeria should be governed. His "knowledge" of Nigeria as "North" and "South" lagers is reminiscent of colonizers" erroneous belief that Africa was a "dark continent" just because they did not know about it Interestingly *Gaddafi shares a lot in common with American (CNN's) perspective of Nigeria as "Muslim North" and "Christian South".* It is in the nature of false heroes that they are the real agents of forces they falsely decry. In 2005 an America's dubious intelligence report predicted a collapsed Nigeria state in 15 years' time. It is a paradox that it takes a Gaddafi to legitimize a CIA's desire. The profile of Mammar Gaddafi as a CIA agent will be exciting to read. He ironically shares a lot in common with the late President Ronald Reagan who nearly criminally bombed him out of existence in 1986 on the ground that he was sponsoring terrorism. As a Hollywood actor, President Reagan throughout his tenure spoke from film scripts which explained why he once jokingly claimed to be bombing former USSR on a telephone line. Gaddafi is driven by megalomania which could explain how audaciously he could verbally dismember a nation so casually. He claimed to be reacting to the crisis in Plateau State. Nonsense! There was no "religious" divide in Liberia and Sierra Leone before Gaddafi fuelled anarchy in those countries. The regional anarchy tasked Nigeria and ECOWAS resources to halt. Gaddafi's latest verbal missile is part of his heritage of cheap and unearned heroism. The Libyan leader had not visited the UN since he took power in 1969. He however made a disastrous outing last year. Gadhafi was as conscious of the impact assessment of his rhetoric after a long absence "and clearly wanted to make up for it by giving his views on the past four decades of history." But witness Obama's clear and audible few words and compare to Libyan leader's lorry (or is it camel?) load nonsense which tasked listening capacity and certainly proved uncountable. He reportedly talked through some hand written pages which in turn reportedly exhausted an Arabic translator who had to be relieved by a colleague. His empty styles (witness his symbolic tearing of the UN charter) went down as the lowest moment in UN history.

The Senate President David Mark has rightly described the Libyan leader as a "mad man". But if a mad man removes your cloth while you are swimming in a river, you need a superior wisdom to get out and get your cloth back otherwise the difference would be in the degree of exhibited madness. Gaddafi's rascality is a rude reminder that Nigeria must wake up to the challenge of good governance. In 1976 the late Murtala Muhammed was assassinated by coup plotters. Nobody ever imputed motives to the death of Murtala as a Head of State while the nation moved with Obasanjo as his successor. On the contrary Murtala was celebrated as a national patriot nationwide while the coup plotters were summarily treated for what they were: criminals. That was a developmentalist Nigeria which we must bring back. It is sad that today Plateau state crisis is given a wrong religious interpretation when indeed it is purely a crisis of governance. It is this diversionary interpretation by Nigeria media in particular and the Western media in general that capture the false imagination of the false heroes like Gadhafi. The burden is actually on us not on Gadhafi who in any case emerged out of crisis and muddles through crisis anywhere. Let us rid ourselves of crisis of governance and get Gadhafi out of business.

Israel: Flotilla is not an exception*

Almost every day, the global media bias manifests in permanent smear reportage that casts both Iran and North Korea, as the world's remaining *rogue states.* The discredited Bush administration even feverishly enlisted Cuba as part of its notorious Axis of evil smear campaign. But somehow (and definitely and unarguably so), Israel as the undisputed world's standing *real rogue state* has proved to be more than just a media made, no thanks to its globally acknowledged historic systemic violations of known global rules. Avi Shlaim is an Oxford professor of international relations who paradoxically "served in the Israeli army and has never questioned the state's legitimacy". He is also the author of *The Iron Wall: Israel and the Arab World and of Lion of Jordan: King Hussein's Life in War and Peace.* In the wake of mass killings of Palestinians during the 2009 Gaza conflict, he wrote among others to define a rogue state as that: "state that habitually violates international law, possesses weapons of mass destruction and practises terrorism - the use of violence against civilians for political purposes." He then concluded that, "Israel fulfils all of these three criteria; the cap fits and it must wear it." Over 60 years after its existence, for Israel, it is not yet the end of history of atrocities, aggressions and impunities that are defining characteristics of the Zionist regime.

On Sunday, 31st of May, Israeli naval forces, in a gangster-approach identified with Somalis pirates intercepted the ships of a Turkish nongovernmental organization (NGO) delivering humanitarian supplies to the blockaded Gaza. The ships had on board unarmed global activists drawn from Turkey, Ireland, Cuba

---

* *Daily Trust,* 7th June 2010

and United States. Given the preponderance of Turkish activist nationals as victims of Israel's terrorism, the aftermath of Israelis' attack on the international aid flotilla is being presented falsely as a set-back for the renewed diplomatic relations between Israel and Turkey. The truth however is that Flotilla carnage is more than a diplomatic row between Turkey and Israel. It further brings out the character of Tel Aviv regime as a rogue regime that moves against the tide of history by consistently denying the right of Palestinians to their home land and willing to take on the world to pursue narrow Zionist, (not necessarily Israelis people's agenda). Flotilla under Prime Minister Netanyahu Benjamin is not an exception to generalised Israeli atrocities. Ariel Sharon, the former Prime Minister was equally once a crime minister of sort proudly presided over the massacre of Palestinian refugees in Sabra and Shatila camps in Lebanon in 1981. Sharon even regretted not having liquidated Yasser Arafat who was held up in the siege in southern Lebanon. The Israeli occupation of the West Bank and the Gaza Strip in the aftermath of the June 1967 war, just like the latest Flotilla had very little to do with security but everything to do with territorial expansionism of the Zionist regime. "The aim was to establish Greater Israel through permanent political, economic and military control over the Palestinian territories. And the result has been one of the most prolonged and brutal military occupations of modern times".

Israel at different times had reacted with extreme violence to the resistance of Palestinian people but "the flotilla carnage is the first direct and officially declared attack by the Israeli army on foreign activists - taking Israel's reaction to solidarity activities to a new and unprecedented level". Even the Israeli claims that Turkish activists "resisted" its takeover of the ships only increased the noise level of the pettiness of Israeli regime as a rogue regime that dared to use armed operation against unarmed activists who were trying to deliver food and medical supplies to the besieged Palestinian population. The world understandably hailed the humanitarian activists that included a Nobel prize laurel while understandably the world condemned the Israelis actions. The fact that Israeli naval personnel were beaten to retreat not to further attack the subsequent Malaysia-funded Irish ship, the *Rachel Corrie,* and beaten to release the activists proved that the initial criminal attacks remains criminal and proves an unsustainable method in an increasingly civilized world. It also shows a triumph of non-violent approach of the activists over the predictable violence and deaths of the Zionist regime. Israel must relook at its out-dated concept of security that has its root in the old cold war era. You cannot deny the most elementary security to the other community (Palestinian) and sustain your own peace. The only way for Israel to achieve security is not through shooting but through talks with Palestinians regardless of party affiliations. With global strong reactions to the Gaza flotilla raid of 31 May 2010, Israel, not Palestinians is the looser. Many countries have rightly called for an international investigation. Unofficial responses included civilian protests against Israeli action following reports of the deaths aboard the *MV Mavi Marmara.* Four countries downgraded their diplomatic relations with Israel and/or withdrew ambassadors: Ecuador, Nicaragua, South Africa, and Turkey. Twelve Latin American countries condemned Israeli actions: Argentina, Bolivia, Brazil, Chile, Cuba, Ecuador, Mexico, Nicaragua, Paraguay, Peru, Uruguay and Venezuela. Israel had developed significant bilateral relationships with seven of them. Twenty-one European countries condemned or protested Israeli actions: Albania, Azerbaijan, Belarus, Bosnia and Herzegovina, Bulgaria, Croatia, the Czech Republic, Estonia, Finland, France, Greece, Iceland, Ireland, Italy, Luxembourg, Norway, Portugal, Russia, Spain, Sweden and the United Kingdom.

Israel was widely condemned in the Arab world. Twelve non-Arab Asian countries condemned Israeli actions: China, India, Indonesia, Iran, Japan, Malaysia, Maldives, North Korea, Pakistan, Sri Lanka, Turkey and Uzbekistan. Israel was also condemned by: Australia, Kenya, New Zealand and South Africa. Eighteen countries focused their statements on expressing regret over loss of life: Israel (also!), Argentina, Australia, Azerbaijan, Bangladesh, Canada, Czech Republic, Croatia, Egypt, Estonia, Greece, India, Ireland, Japan, Sri Lanka, the United Kingdom, the United States. So far, Nigeria's voice has not been heard either for or against, the Flotilla carnage. With a substantive, (not acting), healthy (not sick!) President Goodluck Jonathan, a substantive Foreign minister, Odein Ajumogobia and a Minister of State, Aliyu Idi Hong for foreign Affairs, Nigeria is certainly does not lack officials handsomely paid to covey our legitimate national feelings in a global arena! Are they really on duty or are they busy organizing new rounds of global trips?

Nigeria at 50 - How (Not) To Celebrate*

Ghana was the first African country that fought and won independence from British imperialism in 1957. Former Tanzanian President, Late Julius Nyerere, underscored the significance of Ghana's Independence on the 6th March 1957. In 1997 Nyerere succinctly observed that:

> "Ghana was the beginning, our first liberated zone. Thirty-seven years later – in 1994 – we celebrated our final triumph when Apartheid was crushed and Nelson Mandela was installed as the president of South Africa. Africa's long struggle for freedom was over."

It is one naughty historic fact; no country is eminently positioned to set the benchmark to mark the Golden Jubilee anniversary than the country which dared to lower the century long oppressive Union Jack and in place proudly raised the Ghana's flag that has been a pride of the continent since. Ghana's (and indeed Africa's) founding father late President Osagyefo Dr. Kwame Nkrumah on that faithful day 53 years ago at the Old Polo Ground in Accra was conscious of the pan African impact of Ghana's breaking of the colonial chain. Witness his quotable quote: "*Our independence is meaningless unless it is linked up to the total liberation the African continent.*" Nigeria and score of other African countries, that include Cameroun, Congo, Zambia, followed Ghana's historic footstep, won liberty in quick successions making them worthy Golden celebrants this year. We can debate how each of the independent countries had fared 50

* *Daily Trust*, 27th September 2010

years after liberation, but there is no doubt that so far Ghana's historic Golden Jubilee celebration three years ago is not yet rivalled. Somalia was 50 years on the 1st of July this year. It is an open sore to see Somalia suffocating under the spell of factional suicidal rogue clans which not only daily maim its citizens, pirate others but "celebrated" its independence by sponsoring terrorism in Uganda early this year. Comparing Ghana with Somalia at celebration is comparing model like with unworthy unlike respectively. On the 15th of August, three quarter of the paraded troops at Congo, DRC's celebration were UN peace-keeping forces. So much for Independence, a la Congo DRC. On the 7th of August, Ivory Coast celebrated against the background of divided Republic and disputed election compared to Ghana that has held successfully three elections, two of which led to the democratic retrenchment of two incumbent ruling parties.

Nigeria is in a better position to beat Ghana's record in independence celebration. With scores of political parties contesting for elective offices, no better time to have a robust golden anniversary narrative and agenda setting for the next fifty years. Alas in conceptual framework and historic reflection, our golden anniversary programme miserably fell short of Ghana's informed programme. Ask me the theme of Nigeria's celebration, yours sincerely simply cannot remember. The official *Nigeria @ 50 website* parades a number of "quick links" but not a single theme! Pray if you lack a theme, what is the thrust of a celebration? Three years after, Ghana's theme for its Golden Jubilee anniversary still captures imagination, "Championing African Excellence". The theme flew from the theory according to which Ghana's first President, Osagyefo Dr. Kwame Nkrumah, envisioned Ghana as the "guiding light of African Independence and solidarity -- the Black Star, the lodestar of Africa". With this theme, in 2007 Ghana was an inevitable celebration destination for all Africans. Yours sincerely bears witness as Golden Jubilee pilgrim in 2007. On the 5th of March I arrived in Ghana, (deliberately by road to keep date with history, an experience that constitutes another reflection) for the 50th Independence anniversary. Ghana's theme: *Championing African Excellence* was a clarion call to Africans like me. With what theme are we inspiring

Nigerians at 50 not to talk of attracting other Africans? Devil is in the details. Some details of Nigeria's programme say volume about the values we assign to a historic anniversary. Ten billion naira will be spent by the Federal Government to celebrate the 50th Anniversary of Nigeria's Independence in October.

Some breakdown of the expenditure simply do not add value whatsoever to an anniversary and the items can hardly allow for accountability. Witness these; ₦950 million for anniversary parade including march past, fleet review and aerial display, ₦350 million will be expended on national unity torch and tour, First Lady Mrs. Patience Jonathan spends ₦50 million for a special visit to special homes, orphanages, prisons and selected hospitals, while ₦20 million for a special session of the National Children Parliament, and another ₦20 million will used to organise a party for 1000 children.

The late Premier of the Northern region, Sir Ahmadu Bello, Sardauna of Sokoto spent just 1,250, 000 pounds (₦291,000,000) as an investment seed money to start Kaduna Textile Mill which lasted up to 40 years before it collapsed under our independent official nose.

Nigeria is willing to expend billions for uneventful two weeks programme. Kindly note that Ghana spent far less for a year-long historic programme that includes the following monthly themes; Reflections, Towards Emancipation, Freedom March and Our Nation, Our People. Other themes are Our Wealth and Our Prosperity, Heroes of Ghana, Africa Unity, Diaspora Month, Service to the Nation, Knowledge and Ghana's Development, Health People, a Healthy Nation and then the Final Curtain. Please kindly compare the above Ghana's historic programme to Nigeria's money sharing unstructured jamboree of dubious value: Saturday September 25th: (Children Presentations @ 12 noon & Cultural Night @ 6pm) Sunday September 26th: (National Praise & Worship Service) From 10am Monday September 27th: Lectures & Photo exhibitions Tuesday September 28th: Lectures & Photo exhibitions Wednesday September 29th: Lectures & Photo exhibitions Thursday September 30th: Lectures & Photo exhibitions Friday October 1st: Book Launch, Speeches, Exhibition, Parties Saturday October 2nd: Parties,

Shows, & more Sunday October 3rd: Thanksgiving Services, Praises, Worship, etc.

Arab Protest and Good Governance*

Undoubtedly the spontaneous mass unrest which rightly ousted Tunisia's leader Ben Ali few weeks ago had snowballed to streets of Algiers, Algeria and Sanaa, Yemen. In these countries, thousands of demonstrators are demanding for regime changes. More than anywhere else, the on-going Egyptian protests in Egyptian notable cities of Cairo and Alexandra as fall out of the now famous Tunisian effect have more implications for good governance on the continent. 80 million people with relative high growth rate and development in infrastructure, if this could happen in Egypt, Nigeria's reality is then better imagined.

The theme of the 8th Daily Trust Dialogue is; *The Challenges of Good Governance in Africa.* Very apt and timely theme indeed! *Trust Dialogue* held on the eve of *Friday of Wrath* in most Egyptian cities when North African masses legitimately thronged to the streets, pushing in an unprecedented manner, to demand for immediate and practical good governance. Surprisingly invited speakers at the Dialogue kept mute on the implications of Arab revolts for good governance on the continent. This is in spite of the fact that Trust's Chairman/ CEO, Kabir Yusuf had rightly cited the *"explosion in stable Tunisia*" as one of the momentous events in the continent. Not a single selected speaker at the Trust Dialogue frontally addressed the implications of events in North Africa. Ms Arunma Otteh, the Director General of SEC, the second speaker was once a former Vice President of African Development Bank (ADB) based in Tunis, (now with benefits of hide-sights, the capital city of dictatorship and bad governance) which still hosts the headquarters of ADB. Undoubtedly

* 31st January, 2011

it was a crisis of governance and development that triggered the Tunisian revolts from which other similar regimes in bad governance might not recover. It started with a 26-year old young man, Mohamed *Bouazizi* a university graduate without a steady job who out of desperation for survival set himself on fire, after police confiscated the fruits and vegetables he sold allegedly without a permit. How many of *Bouazizis* do we have on the streets on Nigeria riding Okada or roaming about in search of jobs after living schools? Now that we have job suicides on our hands, may be what our governments need urgently are advisers on mass job creation not advisers on terrorism. The self-immolation of *Bouazizi* which left him in intensive care, wrapped head to toe in white bandages - shocked the North African nation and sparked protests over unemployment. It eventually led to the sacking of the government of President Zine El Abidine Ben Ali, who has ruled Tunisia with an iron fist since 1987. What are the implications of this development for good governance in Africa? The International Monetary Fund had long praised Tunisia for economic prosperity. It is even dubbed the *Singapore of Africa.* The events of recent weeks show that a disconnection between impressive figures of growth and the reality of jobless growth, deprivations and lack of freedom of expression in Tunisia. The dramatic singular historic event in Tunisia and its contagious effects on Egypt have raised the issue of how we remove tyrants and sit-tight leaders in Africa. Ben Ali's government, just like Hosni Mubarak's regime, tolerates little public dissent and no wonder they got drown by mass discontent.

It was unfortunate that Mo Ibrahim fell for Malaria and was unable to attend and provoke genuine debate about leadership and good governance in Africa. It would have been nice to ask him that the implications of Arab masses' revolt for leadership crisis in Africa? Do we need to attract plausible sit-tight leaders to step down through monetization or dollarization or we simply encourage masses to take to the streets as did in Tunisia and as they are currently doing in Egypt? MO Ibrahim Prize for Achievement in African Leadership was initiated three years ago by Mo Ibrahim, the Sudanese-born mobile phone tycoon. The plum prize amounts to some $5 million (almost a billion naira) plus $200,000 salary for the rest of the recipient's life who must have been a former president or head of state who has stood down from office in the previous three years. Mo Ibrahim's effort is conceptually driven by a commendable tested assumption according to which without development, there cannot be good governance in Africa.

With the events in North Africa, it is time to interrogate prize for leader component of Mo Ibrahim good governance agenda. In the last two years, it was bad enough that favourites for the award, never scaled through. But it was worse enough that dictators like Ben Ali and Mubarak were never attracted to step down by the dollars on offer! Yet within weeks the masses of North Africa had achieved what MO's dollars cannot achieve; getting rid of dictatorship and bad governance. We must demonetize public office and make leadership as selfless as it should be. To whom much had been given in terms of power and authoritative allocation of resources in Africa, please do not let anybody further generously throw additional money and power at him. Mo Ibrahim was born the son of a Sudanese clerk in 1946. Interestingly, the 1940s and 1950s he was born was the period of great changes and development that threw up selfless and indeed prizeless leaders in Africa. A prize for Kwame Nkrumah, Sekou Toure (who effortlessly shared co-presidency with Nkrumah after the latter was overthrown), Aminu Kano, Amilcal Cabral or Ahmadu Bello and in dollar or pound sterling denominations would have been deemed cheeky and definitely rejected. Of course, Nelson Mandela — who modestly served only one term after becoming the first democratically elected leader of South Africa in 1994 could not have gone to prison for 27 years to be awarded a prize by a mobile business Mongol! Mandela actually told the Apartheid hangmen that he dared to die for freedom, the unquantifiable prize indeed. Please don't let us make fetish of our leaders through silly and cheap prizing when we can boldly engage them to be accountable and if they refuse we can be on the streets to collectively throw them out. The pitiful state of democracy in Africa is due to the fact that we unduly privilege leaders while the real "kings" are the masses in a democracy. To therefore further privilege our leaders with take away lump sum for stepping down when they must is to further privilege the powerful. The money we saved from our leaders could be used to encourage the mass to stay outdoor in protest against dictatorship or fight malaria which denied us Mo Ibrahim's refreshing thoughts on leadership at the Trust Dialogue last Thursday.

Reading Hosni Mubarak's Mind*

At the best of times, having a true appreciation of the real workings of a non-transparent, unaccountable and repressive dictatorship would prove a tall order. This is certainly not the best of times for a three decade-long Egyptian dictatorship daily and rightly tormented by serial mass protests, 14th day of protests today. Discerning the mind of dictator, Hosni Sayyid Mubarak; the fourth President of the Arab Republic of Egypt at this worse of times must therefore prove an exercise in frustrations. Yet given his obstinacy to hang on, a psychological profiling of a man who dares to sit atop of a volcanic political eruption two weeks long might have some heuristic value. What for instance are Hosni Mubarak's motivations? What are his methods? True to character trait of an oppressor dictator, Hosni Mubarak is undoubtedly motivated by *self-love* and *self love* alone. Since the outbreak of the uprisings, on the 24th of January, in panic he has retrenched the cabinet, feverishly appointed a former intelligence chief Omar Suleiman as Vice President. Hundreds of protesters reportedly killed. A thousand injured when official thugs moved against peaceful protesters last Wednesday. Top members of the ruling National Democratic (sic!) Party, including his son Gamel Mubarak (who must have been planted therein out of self love) had resigned. Yet Mubarak still holds on tenuously to a precarious power of dubious legitimacy proving that he loves himself more than his cabinet, his party and indeed than his country, out of self-love and self-love alone. Like many dictators before him, Mubarak at this hour plays last minute indispensability, even when he summarily dispensed with his countrymen through his officially orchestrated violence. He

* 7th February, 2011

has announced that he will not seek re-election in Egypt's upcoming September election. The motivation here is again nothing but self. The people say Mubarak should live now. What then has taunted September election got to do with a million matchers who are insisting on democracy now and end to three decade dictatorship? Whoever voted for him in previous sham elections in which in any case votes were never counted? President Mubarak has been "re-elected" by self-help "majority" votes in a referendum (note; not elections!) for successive terms on four occasions: in 1987, 1993, 1999 and 2005 in which he was a lone candidate. No one could run against him according to the Egyptian Constitution in which the People's Assembly played the main role in electing the President of the Republic.

14th day after Egypt is avoidably getting deep in unprecedented uprising with clashes intensifying after Mubarak's desperate self-preservation measures. Mubarak's method in dealing with the uprisings so far fits into oppressor regime styles over the ages; sentiments arms twisting and sheer repression. At sentimental level Mubarak plays on "national stability" and "peace", twin critical national success factors, his long reign of repression had put in jeopardy. The dictator's mind set is again true to type of how oppressor regime perceives the oppressed when they rise against oppression. The rising oppressed Egyptians are seen as "subversive", "violent", "destabilizing" and "disorderly". Interestingly Mubarak's allies in Israel, Europe and USA also reinforced this Mubarak's patronizing/dictatorial mind set of "stability" without democracy and social justice given their hypocritical posturing and double faced self-serving approach to the Egyptian crisis. According to Mubarak, his

> "primary responsibility now is security and independence of the nation to ensure a peaceful transfer of power in circumstance that protect Egypt and the Egyptians and allow handing over responsibility to whoever the people choose in the coming presidential election."

Appointed Vice President as far back as 1975, he ascended the Presidency on October 14, 1981, following the assassination of President Anwar Sadat. There is certainly something sinister, seemingly deceptive about a ruler who in the wake of an unprecedented unpopular uprising against his sit tight regime playing "stability" and "peace" cards with his people in place of dignified resignation and apology. It is amazing how Mubarak, longest-serving Egyptian ruler (since Muhammed Ali Pasha) has turned a slave of his own power. An Egyptian proverb has it that; "*the tyrant is only a slave turned inside out*". Interestingly, the pictures emerging from Tahir (Liberation) square show orderly protests of oppressed people asking for an end to dictatorship, demanding for mass jobs and good governance. With Mubarak's regime, it has been a peace of the graveyards in which as many as 30,000 have been imprisoned on politically motivated charges. The recent desperation to terminate internet service and prevent social networking of the Egyptian people was one exercise in oppressive power. Undoubtedly Mubarak recorded significant economic growth rate for Egypt, albeit jobless growth which is at the root of the current mass protest. To his credit notwithstanding mass protests uninterrupted light illuminates better at the Liberation (Tahir) square than Nigeria's Eagle Square! Even at that, Mubarak's success at the level of the economy is far from being selfless. His estimated wealth and that of his family reportedly range from US$40 billion to $70 billion, competing with GDP of Egypt itself. With alleged mass accumulation of this proportion indispensability mentality of Mubarak is better appreciated.

Mubarak: Resignation or Humiliation?*

Last Friday, three decade old dictator of Cairo reportedly resigned from office. In the next thirty years, for generation of future Africans to appreciate whether Hosni Mubarak truly honourably "reigned" or legitimately humiliated out of office we must come to terms with how a 30 year dictator of Egypt, Hosni Mubarak was forced out of office. Thanks to, 18 days of rage and protests that brought out the best of the ancient people; resistance and demand for freedom! This is the daily chronicle of Egyptian resistance and protests as reported by news agencies. In January inspired by the spontaneous uprising in Tunisia, activists in Egypt called for an uprising in their own country, to protest against poverty, unemployment, government corruption and the rule of president Hosni Mubarak. On January 25, Egyptians took to the streets. It was aptly tagged a "day of rage". Thousands marched downtown Cairo, Mediterranean city of Alexandria, the Nile Delta cities of Mansura and Tanta and in the southern cities of Aswan and Assiut as well as other towns.

They marched towards the offices of the ruling National Democratic Party, as well as the foreign ministry and the state television. After the initial relative peace, demonstrators clashed with the police who fired tear gas and used water cannons against demonstrators crying out "Down with Mubarak" in Cairo's main Tahrir Square. Mubarak tried to blame the Muslim Brotherhood, for fomenting the unrest. Officially three protesters reported killed during the anti-Mubarak demonstrations.

---

* 14 February, 2011

January 26: Protests continued with demonstrators pelting security forces with rocks and firebombs.

Police used tear gas, water cannons and batons to disperse protesters in Cairo. In Suez, the protest was bloody clashes as the police and protesters clashed.

January 27: Mohamed ElBaradei, the former head of the UN nuclear watchdog turned democracy advocate, arrived Egypt to join the protests while protests continued across several cities. Hundreds arrested, but the protesters insisted to continue until Mubarak leaves office. Professionals like Lawyers staged protests in the Mediterranean port city of Alexandria and the Nile Delta town of Toukh, north of Cairo. Mubarak regime disrupted Face book, Twitter and Blackberry Messenger services in a desperate attempt to scuttle the protest.

January 28: Major disruptions to internet services were reported as the country prepared for a new wave of protests after Friday prayers. Egypt's interior ministry threatened "decisive measures", but the protests persisted. Eleven civilians reportedly killed in Suez and 170 injured. At least 1,030 people get injured countrywide.

January 29: Fire engulfed the ruling party headquarters next door on Friday night, set ablaze by anti-government protesters.

For the first time in three decades, the dictator Hosni Mubarak appointed a vice-president, Omar Suleiman, the country's former spy chief, who has been working closely with Mubarak most of his reign of terror.

January 30: Thousands of anti-government protesters in Cairo's Tahrir Square stood their ground, despite troops firing into the air in a bid to disperse them.

January 31: President Hosni Mubarak still clung to power, refusing to step down, amid growing calls for his resignation. Protesters continued to defy the military-imposed curfew. Thousands gathered in Cairo's Tahrir Square and hundreds marched through Alexandria.

Egypt's new vice-president promised dialogue in order to push through constitutional reforms.

Protesters called for a "million man march" and a general strike on Tuesday to commemorate one week since the protest movement began. The military reiterates that it will not attempt to hurt protesters.

As 250,000 gathered around Cairo's Tahrir Square on Monday, Mubarak asked his new prime minister, Ahmed Shafiq, to start talks with the opposition.

Mubarak named his new crisis cabinet on state television. Former US president Jimmy Carter called the unrest in Egypt an "earth-shaking event", and said Hosni Mubarak "will have to leave".

Paradoxically or interestingly Israel urged the world to tone down Mubarak criticism amid Egypt unrest to preserve stability in the region!

February 1: Hosni Mubarak announced in a televised address that he will not run for re-election but refused.

Mohamed El Baradei, the Egyptian opposition figure said Mubarak's pledge not to stand again for the presidency was an act of deception. US President Barack Obama in a speech at the White House praised the Egyptian military for their patriotism and for allowing peaceful demonstrations. Khalid Abdel Nasser, son of the former Egyptian president Gamal Abdel Nasser, too joined the protest in Tahrir Square.

February 2: Demonstrations against President Hosni Mubarak's regime continued. Violent clashes raged for much of Wednesday around Tahrir Square in central Cairo. Up to 1,500 people were injured, some of them seriously, and by the day's end at least three deaths were reported by the Reuters news agency quoting officials.

February 3: Bursts of heavy gunfire early on Thursday aimed at anti-government demonstrators in Cairo's Tahrir [Liberation] Square, left at least five people dead and several more wounded, according to reports from Cairo.

February 4: Hundreds of thousands of anti-government protesters gathered in Cairo's Tahrir Square for what they have termed the "Day of Departure".

February 5: Thousands remained inside Tahrir Square fear an approaching attempt by the military to evacuate the square.

The leadership of Egypt's ruling National Democratic Party resigned, including Gamal Mubarak, the son of Hosni Mubarak but the dictator sat tight.

February 6: Banks officially re-opened for 3.5 hours, and traffic police were back on the streets in Cairo, in attempts to get the capital to start returning to normal.

February 7: Thousands were camping out in Tahrir Square, refusing to budge. While banks have reopened, schools and the stock exchange remain closed.

Egypt's government desperately approved a 15 per cent raise in salaries and pensions in a bid to appease the angry masses and cultivate Egyptian labour movement.

February 8: Protesters continued at Tahrir Square, which now resembles a tented camp. Protesters in the capital also gathered to protest outside parliament including Egyptians who have returned from abroad. Omar Suleiman, the Egyptian vice-president, warned that his government "can't put up with continued protests" for a long time.

Ban Ki-moon, the UN chief, said genuine dialogue was needed to end the current crisis, adding that a peaceful transition was crucial.

February 9: Labour unions joined protesters in the street, with some of them calling for Mubarak to step down while others simply called for better pay. Massive strikes started rolling throughout the country.

February 10:

The Egyptian prime minister formed a committee that will gather evidence on "the illegitimate practices" that resulted from the events of recent weeks

February 11

Mubarak "resigned" or rightly and legitimately forced out?

Gaddafi's Grey Book*

At the height of the mass Tahir square uprisings against the 31 year oppressor of Cairo, my attempted psychological profiling of an erstwhile Egyptian dictator, Hosni Mubarak; the popularly dethroned fourth President of the Arab Republic of Egypt proved a tall order. It might therefore appreciation of the real workings of a more deadly unaccountable and repressive dictatorship like that of Muammar Al Gaddafi might even be more frustrating. Paradoxically compared to Hosni Mubarak and Ben Ali and even ever brutal sit-tight Robert Mugabe, Al Gaddafi more than other dictators espouses his world outlook. We need not agonize about Gaddafi's mind when we can simply discern the way he thinks through his articulated views. In the wake of the global climate change, green colour has assumed special significance and importance. But Al Gaddafi must be credited with the singular honour of promoting green consciousness at a time it was not fashionable to do so. I am privileged to have an autographed copy of Gaddafi's *Green Book*. That was in 2009 at the Congress of Organization of African Trade Union Unity (OATUU) during which we were treated to some hours of incoherent ranting on African and global affairs by Brother Gaddafi. *Green Book* "is a three-part collection of political thoughts, social and economic theories and day-to-day how-to guides by Libya's Muammar el Gaddafi". The book sums up Gaddafi's "Third Universal Theory," designed to be an alternative to capitalism and "atheistic communism." It also expounds on the role of women, men, "black people," music and education in everyday life. In Gaddafi's words, "THE GREEN BOOK presents the ultimate solution to the problem of the

* March 14, 2011

instrument of government, and indicates for the masses the path upon which they can advance from the age of dictatorship to that of genuine democracy. Interestingly Gaddafi's inspirations originated from Egyptian leader Gamal Abdel Nasser's *Philosophy of the Revolution* (1954), where he Nasser lays out his ideas about pan-Arab nationalism and his intention to be not only the Arab world's leader, but Africa's, too. The *Green Book*, is a compulsory reading in Libya. But as the saying goes *Never judge a book by its cover.* Thanks to the ongoing mass resistance against Gaddafi's 42 year old dictatorship, Gaddafi's *Green Book* has turned some what a *Grey Book*.

A collection of three volumes, Green Book was published between 1976 and 1979. Book One: Published in 1976, the first volume, espouses the "The Authority of the People," The volume expounds on the failure of parliamentary democracy and in place makes a case for what Gaddafi calls "Popular Conferences and the People's Committees." The events of recent weeks show that the so called people's committees have not been a factor in Libya's development. On the contrary what we have is singular leader dictatorship/nepotism, worse than parliamentary democracy Green Book decries. The star defenders of Gaddafi are his notorious children with Saif al-Islam, long regarded as Gaddafi's heir apparent, as the arrow head and not the peoples' committee.

The second volume of the Green Book entitled, "The Solution of the Economic Problem: Socialism," was published in 1978. "It calls for the end of a wage- and rent-based economy, to be replaced by self-employment or economic partnerships".

"Wage-earners are but slaves to the masters who hire them," Gaddafi writes. The solution? "The ultimate solution lies in abolishing the wage-system, emancipating people from its bondage and reverting to the natural laws which defined relationships before the emergence of classes, forms of governments and man-made laws. These natural rules are the only measures that ought to govern human relations."

Many can hardly know what Gaddafi means by abolishing wages resulting from "production". But the events of recent times in Tripoli show that there is a huge gap between Gaddafi's theoretical rhetoric and the reality of wage system. In an attempt to undermine the mass revolts against his regime just like in Egypt Gaddafi has further legitimised the wage system by generously massively increase wages to bribe off resistance. The third volume tries to lay bare the "The Social Basis of the Third International Theory," was published in 1979. Interesting most of the actions of Gaddafi in the past 42 years of rule do not flow from the Green Book. Like some leaders in Africa – Nkrumah, Nyerere, Kaunda, Gaddafi devoted much time to pan-Arabism and pan-Africanism. But no one has undermined the very cause of continental unity than Gaddafi himself. With disastrous adventures in Chad, Liberia, Sudan and Sierra Leone over the years, and verbal aggression against Nigeria which he wished is balkanized along religious line and his latest disastrous responses to the pressures for reforms by his own people, all leading to deaths of some thousands of Africans, Gaddafi's Green Book has truly turned grey!

Reading the News*

President Goodluck Jonathan has reportedly ordered a review of Nigeria's foreign policy. Nothing could be timely. Better late than never. Not long ago, down town Ugandan capital stones were reportedly thrown at a car carrying President Goodluck Jonathan to the 4th inauguration of President Yoweri Museveni. What a one chance-President Goodluck Jonathan was doing with an upth time dictator Museveni beats national and international imagination. Ugandan trip by the President simply did not add up for Nigeria. Here is Nigeria coming to terms with the challenges of democratic consolidation through attempted free and fair elections, one woman, one vote, multiple choices of candidates and parties. Conversely we have Uganda being suffocated by dictator Museveni, who has been in power for 25 years, moving against the global wind of democratic renewal, being "sworn" in for a fourth term in office after "winning" February's elections that were never judged to be free or fair. True to the character of President Jonathan's spokesman Ima Niboro he had since been on the defensive and hard put convincing nobody that "there was no attack on the president [Jonathan] in Uganda". Pray, must a visiting President in any country be embarrassed at all? What the President's spokesman should tell Nigeria (proactively, not reactively) even well before the alleged mob accident in Uganda, is what the President was billed to do in Uganda. Was it to celebrate democracy or simply dignify an unrepentant and arrogant dictator like Museveni? Foreign policies must reflect domestic policies of the nation? Nigeria is already converted to democratic process, we must learn to advance democratic process on a global scale. Patronizing

---

* May 23, 2011

the likes of Museveni and Mugabe who serially trample democracy undermines democracy in Africa. Next time Museveni is being "inaugurated" for the fifth time, let the sit-tight and die-likes like Muammar Gaddafi, who has ruled Libya since 1969, and Robert Mugabe of Zimbabwe, who has been in power since 1980 attend not President Jonathan who has made a pledge in deference to Nigeria's democratic pressures not spend more than one time in office.

The much awaited President Barrack Obama's speech on the Arab Uprising turned out not be earth breaking like the mass uprisings that are changing our world for the better. Revolutions are certainly not dinner parties! Revolutions are not speech making either! Whatever it is worth the remark of President Obama on Bin Laden did not logically add up. Hear President Obama:

> "Bin Laden and his murderous vision won some adherents. But even before his death, al-Qaida was losing its struggle for relevance, as the overwhelming majority of people saw that the slaughter of innocents did not answer their cries for a better life. By the time we found bin Laden, al-Qaida's agenda had come to be seen by the vast majority of the region as a dead end, and the people of the Middle East and North Africa had taken their future into their own hands."

The question is: If Bin Laden was already ideologically and spiritually dead well before Operation why then an over kill, sorry in Obama's words "…a huge blow by killing its leader - Osama bin Laden" by United States combined forces. Why must USA violate the sovereignty of Pakistan in an attempt to get at Bin Laden who USA said was long dead ideologically?

Still read President Obama:

> "Bin Laden was no martyr. He was a mass murderer who offered a message of hate - an insistence that Muslims had to take up arms against the West, and that violence against men, women and children was the only path to change. He rejected democracy and individual rights for Muslims in favour of violent extremism; his agenda focused on what he could destroy - not what he could build."

Why on earth should President Obama and indeed the USA spend so much energy and dissipate so much heat over a non-

Martyr. It is the greatest paradox of Bin Laden that his killers (at least verbally) made martyrdom out of him.

What on earth is all the noise about Monsieur John Campbell a notorious former US ambassador to Nigeria (from 2004 to 2007) being denied a visa to Nigeria? The former ambassador, currently said to be a Ralph Bunche Senior Fellow for African Policy Studies at the Council on Foreign Relations in United States had predicted a failed Nigerian state if April polls did not follow the logic of his failed analysis. Campbell's 1000 political terror word counts aggravated the country's political blood pressure (PBP) more than the anything else before the election. Witness him: "The 2011 elections in Nigeria, scheduled for January 22, pose a threat to the stability of the United States' most important partner in West Africa." What a pessimistic poetic/political terror licence? Now that Nigeria refused to fulfil Campbell's silly ambassadorial prophesy, what is he looking for in Nigeria? You don't apply for a visa to a preferred failed nation, do you John Campbell? Nobody wants to go to Somalia, a proto failed state certainly not a former American ambassador. Those who refuse to work for a successful state in Africa or those who consciously work for a failed Africa through academic terrorism like John Campbell have no business desperately looking for a Visa for another failed analysis.

Paradoxes of Libya*

"*Time undermines us*"! so goes ancient proverb. History and contemporary reality of Libya once again prove the vitality of this saying. Through an army coup in 1969 a 27-year-old signals officer, called Muammar Gaddafi shot himself to power reportedly motivated by some grand ambitions and above all the revolutionary ideas of Nasser's Egypt espoused from Cairo Radio's 'Voice of the Arabs'. Only time could have so casually undermined the reign of Gaddaffi! On the eve of the 42nd anniversary in power through jack boot, he was in turn paradoxically shot out of power by some combined forces of Libyan rebels and opportunistic big imperial NATO brothers with an eye on Libyan oil rather than Libyan liberty. Ruth First was a South African liberation fighter and a Pan-African intellectual activist. She was killed in 1981 in Mozambique by a letter bomb sent by the then racist Apartheid hangmen in South Africa. She wrote a classical book in 1974 entitled Libya; *The Elusive Revolution.* Very few students of Gaddafii's vision of society, called the Third Universal Theory (purportedly providing an alternative to decadent capitalism and atheistic communism) could have agreed with Ruth First that Libya's Revolution was indeed elusive, not sustainable. Very few could have imagined that the three volumes of Gaddaffi 'Green Book' (made a compulsory read in Libyan garrison schools) could have turned so Gray a book! Libya throws up scores of paradoxes of profound academic interest. What a "perverse" revolution which promised a new social order by overthrowing a monarch (King Idris) but turned out to make a proud "King of Kings" of a signal soldier? An oil-rich state with a revolutionary

* September 5, 2011

promise not to be another conservative sheikhdom turned out to be a conservative personal dictatorship. The author of the Green Book came to power without firing a shot in 1969 (deposed King Idris was absent on a visit to Turkey). But Gaddaffi's removal has left in its trails a civil war, thousands dead and imperial NATO forces on African continent. What a perverse revolution led by 11 young unrelated soldiers and compatriots claiming to represent a mass-based popular revolution (with one notorious Major Jaloud) but ending up with Gaddafi and his almost 11-member nepotistic family cabal? What a paradox of a false hero who historically committed a regicide against a deposed King but is on the run with family (family members alone) in the wake of rebels' invasion? For as long as it lasted Gaddafi lived on make ups in literal and generic terms. Literally he had female make-up body guards just as he paid lip-service make ups, first to pan-Arabism and later opportunistically later-day pan-Africanism which distorts the pan Africanism of Nkrumah of Ghana and Nasser of Egypt. Gaddafi's scores of failed proposals designed to forge Arab unity 'from the Atlantic Ocean to the Gulf' could fill a *Ghana-must-go* diplomatic bag! Barely three months after he seized power he proposed Tripoli Charter aimed at linking Libya's destiny with Nasser's Egypt and Numeiri's Sudan. In 1971 there was the Benghazi Treaty linking Libya, Egypt and Syria. "In 1973 he threw up the Hassi Messaoud Accords linking Libya and Boumedienne's Algeria. In 1974 came the Djerba Treaty linking Libya and Bourguiba's Tunisia." All these schemes went the ways they came via personal impulse and collapsed well before Gaddafi's collapse! Gaddafi projected the image of a philosopher King who sought African unity and was indeed briefly AU chairman. Before then in engaged in war of attritions in Chad (remember Aozou Strip!) that left millions dead in the 1970s/1980s. Yet as a chieftain of AU he audaciously recommended that Nigeria be split into some religious enclaves. It is a paradox indeed that it is Gaddafi's Libya that has split into smithereens of no clear-cut ideological or political patterns beyond the rebels and the oil fields. In 2009 Gaddafi's empty styles climaxed in a symbolic tearing of the UN charter during a long, long incomprehensible speech that went down as the lowest moment in UN history. Any further evidence the world unanimously backed the notorious security council resolution 1973 (2011) the cover for NATO's wholesale intervention in Libya? Paradoxically the Libyan crisis has brought to the fore the increasing bankruptcy of Nigeria's foreign policy. I agree with my friend, the Presidential Spokesman, Reuben Abati, who said Nigeria needs not worried at the criticism from South Africa over its quick recognition of the Libyan interim government. After-all when South African government under the discredited President Mbeki was in bed with power usurper Laurent Gbagbo of Ivory Coast, nobody took South Africa government to the cleaners for meddling wrongly in West African Affairs. However I disagree with Abati, that "the position of Nigeria on Libya is consistent with its principles as a nation". It is a paradox for a country like Nigeria which fought a civil war and defeated rebels at a great cost of a million lives to be trigger happy to accord uncritical recognition to some rebels in Tripoli that have not sought our support! Senate committee on foreign affairs must conduct a public hearing on this foreign policy misadventure in Libya. We can get rid of dictators without compromising African sovereignty and undermining democracy.

The Minister of Foreign Affairs, Ambassador Olugbenga Ashiru, got it wrong when he said last week that national interest informed a quick recognition of the Transitional National Council in Libya, which in collaboration with NATO forces (not AU forces) overthrew the 42-year regime of Col Muammar Gaddafi. We pride ourselves of promoting democracy as means of popular governance in Africa. It is a paradox that Nigeria will be eager to lead scores of members of African Union to recognize a transitional council in Tripoli financed and promoted by NATO through arms and killings as road to effect regime change in Africa. Libya under Gaddafi was on top of UNDP development index. The greatest paradox is that development under dictatorship is elusive and unsustainable.

Libya, a Day After[*]

After the death of Muammar Gaddafi, Libya's four decade long last Thursday in his hometown of Sirte after captivity, the interest of yours sincerely is pure academic. The gory globalized and celebrated pictures of the fallen Libyan leader reopen the critical question of celebrated killings and murders (and indeed the methodology of fighting or armed conflict as mode of political engagement). It is now an open knowledge that from all accounts (including the untidy white washing official story of the leadership of the ruling National Transitional Council (NTC)) the former Libyan leader was literarily lynched and murdered. The seemingly global acceptable reactions to the mob justice meted to Gaddafi has dragged whatever is remaining of our humanity to the mud. Apart from President Jacob Zuma who on Friday while addressing a joint media briefing with Equatorial Guinea President Teodoro Obiang Nguema Mbasogo at the Union Buildings in Pretoria interrogated the nature of Gaddafi's death, most African leaders by their loud silence and indifference seem to have accepted televised mob justice for a fleeing Head of state. According to Zuma:

> "Given there was a warrant of arrest against Gaddafi, those who found him should have arrested him and handed him to the ICC," "We expected him to be captured, given that everybody knew there was a warrant of arrest issued against him."
>
> "There is a trend across the world where former leaders accused of injustice are not given an opportunity to stand trial in a court of justice. That is surprising. I think even those who accused him [Gaddafi] would have wanted to see him become answerable," he

[*] October 24, 2011

said.

We have read the thought process of South African leadership about the tragedy of Libya, pray what is President Jonathan's attitude to Gaddafi's summary mob liquidation?

Certainly it is an open knowledge that while Gaddafi was in the saddle as the "King of Kings" he was definitely no respecter of due process or due justice for his opponents. From his murderous expansionist adventures in Chad in the 1980s (occupation of Aozou Strip) in which some hundreds of thousands were killed, readiness to use bribery and violence to pursue his self-appointed ideological cause, some can say Gaddafi was hunted by the spectre of his bloody methodology to the end. Indeed if we add Gaddafi's dubious legacy of support for murderer leaders like Idi Amin of Uganda, Charles Tailor of Liberia and hand/limp cutters of Sierra Leone, not few might agree former Sudanese military leader, Numeiri who after accusing Gaddafi of supporting a bloody coup against him in 1976 described Gaddafi as "*a split personality- both evil*" . Whatever the dark side of Gaddafi's dictatorship, there is no excuse for the indifference of our humanity to clearly exhibited jungle justice of Libya under the guidance of the "civilized world" and NATO commanders. President Obama in his celebrated Cairo speech audaciously quoted reminded the world that killing a human without justice amounts to destroying a whole humanity. The American President however literarily supervised and hailed the serial murders and lack of due process in Libya in recent weeks. Not until UN promised an inquiry into the death of Gaddafi, President Obama never demanded for accountability with respect of the slain of fleeing members of the old regime. He has actually embraced the news that the former Libyan leader was so killed calling it the end of a long and painful chapter for the country.

The point cannot be overstated. Our humanity must return to civil approach to global governance. We must respect not selectively all the rules of engagements even for the non-respecters like Gaddafi. The world must hold the TNC under the interim Prime Minister Mustapha global Jalali accountable to the promise of non-vengeance and reconciliation. Cathartic bloodletting of the recent months must give way to active reinvention of civil society with vibrant political parties and trade unions which Gaddafi ruthlessly suppressed under his reign. Paradoxically Mustapha Jalali's speech yesterday lacked a new revolutionary social/political and democratic agenda befitting a liberation day speech in this direction. Time however will tell. Meanwhile the question remains; how new is the new Libya?

ANC - Centenary of institution-building*

President Barack Obama of United States made a historic speech to Ghanaian parliament during his equally historic visit to Ghana as the first Africa American President on the 11th July 2009. His quotable quote still hunts the continent like a spectra; *Africa according to him needs strong institutions, not strong men*! The uncritical downloading of Obama's remark about strong institutions further exposed the absence of memory in African discourse in general and in African media in particular. On January 8th, National Congress (ANC), South Africa's ruling party marked 100 years of its existence. This historic fact belies the admonition of the American President. Apparently it is Obama that has to appreciate that Africa is not short of tested strong institutions like ANC after all. ANC was formed in 1912, almost 50 years before President was born and almost 100 years before America produced him as the first African American President. Paradoxically President Obama was not counted at the celebration of a strong African institution that is ANC. Indeed ANC became a strong institution in spite of the Anglo-American conspiracy of silence and active support for half a century long Apartheid regime which ANC fought and defeated with the release of Nelson Mandela from 27 year imprisonment in 1990. Africa has become a dustbin for received wisdom for about good governance and institution building. History however shows that those who sermonize to Africa are the very people who historically undermined the emergency of strong men and strong institutions in Africa in the past and of course in the present. It was a scandal that when Nelson Mandela visited America in the 90s he was still classified a "terrorist" leading a "terrorist" organization. When the whole world including United Nations saw

* February 6, 2012

ANC as a liberation movement, Britain and America in collaboration with the Apartheid regime saw ANC as an outlaw.

Nigeria interestingly was one of the frontline states which pushed for the unconditional support for ANC in its struggle against Apartheid. The British Prime Minister Mrs. Thatcher, under the guise of constructive engagement with Apartheid together with President Regan of America denied talks with the ANC. The ANC, is the oldest liberation movement in the continent formed in 1912. It has had 12 Presidents since then namely John Langalibalele Dube from 1912-1917, Sefako Makgatho from 1917 to 1924, ZR Mahabane served his first term from 1924 to 1927, Josiah Gumede from 1927 to 1930, Pixley ka Isaka Seme from 1930 to 1936; ZR Mahabane's second term from 1937 to 1940, AB Xuma from 1940 to 1949, James Moroka from 1949 to 1952, Albert Luthuli from 1952 to 1967, Oliver Reginald Tambo from 1967 to 1991, Nelson Mandela from 1991 to 1997, Thabo Mbeki from 1997 to 2007 and Jacob Zuma from 2007. Only the last three have held executive presidential power. The lesson here for Nigeria's political party building is the need for continuity and perseverance in institution building. President Zuma underscored the significance of ANC as a liberation movement when he said that:

> "The national liberation struggles were fought to achieve an Africa in which people were free from colonialism, racism, paternalism, patriarchy, poverty and all forms of social and political ills.
> Given our common history as a people that were oppressed, we share the belief in democracy, justice, human rights and all freedoms that a free people should enjoy. Most importantly we share the passion for achieving the unity of the African continent. The ANC has worked for the unity of the continent for many decades...As Africans we share the quest for prosperity and a better life for all the African peoples, a passion the ANC has had for almost a century now."

Beyond Yellow fever Diplomacy*

After a four-day stand-off between Nigeria and South Africa over alleged possession of fake yellow fever vaccination document by the citizens of the former, the interest of yours sincerely remains purely academic. As at the last count the degenerated yellow card diplomacy led to mutual deportation of as many as 300 nationals of the two countries. We were told that at the root of the crisis was the deportation of 125 Nigerians by South African immigration officials over alleged fake yellow cards. The Federal Government of Nigeria did feel some diplomatic humiliation. In turn it threatened retaliation and actual turned back some 128 South Africans from the country. South Africa and Nigeria were both 2010 World Cup qualifiers in South Africa that some-how miserably crashed out of the recently concluded Africa Cup of Nations in Gabon and Equatorial Guinea. Both Nigeria and South Africa blamed others rather than their poorly organized soccer for crashing out of the Cup of nations. Nigeria reportedly blamed a faith healer and South Africa the head-to-head rule for missing out. Some mischievous foreign policy observers noted that if there was no alleged fake yellow fever vaccination row, both South Africa and Nigeria could have invented one anyway, arguing that both countries suffered from Cup of nation crashing out syndrome, adding that what we witnessed last week was some contest for cup of nations relevance by some diplomatic means. For as long as this diplomatic contest lasted Africa's spectators were truly entertained. Many thanks to South Africa, for initiating a process that ended the unfortunate altercation through a historic diplomatic letter of apology. South Africa's Archbishop Desmond

* March 12, 2012

Tutu had long written that there is No Future Without Forgiveness. According to the chairman of the South Africa's Truth and Reconciliation Commission, "It is crucial when a relationship has been damaged or when a potential relationship has been made impossible, that the perpetrator should acknowledge the truth and be ready and willing to apologise. It helps the process of forgiveness and reconciliation immensely." It is gratifying that the issues around the yellow fever card controversy, which led to a strain in relations between both countries would be resolved through the standing Bi-National Commission (BNC). The psychic victory might be Nigeria's that extracted a diplomatic apology but the real victory goes to South Africans who ignored the cheap denial mode and opted to bold responsibility and apology. Witness Deputy Minister of the South Africa's Department of International Relations and Co-operation DIRCO, Ebrahim Ismail Ebrahim who disclosed that he was

> "confident that the steps that were agreed upon would ensure that travel to and from Nigeria returns to normal. We apologise for this unfortunate incident and we hope this matter will not in any way affect our bilateral relations...We've put into place certain mechanisms to ensure this doesn't happen again, and we believe that this matter is closed."

The frosty relations between the two countries have raised the naughty issue of the human dimension of the taunted new globalization. While capital and money electronically move without passports much less yellow fever vaccination cards, it is interesting that human beings (human labour) are being scrutinized at global borders. It is interesting that feverish hot hourly capital flight often from Nigeria to South Africa faces no restrictions compared to human travellers. It is truly a globalization of capital! It also interesting and, indeed, remarkable that despite the much talk about reprisals against business interests of respective countries, nationals of the two countries were the instant victims of the avoidable diplomatic row. It is a sad commentary that we appreciate Nigeria and South African diplomatic relationship through yellow fever vaccination. Whence the diplomacy of the tow giants on Libya, Ivory coast and currently Senegal? Lastly must not Nigerians be united by yellow fever in faraway South Africa? For a week we never read about North and South, Muslims and Christians. We were all Nigerians! Is this instant patriotism an enduring commitment or a passing fad?

World Bank's Presidency; Whence the Contest?[*]

After the American Dr Jim Yong Kim has emerged as the new President of the World Bank Group, the interest of yours truly remains as usual; academic! Anybody from the outer space, (certainly not this our planet,) reading the statement of the finance Minister Ngozi Okonjo-Iweala ostensibly congratulating the American Dr Jim Yong Kim "*on his emergence as President of the World Bank Group*" would readily salute her for some spirit of sportsmanship in a contest she seems to have lost out. But was there a really contest in the first place? Was there a "battle" for the post of the President of International Bank for Reconstruction and Development (IBRD), otherwise known as the World Bank as we have been made to believe? The truth of the matter is that there was never a contest, no less a contestant from Africa for the post of the presidency of the World Bank. I have not read where the AU passed a resolution on the need for Africa to contest for the Presidency of the World Bank. In Nigeria, at no time was there a resolution of either of the House or the Senate or of the Federal Executive Council for a "battle" for the post of the presidency of the World Bank. So where is the source of all the hype for a contest for which there was no contestant in the first place? Of course there was an open "battle" not long ago for Mrs Okonjo-Iweala to return from the same World Bank to take up an expanded position as Coordinating Minister for the Economy and Minister of Finance. The then World Bank President Robert Zoellick had said in a statement that: "*Her desire to serve her country is truly a big loss for the World Bank but a major gain for Nigeria as it works to craft its*

[*] April 30, 2012

economic way forward." What then suddenly happened to Ngozi's celebrated "*desire to serve*" her country when she so soon she was in for a "battle"" to return to Washington? Will her return not be a " *big loss*" to Nigeria and a "*major gain*" for World Bank? Is anybody doing the transaction costs for Nigeria? Whence then the patriotism in this global endeavour? President Jonathan was so up-beat while belatedly swearing in Minister Ngozi. He claimed that foreign Heads of state patted him at the back for getting the former World Bank chieftain to his cabinet. Undoubtedly there were multiple "nominees" for a "selection process" (note; not election process!) that featured Jim Yong Kim of United States of America, José Antonio Ocampo of Columbia and Ngozi Okonjo-Iweala of Nigeria. Even at that José Antonio Ocampo of Columbia withdrew from the selection process With regard to the "selection process" Mrs Iweala demanded for more openness. The assumption here is that the selection process of the World Bank is already open which of course we all know remains closed. Students of internal democracy in corporate organizations would hold that by pretending to participate in a well-known closed selection process, Minister Ngozi has willy-nilly legitimized a clearly undemocratic process. Joseph E. Stiglitz who enthusiastically campaigned for Minister Ngozi knew it was as exercise in futility; there is "a cabal" that runs international financial institutions, who scandalously alternate the top jobs between Europe and America in IMF and World Bank respectively. Not few hold that her admonition for others not to "contribute to a democratic deficit in global governance" is actually meant for her who seemed to have given flawed process some legitimacy through media hype for a non-existent contest. But can we talk of any victory at all not to talk of important "victories" from a contest that never took place in the first instance? It is debatable whether we have actually shown "what is possible" in terms of the future of the World Bank. Minister Ngozi had always been a compliant not a rebel "insider" (with her favoured neo-liberalism) in the World Bank unlike "rebel insiders" like Professor Joseph Stiglitz who had long campaigned for the reform of both the policies and the international financial institutions for which his appointment was terminated as a chief Economist. Mrs Ngozi unnecessarily also makes fetish of "a merit-based challenge". It is precisely the claim for so-called meritocracy as distinct from democracy that makes a closed shop selection process attractive to the big-players in the Bank, who arrogantly define merit in their own terms! If we are for democratized World Bank please let us insist on that and refuse the wrong temptation of pitching democracy against meritocracy. Are we then saying that the new World Bank President lacks the necessary qualifications for merit for the new job? There is a consensus that people are both the means and ends of development. The pedigree of Dr. Jim Yong Kim shows that he had more dealings with people than the other nominees. "Dr. Kim is a co-founder of Partners in Health (PIH) and a former director of the Department of HIV/AIDS at the World Health Organization (WHO). Before assuming the Dartmouth presidency, Dr. Kim held professorships at Harvard Medical School and the Harvard School of Public Health. He also served as chair of the Department of Global Health and Social Medicine at Harvard Medical School, chief of the Division of Global Health Equity at Brigham and Women's Hospital, and director of the François Xavier Bagnoud Centre for Health and Human Rights at the Harvard School of Public Health. He was elected in 2004 to the Institute of Medicine of the National Academy of Sciences—one of the highest honours in the fields of health and medicine—for his professional achievements and commitment to service. He has published widely over the past two decades, authoring or co-authoring articles for leading academic and scientific journals, including the New England Journal of Medicine, Lancet, and Science." What better merit do we need for a global Development Bank? The narrative should remain focused on the process but above all on the policy thrust of the Bank that came into existence even when many African countries were under colonial rule.

The Rise and Fall of Nigeria's Diplomacy*

Since the controversial emergence of the former South African minister, Nkosazana Dlamini-Zuma, as the new head of the African Union Commission in Addis Ababa, Ethiopia, Nigeria's Minister of Foreign Affairs, Ambassador Olugbenga Ashiru, had been hard put to rationalize the abysmal collapse of Nigeria's diplomacy in the face of South Africa's dramatic diplomatic renaissance. In one breadth he claimed that Nigeria was never in contest with South Africa for the Chair of the Union commission. Witness him:

> "You will recall that President Goodluck Jonathan said it many times that this is not a contest between Nigeria and South Africa and that Nigeria is actually not campaigning for anybody. That is the truth. We did not mount any campaign for any country."

But in another breadth he accepted as much that Nigeria did

> "stand by ECOWAS' endorsement of the candidature of (the failed) Dr. Jean Ping the Gabonese foreign minister...and that was it.
> We just took a position which was principled along with our ECOWAS members and we stood by it. But as usual, people can insinuate that once Nigeria was not in the camp of South Africa, it means that Nigeria is against South Africa. We are not against South Africa."

Somebody once observed rather sarcastically that "*Diplomats make it their business to conceal the facts.*" But when the facts are as obvious as stated by Ambassador Ashiru, it is simply unhelpful to

* July 23, 2012

obliterate the obvious. Certainly only the Honourable Minister and President Jonathan would disbelieve the obvious fact that with the endorsement of ECOWAS' candidate meant Nigeria was truly in a contest it miserably lost.

In any case, Minister Ashiru accepted as much as an active contestant (certainly not a passive endorser of a sub-regional candidate) that Gabonese foreign minister Dr Jean Ping (Nigeria endorsed) ran a miserable campaign compared to robust campaign of Ms Chirwa Dlamini-Zuma. Again witness Minister Ashiru:

> "We must admit that South Africa ran a better campaign. You can imagine that South Africa was able to dispatch envoys once or twice to all 51 African states, you can imagine the outcome. If they have worked hard which we must accept, then the result was not a surprise to some of us."

It is certainly honourable to have accepted that South Africa's victory was deserved. However it is unacceptable to engage in diplomatic subterfuge that Nigeria, a leading member of ECOWAS which ran a mediocre campaign was not in the contest. The recent diplomatic double talk, incoherence and wholesale setback for Nigeria in AU underscores the free fall of Nigeria's diplomacy in general from the erstwhile globally acknowledged rise from Independence even up to the formation of the AU in 2001.

Both history and bagful of deserved diplomatic achievements in favour of Africa and Africans spanning five decades qualify Nigeria as an unbeatable African leading nation in Africa Union (AU). AU emerged out of the Organization of Africa Unity (OAU) formed by founding nations that included Nigeria, Ghana, Ethiopia, Liberia, Egypt and other nations in May 25th 1963. South Africa was then not a liberated country and it was indeed under the heels of the hated Apartheid regime. In fact in 1961 the seemingly conservative government of the late Prime Minister Tafawa Balawa had spearheaded the expulsion of South Africa from the Commonwealth as part of the selfless overall objective of ending colonialism and its Apartheid surrogate suffocating the African majority in the Apartheid enclave. In the 1870s and 1980s, Nigeria put its weight behind the liberation of Angola, Mozambique and Zimbabwe. The bold recognition of the major liberation movement, MPLA (the ruling party in Angola today) on November by Nigeria's Murtala regime contrasted with the despicable role of Apartheid regime of South Africa which unconditionally backed the notorious UNITA and FNLA that waged war of attritions against MPLA. Up to the 1980s Nigeria was a frontline state that shared great historic ideals of African liberation with Zambia, Tanzania, Lesotho Botswana and Angola. All these diplomatic successes that accorded Nigeria a great respect were products of good governance and leadership at home and commitment to great ideals of OAU/AU. The recent Nigeria's authority melt down in AU is a reflection of domestic bad governance and clear cut abandonment of pan African development agenda. On what basis is Nigeria's uncritical support for Dr Jean Ping? Are we to just back a candidate just because is from our region or because he stands for greater ideals of the continent on the verge of second decolonization? Was the so-called principled support for the failed Gabonese foreign Minister not an extension of our domestic/regional tribalism that has degenerated into the new Apartheid franco/anglophone divide? Yours sincerely remains a critic of the moribund Gaddafi regime. But if the AU under the leadership of Dr Jean Ping as well as President Zuma of South Africa and President Jonathan of Nigeria had offered leadership, undoubtedly we did not need NATO to democratize Libya. We can only wish Dlamini-Zuma a refreshing tenure from the recent collapse of leadership in AU. She has already started on a modest note.

Margaret Hilda Thatcher; Lest We Forget[*]

Baroness Thatcher the longest-serving British Prime Minister of the United Kingdom in the 20th century died on the 8th of April 2013 at the age of 87. She was better remembered as The "Iron Lady", a nickname paradoxically given to her by a Soviet communist journalist. A paradox because Thatcher, the first woman to be a British Prime Minister, was notoriously anti-communist. Apparently her globally "uncompromising politics and leadership style" captured the imagination of her enemies (the Soviets) who dignified her as an Iron Lady.

In Africa, we are enjoined not to ever speak ill of the dead. Certainly nobody would ever recommend a Thatcher Death party which last Saturday reportedly attracted some hundreds in London, having fun rather than mourning a Prime Minister, whose poverty inducing policies in Britain have come to be known as Thatcherism.

However some of the post mortem exaggerated tributes from Africa are too good to be believed about the Iron Lady. Indeed some tributes by their factual untruths amount to speaking ill of the dead. President Goodluck Jonathan on Monday while condoling the government and people of Britain on the death of its former Prime Minister Margaret Thatcher said in a statement signed by the President's spokesman Reuben Abati, that "The late Baroness Thatcher will always be remembered by the world for her very unique, distinctive and purposeful leadership which restored pride

[*] *Daily Trust*, 15th April, 2013

and respect to her country and made a resurgent Great Britain a force to be reckoned with on the global stage," Jonathan said. These tributes are mere words without historic content and facts. What made Thatcher's leadership "unique", "purposeful" especially for Africa we are not told. The bane of African leadership is lack of memory and accountability. The generous posthumous assessment of Margaret Thatcher once again shows that African leaders are eager to impress outside powers rather than being accountable to their peoples.

Thatcher while in office made two rancorous visits to Africa characterized by protests and condemnations for her notorious racist support for the discredited Apartheid regime as long as it lasted. How can a woman who in defiance of the world unapologetically saw Nelson Mandela as "a terrorist" deserving no freedom from Robben Island maximum prison (instead of a freedom fighter Madiba is) be said to offer purposeful leadership for Africa?

Undoubtedly, the sudden resignation of Mrs. Thatcher as British Prime Minister on November 22, 1989 after her humiliation by her conservative party was one big relief for Africa. Big relief, because long before the war in the gulf, the African policy of Mrs. Thatcher passed for political and economic equivalent of war(s) against a continent. Thanks to the scores of her doctrinaire policies (read: missiles) for which the continent lacked the capacity (read: patriots) to repel.

Among other things, Apartheid in South Africa thrived on Mrs. Thatcher's 'no-sanctions' policy. The popular belief was that both the liberation efforts and sanctions by the international community would bring the racist Boers to reason and therefore to negotiation table. For Mrs. Thatcher, sanctions campaign was 'absurd' and commonwealth-after-commonwealth, she could not conceal her annoyance about the fact that sanctions would not set out 'to relive the poverty and starvation' in South Africa. Successfully, the 'no-no-woman' defied reasoned positions of the Commonwealth's Eminent Persons' Group (EPG) on Apartheid and by doing so, guaranteed British security for the most inhuman system on the globe (still very much so). Not surprising then that her two official 'African' tours of the Prime Minister in office, were marked by significant demonstrations and condemnations too.

Former President Olusegun Obasanjo had long unmasked Mrs. Thatcher's outlook in a personal letter, sent to her published in an edition of *Financial Times*, when he told her thus: "Many people around the world view your continued opposition to sanctions as founded in instinct, not logic and as displaying a misguided tribal loyalty and myopic political vision…" Obasanjo also rightly pointed out that the "mental laager of the Boer seem to be mirrored" in Thatcher's "own attitudes". Anybody who ever doubts that Thatcher has long assumed notoriety as a tribal chieftain should read her views on immigrations as early as 1978. "People" she said "are really rather afraid that this country (i.e. Britain) might be rather swamped by people with a different culture". A black horse from the city of Kano might well be an evidence of "different culture" in London.

Still on freedom, it is on record that Thatcher's UK did not promote any decolonisation policy or initiative on Namibia. Cold war perspective beclouds the policy perception of the legitimate efforts of SWAPO to restore the usurped rights of black men and women. The struggle for Independence was reduced to a 'regional ideological conflict' according to which a 'linkage' existed between the withdrawal of the Cuban troops in Angola and the Independence of Namibia. Indeed, with the unscheduled visit of Mrs. Thatcher to Windhoek in September, 1989, the world nearly had a caricature of UN Resolution 435 on Namibian independence as she displayed colonial bias and wrongly accused SWAPO of 'disrupting' decolonisation process, she never believed in the first instance. For one, it can be said that Africa problem solving was never her specialisation in office.

However, it was on the economic front, the legacy of her tenure remains a naughty obstacle to development of the continent.

Not by design, but the Thatcher period coincided with the worst economic crisis in Africa: balance of payment crisis, collapse of primary goods' prices, poverty and unemployment. These crises are in themselves attributable to the debt crisis. There was no doubt that Mrs. Thatcher was committed to debt collection and the better if the structural 'adjustment' programme lacks a human face. Britain remains the home of the 'Club of private creditors'. The Prime Minister was committed to free enterprise at home and did not hesitate to export same abroad through the support for IMF and World Bank reforms. Thus the continent became a showcase of mutually exclusive policies of devaluation, liberalisation, privatization and cuts in public spending. The results: unemployment, brain drain, decline in income, and 'perverse flow of resources' through debt repayment.

The defunct *West Africa Weekly* summed up Mrs. Thatcher's tenure thus: 'Mrs. Thatcher never developed a coherent policy that remotely took account of the genuine interests of African people…and reported to have said: "South Africa is not going to come to Addis Ababa to run the AU. It is Nkosazana Dlamini-Zuma who is going to come to make a contribution," she reportedly told reporters after her election to the post of AU chairperson. Most African leaders who are men are not known for modesty.

It is time we reinvented Nigeria's diplomacy in AU in line with the previous efforts of Nigeria's founding fathers, namely Tafawa Balewa, General Gowon, Murtala Muhammed/Obasanjo Shehu Shagari (in that order of honesty of purpose and commitment to Africa).

Wither South Africa-Nigeria Bi-National Commission (BNC)?*

One critical success (or is it failure?) factor in a nation's foreign policy is the domestic or internal development. A tested thesis on international relations says ultimately, foreign policy is an an abridged version of internal policy. This truism was once again played out recently when President Goodluck Jonathan cut short his Southern African trip to attend to urgent security challenges in the country, the latest then being the killing of some 20 policemen in Nasarawa State by some armed cultists while the most notoriously recurring being Borno and Yobe. The two states together with Adamawa state had since come under the heels of emergency rule. The lesson here is that, governance crisis at home keeps undermining the historic commendable relevance of Nigeria in international relations.

We just must put our house in order before we can have a sustainable foreign policy. It is significant and commendable that the President answered the call of national duty with a nation-wide broadcast that among others reaffirms commitment to an indivisible Nigeria based on law and order.

Notwithstanding, the insecurity factor which necessitated the President Goodluck calling off the Namibia trip, the significance of the recently concluded President Jonathan's cuts trip to South Africa South cannot be overstated. Both Nigeria and South Africa are like twin nations, albeit non-identical ones. In land mass, the two countries are among the biggest. South Africa occupies some 1,221,037 km2. Nigeria is also a huge land mass of some almost 1,000,000 surface area (square kilometres). South Africa's

* *Daily Trust*, 20th May, 2013

Population of some 48,810,427 is a third of Nigeria's population of 165 million. The two are regional powers of ECOWAS and SADCC.

They are also football loving nations. Nigeria is three times winner of Africa Cup of Nations championship hosted by South Africa. SA won the cup in 1996 again hosted by South Africa boycotted by Nigeria, no thanks to the Abacha dictatorship.

In terms of economics, South Africa paraded an estimated gross domestic product (GDP) of $368 billion in 2011 as Africa's biggest economy, while Nigeria Africa's second biggest economy by GDP, recorded some $232 billion. The forecast is that with Nigeria's growth rate of seven percent, Nigeria could even overtake South Africa's economy by 2015. The growth drivers are almost the same; export of raw materials. In the case of Nigeria, crude oil and gas, while South Africa has gold and diamonds. Of course unlike Nigeria that has regrettably been pushed back to de-industrialisation with just less than 4 percent manufacturing value added to GDP, South Africa parades good and the highest manufacturing value added number of 24 percent being the leading industrialising nation in the continent. Over 100 South African companies are doing business in Nigeria in real service sectors such as Telecommunications, Banking, property development and entertainment industries like the DSTV. Conversely reportedly 100 000 Nigerians live in SA doing God-knows-what. President Jonathan acknowledges the unfavourable balance of trade in favour of SA, but no practical proposals to reverse the trend. Like in football Nigeria seems excited to collect the trophy while SA counts the dollars as a permanent host of global tournaments with superior infrastructure.

The relations between two countries has historically been characterised by contestation and cooperation. During the discredited Apartheid order, Nigeria under the leadership of Tafawa Balewa in the 60s put pressure on South Africa to withdraw from the Commonwealth. Conversely (and indeed ironically,) Nigeria was suspended from the Commonwealth at a summit in 1995 attended by South African President Nelson Mandela following the execution of Nobel Peace Prize nominee Ken Saro-Wiwa by Abacha regime. However, the sustained legitimate struggle against Apartheid conferred moral and political claim to Nigeria. It is commendable that President Goodluck Jonathan extensively brought to the fore the details about the sacrifices of Nigeria and Nigerians in the total liberation of the Southern African countries of Namibia, Angola and Mozambique at a time all weather friend nations in Europe and America were in bed with the most inhuman Apartheid order.

While welcoming President Jonathan, President Jacob Zuma, South African President commendably singled out the historic role of Nigeria. According to him; "Nigeria was one of the foremost supporters of the South African liberation struggle. We remain grateful for the solidarity and support during that most difficult period in the history of our country and people, the fight against Apartheid colonialism." But Godliness is even more in the details of Nigeria's sacrifices, as captured by President Jonathan during his speech to the South African Parliament in Cape Town, on the May 7, 2013.

Witness him:

> "In those dark seasons, Nigerians stood by their South African brothers and sisters, because we shared your pain and concerns...Suffice it to say that throughout the long-drawn, anti-Apartheid struggle, although we were not geographically contiguous, Nigeria was, nevertheless, considered a Frontline State, by the sheer fact of our commitment to the just struggle for freedom in Southern Africa... It was for this reason the Southern African Relief Fund (SARF) was created.
>
> This was funded with deductions from the salary of every Nigerian worker, irrespective of rank, both in the public and private sectors as well as donations from ordinary Nigerians in all walks of life, including students. This fund was placed at the disposal of the liberation struggle...Nigeria provided scholarships for students from South Africa. Our musicians waxed albums in support of the anti-Apartheid struggle, a memorable one in this respect being Sonny Okosun's timeless piece, "Fire in Soweto". ...At the international level, Nigeria gave leadership at the United Nations, the Organization of African Unity, as it then was, the Commonwealth and several other forums in the fight against Apartheid. For instance, we chaired the UN Special Committee Against Apartheid (UNSCAA) for most of its existence."

OAU At 50 - Revisiting Kwame Nkrumah's Speech In 1963*

Almost by conspiracy of omission, scores of contemporary global books of great speeches by World leaders conspicuously miss out the great speeches of great African leaders. It was as if the continent lacks historic leaders with great speeches. Yet Africa parades great motivational leaders like Amílcar Cabral (Weapon of Theory), our own late General Murtala Muhammed of Africa Has come of Age (speech that courageously set the tone for the liberation of Angola and Mozambique) the great war speeches of the late Egyptian President Gamal Nasser and of course, Nelson Mandela's Rivonia Trial speech.

Organization of African Unity (OAU) just marked its 50th anniversary. There is no better time than this OAU anniversary period to revisit the greet speech of Ghana's then president, Kwame Nkrumah. It was on the 24 May 1963, 32 then independent African countries met in the Ethiopian capital, Addis Ababa, "to find ways to unite the continent." Kwame Nkrumah gave what has come to be "one of the greatest speeches of his life, a speech which has since become the definitive blueprint for a strong, but so far sadly elusive, African unity". In the absence of any quotable quote from Addis Ababa where some 52 heads of state made three minute anniversary speeches, the nostalgia for Kwame is irresistible. Here are some extracts.

> "I am happy to be here in Addis Adaba on this most historic occasion. I bring with me the hopes and fraternal greetings of the government and people of Ghana. Our objective is African union now. There is no

---

* *Daily Trust*, 3rd June, 2013

time to waste. We must unite now or perish. I am confident that by our concerted effort and determination, we shall lay here the foundations for a continental Union of African States. A whole continent has imposed a mandate upon us to lay the foundation of our union at this conference. It is our responsibility to execute this mandate by creating here and now, the formula upon which the requisite superstructure may be created.

On this continent, it has not taken us long to discover that the struggle against colonialism does not end with the attainment of national independence. Independence is only the prelude to a new and more involved struggle for the right to conduct our own economic and social affairs; to construct our society according to our aspirations, unhampered by crushing and humiliating neo-colonialist controls and interference.

From the start we have been threatened with frustration where rapid change is imperative and with instability where sustained effort and ordered rule are indispensable. No sporadic act nor pious resolution can resolve our present problems. Nothing will be of avail, except the united act of a united Africa. We have already reached the stage where we must unite or sink into that condition which has made Latin America the unwilling and distressed prey of imperialism after one-and-a-half centuries of political independence.

As a continent, we have emerged into independence in a different age, with imperialism grown stronger, more ruthless and experienced, and more dangerous in its international associations. Our economic advancement demands the end of colonialist and neo-colonialist domination of Africa.

...African unity is, above all, a political kingdom which can only be gained by political means. The social and economic development of Africa will come only within the political kingdom, not the other way round. Is it not unity alone that can weld us into an effective force, capable of creating our own progress and making our valuable contribution to world peace? Which independent African state, which of you here, will claim that its financial structure and banking institutions are fully harnessed to its national development?

In independent Africa, we are already re-experiencing the instability and frustration which existed under colonial rule. We are fast learning that political independence is not enough to rid us of the consequences of colonial rule. The movement of the masses of the people of Africa for freedom from that kind of rule was not only a revolt against the conditions which it imposed. Our people supported us in our fight for independence because they believed that African governments could cure the ills of the past in a way which could never be accomplished under colonial rule.

Our continent certainly exceeds all the others in potential hydroelectric power, which some experts assess as 42% of the world's total. What need is there for us to remain hewers of wood and drawers of water for the industrialised areas of the world? It is said, of course, that we have no capital, no industrial skill, no communications, and no internal markets, and that we cannot even agree among ourselves how best to utilise our resources for our own social needs. Yet all stock exchanges in the world are preoccupied with Africa's gold, diamonds, uranium, platinum, copper and iron ore.

Our capital flows out in streams to irrigate the whole system of Western economy. Fifty-two per cent of the gold in Fort Knox at this moment, where the USA stores its bullion, is believed to have originated from our shores. Africa provides more than 60% of the world's gold. A great deal of the uranium for nuclear power, of copper for electronics, of titanium for supersonic projectiles, of iron and steel for heavy industries, of other minerals and raw materials for lighter industries – the basic economic might of the foreign powers – come from our continent.

We have the resources. It was colonialism in the first place that prevented us from accumulating the effective capital; but we ourselves have failed to make full use of our power in independence to mobilise our resources for the most effective take-off into thorough-going economic and social development.

...Unite we must. Without necessarily sacrificing our sovereignties, big or small, we can here and now forge a political union based on defence, foreign affairs and diplomacy, and a common citizenship, an African currency, an African monetary zone, and an African central bank. We must unite in order to achieve the full liberation of our continent. We need a common defence system with African high command to ensure the stability and security of Africa. We have been charged with this sacred task by our own people, and we cannot betray their trust by failing them. We will be mocking the hopes of our people if we show the slightest hesitation or delay in tackling realistically this question of African unity."

Reading the News; Mandela's Health*

Quite remarkable how the ever "critical but stable" condition of former South Africa's President Nelson Mandela, Jacob Zuma has elicited such global outpour of solidarity, prayers and sympathy. In recent times, as he ages (he will be 95 on July 18th) once Madiba shows some signs of an ailment, the world seems to be on the edge. However since the great iconic first South Africa's democratically elected president (following defining collapse of the discredited SA's Apartheid order) was admitted to hospital on 8 June, the world has not been the same! The only breaking news worthy of attention seems to be Mandela's recovery. Indeed there is a speculation that the inevitable loss of the great global citizen might affect the South African economy. Some are concerned that the death of Mandela, the man who led a peaceful transition from Apartheid to democracy in South Africa, could shake the nation's economy. Even the celebrated Obama's second African tour has been overshadowed by Mandela's health. Mandela has been susceptible to respiratory problems since he reportedly contracted tuberculosis during his 27-year imprisonment. He has been hospitalized four times since last December. Interestingly, the condition of former South African leader Nelson Mandela was a star topic at the Town Hall style meeting University of Johannesburg in Soweto, happily not gay rights! Obama not only praised the ailing anti-Apartheid icon in "emotional terms" but confessed that Mandela's personal courage and South Africa's historic transition are a personal inspiration to him and to the world. History will record it that during his second visit to African continent (during which he again ignored 165 million-

---

* *Daily Trust*, 1st July, 2013

Nigerians for bad governance (his words!) Obama was almost on the trail of Mandela's footsteps. He met his family members; daughters and grand children and his wife Graca Machel! President Obama also visited Robben Island in South Africa on Sunday, the prison where Mandela spent nearly 27 years for fighting to overturn the country's Apartheid regime. As a matter of fact, Mandela's Get-Well cards can make a library! What then are the lessons for the state of Mandela's recovery from world begging for leadership at all levels? Who then leads like Mandela to in turn command such significant multi-racial and inter faith global followership? Which leader in Africa in particular wants to end like Mandela?

Mandela's deserved freedom after 27 years in prison proves that time is longer than the Apartheid rope. Mandela is credited with scores of leadership virtues. They include courage, principle, sacrifice, forgiveness, love and reconciliation and non- vengeance among others. The way Mandela generously forgives and reconciles with his white racist tormentors shows that we can forgive and move on even if we do not forget.

Another singular leadership quality of Madiba, (the "old man") is "making oneself dispensable", i.e. dispensability of leaders. In a continent reputed for sit tight leaders (Egypt's Mubarak, Zimbabwe's Mugabe, Libya's Kaddafi, late Bongo of Gabon and President Museveni of Uganda) Mandela shows that it is not how long power is exercised but how it is creatively humanly used to uplift peoples and societies. His one term 5-year tenure (1994-1999) as the President of a non-racial, democratic Republic offers lessons in leadership for Federal Republic of Nigeria. Given the current crisis of leadership, Nigeria's leaders must emulate Mandela's model of representation and delegation and even resignation. In 1996, two years he assumed power, Nelson Mandela said that "I must step down when there are one or two people who admire me." Nigeria's leaders must accept the reality of exit once they assume power. The protagonists/antagonists of 2015 agenda must reflect on the Mandela's spirit if they must be celebrated like Mandela.

Former President Olusegun Obasanjo refused Mandela formula. Today he is permanently discredited as a sit-tight greedy/power mongering leader, while Mandela is credited with modesty in exercise of power.

Paradoxically Nigeria among other countries fought for the liberation of South Africa. Leadership lessons expectedly should rather flow from Nigeria not from South Africa. Two years before he left office in 1999, Nelson Mandela stopped chairing cabinet meetings. His then Vice President, Thabo Mbeki was reportedly in charge. He had a good rapport with Vice President Mbeki such that he was reported at different forums celebrating him (Mbeki) as a better administrator than himself. He indeed modestly attributed many great ideas he championed to his Vice President, Tambo Mbeki. Our leaders should learn the virtues of comradeship from Mandela. Governors in Nigeria who engage their deputies in wars of attrition are not acting in the spirit of Mandela.

His presidency was inaugurated in 1994. He took pride in the knowledge that ANC boasts of scores of leaders that can rule South Africa. Madiba related cordially even with his political rivals. During his historic presidency, Mandela even allowed his arch rival and die hard apologist of Apartheid regime, Mr Mangosutu Buthelezi as Acting President while he was on overseas trips that also involved his Vice President, Thabo Mbeki. He is a living voice for Africa and the world.

President George W Bush and Vice-President Dick Cheney of America criminally invaded Iraq in 2002. Nelson Mandela's comment on the war was as resonant as the invaders' bombs. According to Mandela, Bush administration's advisers were like "dinosaurs" who did not want President Bush to "belong to the modern age" adding that US was a threat to world peace given its penchant for impunity and unilateralism. The eventual withdrawal of US troops from Iraq under Obama vindicates Mandela's timely moral intervention. Africa is indebted to Mandela for his campaign for 2010 hosting right of FIFA soccer tournament on the continent.

Most elders are conservative and shy to talk about HIV/AIDS. Nelson Mandela was the first to openly disclose that he lost his son to HIV/AIDS and called for an open fight against the scourge. He combines old age with refreshingly new modern ideas. He is a lover of sports (soccer)? However said, have all the Mandela's enthusiasts (who are almost praying for the impossible; a Mandela immortality) read Nelson Mandela's views on death? As far back as 1996 Nelson Mandela said:

> "death is something inevitable. When a man has done what he considers to be his duty to his people and his country, he can rest in peace. I believe I have made that effort and that is, therefore, why I will sleep for eternity."

Madiba also once reported said "There will be life after Mandela."

No Lessons from Egypt*

Since Egypt's military ousted President Mohammed Morsi in an unacceptable coup d'état and handpicked its puppet chief justice Adly Mansour as the nation's interim president, not few have itemised some lessons of Egyptian revisionism for Nigeria and indeed Africa. But in truth, there is no lesson from Egypt. On the contrary, it is Egypt that must retrace its false steps in the direction of dictatorship, learn from the rest of Africa (including Nigeria) where democratic transition of power from civilians to civilians is becoming a norm not an exception. Since the spontaneous mass unrest which rightly ousted Tunisia's leader Ben Ali Egypt's Mubarak and Yemen's Alli Abdullah Saleh as well as Libya's Gaddafi, some observers have recommended some Arab protest-style of regime change in Africa. Such recommendation betrays deep knowledge of democratic process and at best distorts the history of democratic process in Africa.

From the late 1970s through to the 1990s when the Arabs were romanticizing dictators, peoples of Nigeria, Ghana, Zambia, Benin Republic, Zimbabwe, South Africa among others (with enormous sacrifices even to lives) were commendably up in mass protests against military rules and one party-states. Better late than never, that the Arabs at the turn of the 21st century had woken from their slumber to confront dictatorships which other Africans from early 20th century had tried to consign to dustbins of history. Whatever analysts make of our ever disputed elections, Nigeria in recent times remains truly a Democracy Destination. With as many as 73 million voters (almost the population of Egypt!), 50-plus political parties (and

* *Daily Trust*, 8 July, 2013

we are still forming and commendably merging!), more than 20 presidential candidates during 2011 election, our problem unlike Egypt was choice not absence of choices! Democratic struggles had been the norms in Nigeria. Democratic forces in varying political parties and trade unions fought against British colonial order before the eventual Independence in 1960. The decision to have independence in 1960 was made through free elections and debates conducted by various regional political parties. With all the limitations of the second Republic, the disputation against the result of the 1979 elections was constitutional (the famous two-thirds of 19!) not electoral (the vote and the votes counts were never disputed!). The distortion of Nigeria's democratic aspiration started with the criminal annulment of 1993 June 12 free and fair elections. Since that event of 1993, election riggers had perfected the art of violations of peoples' mandates through varying subterfuges that included ballot snatching, falsifications of election results as we witnessed in 2003 and 2007 elections. With this rich democratic heritage, Egyptians have a lot to learn from Nigeria. They must learn to follow the rules of democratic engagements. For one both the electorate and the military must respect the sanctity of democratic tenure. Putting elected President Morsi under house arrest at an undisclosed location, arresting more than 300 ranking members of the Islamic Brotherhood, including journalists, shutting down broadcast stations and other news outlets with connections to the Brotherhood and Morsi is illegal and unacceptable. It is the way of the dictatorships of the recent past which Nigeria and other emerging democracies had discovered to be futile and unsustainable for national stability and development. It is commendable that the Federal government, the Africa Union, the street protesters in Egyptian cities and the democratic forces world-wide have condemned the undemocratic removal of Egypt's democratically elected President, Mohammed Morsi from office by the military and subsequent imposition of an unelected and probably unelectable interim President Adly Mansour.

The Egypt's military must respect the sanctity of democratic tenure and return Egypt to democracy under the constitutionally elected President. Progressive world should also hold the Egyptian military responsible for any avoidable deaths and casualties in Egypt following protests and deadly street battles occasioned by their meddlesomeness in power. Its time African electorates and elected leaders respect democracy and constitutionalism even when we have problems and challenges with democratic process and democratic outcomes. President Morsi was accused of trying to exceed his democratic mandate through dictatorial tendency. However the solution is to democratically remove him not for an opportunistic military return Egypt to the dark and discredited days of Hosni Mubarak and military dictatorship. In a democracy, people can definitely make a foolish choice. The beauty of democracy is that they have another choice to correct their mistakes and make another choice.

The African continent has made remarkable progress in fostering democratic governance after wasted years of military dictatorship and attendant underdevelopment. The challenge is to deepen democracy in the continent and not to reverse it. The Egyptian military lives in the past if it refuses to accept the truth that nobody dares to rule Africa again without a democratic mandate.

All democratic forces must therefore support the Egyptian protesters calling for the return of President Morsi to office and commend them for their abiding faith in democracy. We join the global calls for the immediate restoration of the democracy order in Egypt and urge the Egyptian Armed Forces to allow the democratic culture to thrive in the country.

Mandela at 95 - Celebrate, Organize, Agonize not*

"I am not sick, I am old" remarked Madiba in Johannesburg on 27 January 2011 after his admission in a Johannesburg hospital for some "specialized tests". Undoubtedly the former South African President had faced a number of health challenges in recent times, notably "respiratory infections" not unconnected to the condition at the notorious Robin Island prison in the 1980s, where the legendary leader contracted tuberculosis. Mandela's remark two years ago remains a worthy reminder to us all that a man in his 90s is certainly not young even if not hunted by any affliction.

Nelson Mandela turns 95 on Thursday, 18th of July. The occasion of Mandela Day on July 18 (an annual international day commendably adopted by the United Nations) offers an opportunity to re-echo the legend that he is truly old not necessarily sick. Or better still reminding ourselves that Madiba suffers a natural inevitable illness; old age and that other ailments only compliment this obvious sickness. This message assumes much relevance today because not few of his millions of admirers (including yours comradely) almost gave in to despair and some agonizing since he was admitted more than a month in the hospital with all the attendant global hysteria. It is ever refreshing to read that Mandela is responding to treatment with a condition that is "critical but stable". But it is time that admirers of the global icon accepted that immortality is not the way of Nelson Mandela and that what matters in the final analysis is Mandela's deeds not his mortal. Immortality belongs to God! Talking about immortality, (ability to live forever, or

* *Daily Trust*, 15 July, 2013

eternal life) there are as many quotable quotes of Nelson Mandela on the inevitability of death and his preparedness for it perhaps as much as his words on the marble of freedom, liberty and struggle.

The famous speech by Nelson Mandela was at the 1964 Rivonia Trial which sentenced him and others to life imprisonment for daring to overthrow the Apartheid order. That historic Speech alluded to the inevitability of death as much as the desirability of freedom and liberty. He concluded the famous speech thus; "During my lifetime I have dedicated myself to this struggle of the African people. I have fought against white domination, and I have fought against black domination. I have cherished the ideal of a democratic and free society in which all persons live together in harmony and with equal opportunities. It is an ideal which I hope to live for and to achieve. But if needs be, it is an ideal for which I am prepared to die." It is a great paradox of fate that though he prepared to die, he indeed actually realized the vision of a free and democratic South Africa though with personal sacrifices of 27 years in prison. We should however remember that hundreds of thousands killed during Apartheid were actually not as 'lucky" as Nelson Mandela.

In 1996 in Documentary, Mandela said; "Death is something inevitable. When a man has done what he considers to be his duty to his people and his country, he can rest in peace. I believe I have made that efforts and that is, therefore, why I will sleep for the eternity." And that is precisely what UN Mandela Day is all about; let's put up some efforts for our people and country so that we can sleep for eternity. The overreaching "objective of Mandela Day is to inspire individuals to take action to help change the world for the better, and in doing so build a global movement for good. Ultimately the day seeks to empower communities everywhere". At 95 Nelson Mandela even on a sick bed remains a living moral authority with such global outreach that many a canonized saint hardly covered. There are scores of retired and even serving Heads of states whose birthdays and even health conditions are of no relevance to humanity. What then makes Nelson Mandela special? It is remarkable that though Mandela was the President of South Africa from 1994 to 1999, he is less remembered for his presidency (which he commendably left after an eventful one term, not third term!). His enduring legacy was his unique ability to forgive those who jailed him for 27 years and for being a symbol of reconciliation in a nation polarized along ethnic, racial and class cleavages. Though South Africa still remains a polarized country, the Mandela brand has become a metaphor linking all the polarities in the country together and somehow reminding each of the contending elements of the virtues of sacrifice, forgiveness and reconciliation. This is his greatest legacy to South Africa in particular and to mankind in general. We are enjoined to spend 67 minutes on Thursday to do something positive to serve humanity as part of Mandela Day activities. Here at home, it will be healing for Nigeria's democracy if President Goodluck Jonathan and Governor Rotimi Amaechi embrace, truly reconcile and resume statesmanship in the spirit of Nelson Mandela 95th birthday celebration. And this peaceful gesture to serve humanity by all our warring politicians can be done less than 67 minutes. Happy birthday in advance Madiba!

Mugabedom, Not Yet Zimbabwe*

Okello Oculi's entitled 'Mugabe Shames Tsvangirai and Western Backers' on Friday, 9 August 2013 is more of a heat rather than illuminating light on the worsening democratic process in Zimbabwe. The shame of the continent is not "Tsvangirai And Western Backers". Africa's shame is reading for the 7th time that Robert of 18th April 1980 has succeeded Mugabe (read; Robert Mugabe) in August 2013, (33 years after) as the President of a country of 13.7 million people. Yours comradely together with other African compatriots stormed the British Consulate in 1979 in an ABU students mass action demanding for the immediate independence of Zimbabwe and British respect for the popular votes of ZANU led by Robert Mugabe against the likes of colonialist Ian Smith and his Western backers. We did participate in that singular historic legitimate protest for the liberation of Zimbabwean peoples not for an enthronement of a Mugabedom led by a King Mugabe. Even for an unelected monarch 33years seem a long reign! 33years of sorrow, tears and blood under the reign of Mugabe is even a double jeopardy. Mugabe is the real shame of the continent for leaving Zimbabwe with a political choice like Morgan Tsvangirai who is half his age having presided over the political and virtual demise of veritable contenders and great names like Joshua Nkomo, Herbert Chitepo, Josiah Tongogara, Ndabaningi Sithole, Abel Muzorewa, Edgar Tekere, Byron Hove, Margaret Dongo, etc. I am surprised that my teacher Okello Oculi who taught us the virtues of objectivity in social inquiry explained Mugabe's woes in terms of some conspiracy theories nurtured by the West. Even Structural Adjustment Programme

---

* *Daily Trust*, 12 August, 2013

(SAP) which the then UK Knighted Robert Mugabe willingly plunged Zimbabwe into so as to be accepted when it was fashionable was attributed to the forces opposed to liberation (already won a decade earlier)! In the face of mass opposition by the trade union movement, Mugabe pushed millions into poverty with neo-liberal policies of devaluation, downsizing and subsidy removal. It was a regime of Mugabe's imposed sanctions against his own people. And that was well before the politically motivated and self-perpetuating strategy of land reforms. But who perpetrated the atrocities in the Matebele land in the 90s with the notorious brutality of the North Korean Fifth Brigade and of course their Western backers? Of course it was Mugabe who shamed the continent killing opposition members and bullying them into submission rather than engaging them for consensus. What should worry us is that independent African states courted sanctions not to make a case sanctions against bad political behaviour such as serial Mugabe's brigandage. It is delightful from Okello's account that President Obasanjo is not an observer after all but an active participant in a process characterized by permanent ethnic majorities, voter fatigue and voter apathy and limited political choices. But assuming President Obasanjo's claim that the election was "fairly fair" is true, is the outcome that permanently produces Mugabe"s as a permanent winner in country of 13 million people fair?

Indeed we are all beginner-witnesses to Zimbabwe's story which daily and hourly alternates between some trilling comedy and scaring tragedy or both, tragi-comedy. Yours sincerely thought I had gotten it right when I proclaimed Mugabe as history following 29th March 2008 polls in which the opposition won as many as 105 seats in the 210-seat parliament, leaving ZANU-PF with 93 seats. Watching the 89year old President casting his votes again in an apparent no-contest election (opposition was I'll prepared), it was clear that as far as Mugabe was concerned, it was not yet the end of history as we knew it with great statesmen of honour such as Nelson Mandela, President Sam Nujoma of Namibia and President Kenneth Kaunda who knew when to bow out when the political ovation was loud. As a matter of fact, as far as Robert Mugabe is concerned, it is the beginning of history of sheer profanity and brigandage for which he's fully prepared.

Until recently Mugabe polarized the Africa continent and indeed the world either for (in support of the land reform) or against Zimbabwe (for free and fair elections). No thanks to the combined forces of Tony Blair/George Bush who concealed their racist uncritical support for few white land owners opposing land reform while remaining hard on politics of free and fair elections. But today it is Zimbabwe versus the whole world as Mugabe digs in into political isolation against the background of global pressures and Euro-American blackmail in particular.

Former President of South Africa, Nelson Mandela, the global surviving moral force, once aptly described the unfolding events in Harare as manifestation of tragic leadership failure. Nothing could be more perceptive. Mandela did not elaborate on this but we can imagine that with respect to Zimbabwe, failure of leadership is not peculiar to Robert Mugabe which is crystal clear anyway. The ambiguity and duplicity of Africa Union to Zimbabwe underscores failed leadership at continental level. Lacking independent criteria to assess Zimbabwe (notwithstanding much taunted pair review machinery of NEPAD), AU was once a willing stick of the Gordon Brown and George Bush with which the duo whipped the entire continent into line to condemn already condemned Mugabe. When Washington and London sneeze from Cairo to Cape Town, there is instant climate change! But think about it. The ambiguity of most of the likes of Obasanjo is clearly understandable. With all its imperfections, Zimbabwe elections are certainly better than Kenya's and Nigeria's elections under Obasanjo.

Robert Gabriel Mugabe (RGM) for Beginners*

It is not clear what sit-tightism had to do with drab speeches of sit-tight leaders. Last Thursday, 22nd August 2013 was another "inauguration" of Robert Gabriel Mugabe. The inauguration word-count of the last old man in the world to be sworn in 7th time for another 5-year time in office was almost 4000. The diatribe dubbed speech tasked the listeners (who are certainly as many as those who boycotted the predictable polls that made him another "winner"). The word count competes with his long reign! Obviously there was truly a long diatribe in Africa before Mugabe and there may very well be after him as long as Africans have no zero-tolerance to dictatorship. Perhaps the late former Libyan leader Moammar Gadhafi at the 64th General Assembly of the United Nations (UN) in New York in 2009 could have beaten President Mugabe's record in incoherence, self-praise, arrogance and demagoguery packaged as an address. In his list of protocols were "Representatives of War Veterans, Detainees, Restrictees and War collaborators." This underscores the biometrics of citizenship in Zimbabwe under Mugabe's 30 years in office. Mugabe with tongue in cheek acknowledged "Former Heads of State and Government" and "Outgoing members of cabinet" . Just think about it; if all former Heads of states were to sit-tight like Mugabe, could there have been "Former Heads of State and Government" and "Outgoing members of cabinet at inauguration?

My findings show that in Nigeria, from President Shehu Shagari in 1980s to President Goodluck Jonathan in 2014, as many as 9

---

* *Daily Trust*, 26 August, 2013

Heads of States had witnessed Mugabe's serial inaugurations and left him behind. If Messieur Mugabe were to be a British Prime Minister through his hide and sit-tight game, the British would not have known such Prime Ministers as Sir John Major, Tony Blair, Gordon Brown and Prime Minister David Donald Cameron. Mugabe came to power almost same time Prime Minister Baroness Margaret Thatcher came to office. Of course if Mugabe were to be a Chinese, Li Xiannia, Yang Shangkun, Deng Xiaoping , Jiang Zemin Hu Jintao, Xi Jinping and the Incumbent XII Li Yuanchao could not have been Presidents of the fastest growing economy in the world compared to impoverished Zimbabwe. Robert Mugabe came to power when Ronald Reagan was in power. The two "Bushes" namely George H. W. Bush, George W. Bush and Bill Clinton met and left him in office. Indeed President Barack Obama was in the college in the 80s when Mugabe was already a President. By Mugabe's design, Obama may very well complete two terms in office before he completes his 7th tenure! If Mugabe were to be a South African, there would not have been a Nelson Mandela to succeed him! We would have been crudely denied a global moral authority on freedom, democracy, reconciliation and peace that Mandela represents. Since Mugabe came to office as many as 7 Presidents had emerged in South Africa. Four actually were democratically elected after Apartheid; namely Nelson Rolihlahla Mandela 10 May 1994 – 16 June 1999, Thabo Mvuyelwa Mbeki 16 June 1999 – 24 September 2008 (Recalled from office), Petrus Kgalema (Kgalema) Mothlanthe 25 September 2008 – 9 May 2009 and Jacob Zuma 9 May 2008 - up to date. Mugabe shared statesmanship with Apartheid Presidents; Pieter Willem (PW) Botha 3 September 1984 – 15 August 1989 (Resigned), Chris Heunis 19 January–15 March 1989; and Frederik Willem (FW) de Klerk 15 August 1989 – 9 May 1994.

Reading the mind of RGM through his inaugural address the continent would have to wait for long to see his back. His speech was certainly not a farewell one. Indeed it might very well be a beginning of history of his elongated rule. A man with selective sense of justice who accepted to be happily knighted in the 1990s by the Queen under Lancaster House constitution, said his new re-election is the "first …under a new home-grown Constitution"! Note the "first", not his last re-election. 33 years after Independence, RGM's selling point was still colonialism, not open unemployment as high as 80 per cent, multiple digit inflation and currency devaluation and unprecedented human drain in modern Africa. Indeed his opponent in the polls was "Lord Lugard the author of this anti-African, neo-colonial notion" (his words!) But it was Sir RGM, not Lord Lugard who brutally suppressed Zimbabwean patriots like Joshua Nkomo, Herbert Chitepo, Josiah Tongogara, Ndabaningi Sithole, Abel Muzorewa, Edgar Tekere, Byron Hove, Margaret Dongo and left 13 million people with a no-challenger called Morgan Tsvangirai.

According to RGM, election was over. His speech was however hunted by the spectre of the very election. He almost defined the world in terms of "Our enemies and detractors"! Even friends were qualified; "Genuine friends". Increasingly xenophobic and insular RGM blackmailed all with the land question. Witness him; "Yes, we regained control over our land and our people are happy. They revel in the ownership of that land which has now come. They are beginning to use it profitably, using it for durable wherewithal." It is an open knowledge that Zimbabwe is less food secured than when he came to power despite his vote-catching land reform. But is RGM' the only land reformer in a country of 13 million people that must cling to power for so long? RGM hinges his sit-tightism to ".... African values" . But it's time we reminded Mugabe of sometime tested African proverbs on the pitfalls of greed, including greed for power; "Greed loses what it has gained." ".If a greedy eater is near a patient, such a patient can never survive"; "The wealth of the greedy ultimately goes to the community."

Essential Nkrumah*

Yours sincerely remains averse to the simplistic personality view of history which holds that a country's historical development is explainable on account of leadership types, styles and methods. Yet the historic reality of Ghana and indeed Africa, shows that the singular energy, visions, ideas and methods of the founding President Osagyefo Dr. Kwame Nkrumah Nkrumah were central to the liberation of Ghana (formerly Gold Coast) and indeed the continent from colonial rule.

Today is Founder Day in Ghana. So named after Osagyefo (which means "redeemer" in the Twi language) who was born on the 21st September 1909 and died on 27th April 1972 in Bucharest, Romania from cancer. After leading decades long mass resistance against British colonial rule following brutal arrests and imprisonments, it was Nkrumah who at 12 noon on 6 March 1957 declared Ghana the first independent African nation. In February 1966, while Nkrumah was on a state visit to North Vietnam and China, his government was overthrown in a military coup led by Emmanuel Kwasi Kotoka and his so called National Liberation Council. The spectre of Nkrumah hunts Ghana and indeed Africa, 47 years after Nkrumah was overthrown. Controversy continues over his role in history, albeit ideologically motivated and certainly needless given his singular enormous sacrifices and contribution for pan Africanism. Not even Nelson Mandela with his larger-than-memory status obliterates the unique role of Nkrumah in the liberation of the continent. On the contrary, Mandela himself noted that the events of 1957 in Accra which led to the pulling down of the

---

* *Daily Trust*, 23 September, 2013

Union Jack of imperial Britain and its replacement by Red, Gold and Green flag of a new Ghana were sources of inspiration for the battle against Apartheid, the last draconian face of colonialism. Africans proudly quote Luther King's speech; I have a Dream. We however must not forget that the inspiration for this historic speech came from Ghana when the pastor attended Ghana's independence in 1957 and saw Nkrumah presiding over an African state. Essential Nkrumah is pan Africanism. He declared in 1957; "Ghana, your beloved country is free forever". But he quickly added; "Our independence is meaningless unless it is linked up to the total liberation of the African continent." The former President of Namibia, Sam Nujoma was right when he described Nkrumah as a "prophet" of a kind. After Nkrumah made this declaration he tireless worked for independence of other countries that included Nigeria and the Congo. The concept of European Union was borrowed from Nkrumah's vision of United States of Africa. Sadly Europe has since integrated while African countries are disintegrating as African politicians get more insular and parochial leaving their peoples with poverty, hunger and wars. The balkanization of Sudan to the North and South did violence to Nkrumah's pan Africanism. He was married to an Egyptian Arab African at a time it was unpopular to do so.

Paradoxically, Nkrumah was a political student of our own Zik of Africa. It was Zik that inspired Nkrumah to nationalism and even encouraged him in search of knowledge for further studies at Lincoln University United States of America, .He graduated nine years after Zik at the same university, "the first university in the Americas to produce the first presidents of two Commonwealth countries."

Ghana was the first African country that fought and won independence from British imperialism in 1957. Former Tanzanian President, Late Julius Nyerere also underscored the significance of Ghana's independence on the 6th March 1957. In 1997 Nyerere succinctly observed that; "Ghana was the beginning, our first liberated zone. Thirty-seven years later – in 1994 – we celebrated our final triumph when Apartheid was crushed and Nelson Mandela was installed as the president of South Africa. Africa's long struggle for freedom was over". Thus there can be no better tribute to Nkrumah than making his birthday a Founder Day.

As noted, Nigeria and score of other African countries, that include Cameroun, Congo, Zambia, followed Ghana's historic footstep, won liberty in quick successions. Many thanks to the audacity of Nkrumah in daring to break the colonial chain. We can debate how each of the independent countries had fared years after liberation, but the virtues of independence cannot be overstated. Colonialism fostered underdevelopment and backwardness. Essential Nkrumah is accelerated development and Industrialization unprecedented in the continent. He strongly worked for industrialised Africa that must add value to its God-given natural resources.

He embarked on an unprecedented aggressive industrialisation by building:

> "factories such as Asutuare and Komenda Sugar Factories, Bonsa Rubber Factory, among others. He established the Black Star Line, State Transport Corporation, State Construction Corporation, Ghana Airways, Bolgatanga, Beef Factory, Kumasi Jute and Shoe factories, Aboso Glass Factory, Kade Match Factory, Pokuase and Pomadzi Poultry Farms, Esiama Oil Mills, Tema Oil Refinery, Nsawam Cannery, GNTC, SIC, among others."

Today's wholesale dumping of imported goods in Africa and wholesale importation of goods and even human labour undermines Nkrumah's vision of an independent self-reliant industrialised Africa. Africans must revisit Nkrumah's economic policy which was to make Ghana productive and increase the country's manufacturing capacity so as to create jobs. Lastly Essential Nkrumah is intellectualism. No African leader has possibly written as much as him on governance and development. His works include the following: *Negro History: European Government in Africa, Ghana: The Autobiography of Kwame Nkrumah 1957,Africa Must Unite, African Personality 1963, Neo-Colonialism: the last stage of imperialism, Axioms of Kwame Nkrumah and African Socialism* and *Voice from Conakry* among others.

My posthumous birthday greetings to the philosopher - King of Africa, Dr. Kwame Nkrumah.

No Lesson from South Sudan*

On July 9, 2010, South Sudan proclaimed independence from the North (Khartoum). Less than three years, South Sudan has degenerated into a new war of attritions between the incumbent President Kiir and his estranged vice-president Riek Machar in a run up to the presidential elections in 2015 elections(2015!sounds Nigerian!). Paradoxically South Sudan at independence was celebrated globally but even more loudly by Europe and America as the "newest" African state. No thanks to the decades long marginalization and oppression by Khartoum in the North, (itself for a long time under the heels of varying dictatorships, the longest and the most notorious being that of the discredited General Numeiri supported by America). The world legitimately supported the struggles of Sudan People's Liberation Movement (SPLM). SPLM was formed in the late 1970s by the late Col John Garang. Interestingly SPLM under John Garang did not call for southern succession or Balkanization of the Sudan. Indeed John Garang until his death in a helicopter crash on July in 2005 stood for a united, secular and socialist greater Sudan. Undoubtedly the emergence of South Sudan trampled underfoot the vision of the founding fathers of Organisation of African Unity (OAU) on the 24 May 1963. Ghana's then president, Kwame Nkrumah and key proponent of OAU had envisioned a continental Union of African States, that by now would have transformed into a United States of Africa. And that was before the treaty of Rome that led to the formation of European Union (EU). The emergence of South Sudan as a newest state in Africa on the eve of the 50th anniversary of OAU (now

* *Daily Trust*, Monday December 23, 2013

Africa Union, AU) did an eternal violence to the memory and great vision of the founding fathers of modern independent Africa. They had envisioned the dismantling of the colonial borders not further Balkanization of the continent into some micro unviable states.

However very few observers of the events in Africa would have predicted that so soon South Sudan would return to the familiar road of cut throat elite competition for power and resources that characterized most post-colonial African states and wars that have been the lots of Southern Sudanese in the old Sudan. Reportedly over 500 people have already died in the violence this week following the disclosure by President Kiir according to which he had uncovered a coup attempt which he blamed on his former Vice Machar's supporters. 500 deaths in a singular violence was significant in a country of 10.84 million out of which as many as some two million had died after two decades of civil war:

> "Fighting has spread from the capital Juba, and violence is now being reported in the majority of the country's ten states with civilians seeking shelter in UN compounds. In recent hours, one UN compound in Akobo, Jonglei State, has come under attack from youths rather than military forces. Three peacekeepers and an unknown number of civilians were killed."

Certainly no lesson for Nigeria in South Sudan even when the political narrative increasingly and dangerously sound similar. South Sudan holds the bulk of Sudan's oil resources discovered in the 1970s which in turn had been the basis of the battle by varying groups and foreign countries including China and USA. South Sudan oil is however dependent on Khartoum in the north for infrastructure needed to export it. Nigeria is also a home of oil the bulk of which is now officially acknowledged as stolen and remaining as sources of corruption and political patronage as distinct from development. South Sudan like Nigeria is set for election in 2015 against the background of suspicions, divisions and dangerous mix of politics with ethnicity, regions and religions. In South Sudan, a dangerous relationship between the political struggle and ethnic competition between Dinka and Nuer tribes have emerged. South Sudan also refutes the claim that a country cannot plunge into civil wars more than once. The current violence which is dangerously assuming a war dimension may very we'll be the third civil war. The lesson for Nigerian political class is to return to win-win politics of development as distinct from zero-sum politics of self, ethnicity and greed that portends violence and wars of attritions. There is certainly no lesson in South Sudan. For those who ever harbour the thought that disintegration and divisions of big nation states into smaller states of so called nationalities would lead to prosperity and peace South Sudan's tragic experience so soon shatters this divisive aspiration. As we have seen, smaller states bring back old historical animosities and grievances that promote violence. It's time that AU puts an end to the new violence in South Sudan and safe Africa another photo clips of refugees and deaths in what once just recently presented as the 'newest' African state.

Ariel Sharon was no Nelson Mandela*

"I have fought against white domination, and I have fought against black domination. I have cherished the ideal of a democratic and free society in which all persons will live together in harmony with equal opportunities. It is an ideal which I hope to live for, and to see realised. But my Lord, if needs be, it is an ideal for which I am prepared to die." - *Nelson Mandela*

"Even today I am willing to volunteer to do the dirty work for Israel, to kill as many Arabs as necessary, to deport them, to expel and burn them, to have everyone hate us, to pull the rug from underneath the feet of the Diaspora Jews, so that they will be forced to run to us crying. Even if it means blowing up one or two synagogues here and there, I don't care." - *Ariel Sharon*

Of course, comparing Nelson Mandela with Ariel Sharon amounts comparing like with unlike. But fate records it that in recent times the two are the most recent former heads of state that passed on. Nelson Mandela was the first democratically elected President of a non-racial South Africa in 1990. After serving an eventful one term of office he died on December 5 2013 at the age of 95 after a brief illness and buried at a state funeral held on 15 December 2013 in Qunu, South Africa. Ariel Sharon was a two-term Prime minister of the state of Israel. Having suffered a comma after a debilitating stroke in 2006, he stepped down, died 7 years after on Jan. 11 this year and buried on the Jan. 13 at his beloved Sycamore Ranch in Israel's southern Negev desert. This is where the similarity between the two late leaders ends.

* Monday 26th January 2014

Even the most benign assessment of Sharon sees him as a controversial long-time political and military leader, known as "the bulldozer" notorious for his aggressive style in governance for which the Palestinians paid dearly in loss of lives and territory. In 1982, as a Defence Minister he spearheaded the Israeli invasion of Lebanon in which many Palestinians in the camps at Sabra and Shatila were massacred the tragedy that provoked the largest protest in the history of Israel against Sharon. Indeed a commission of inquiry, headed by the then Chief Justice of Israel's Supreme Court, Yitzhak Kahan, indicted him as being negligent as a Defence Minister. Ariel Sharon, was the only Israeli Prime Minister to be so described as a Crime Minister of sort following the massacre of Sabra and Shatila. Sharon eventually was forced to resign. Sharon was undoubtedly a Zionist Israeli patriot but even by Israeli's standard of a state of fortress, Sharon was an embarrassment and even a failure that could not achieve peace with the Palestinians.

Conversely Mandela's enemies and his jailers who unjustly put him 27-year long imprisonment agreed he was a liberator, unifier and builder of unprecedented reconciliation among races. Mandela was certainly not averse to controversies but was globally acclaimed for his activism for justice, freedom and fairness to all. Mandela received as many as 250 honours while alive, the most outstanding being the 1993 Nobel Peace Prize he shared with De Klerk, with whom he served in the government of national unity. De Klerk saw Mandela as a remarkable man with the biggest of reconciliation and "a remarkable lack of bitterness" . Certainly Sharon was no Mandela. He was no Menachem Begin (1913-1992) either. Menachem Begin was an acknowledged Israelis statesman and Prime Minister who shared Nobel Prize with President Anwar Sadat of Egypt in 1978 following the unprecedented peace deal between Israeli and Egypt. Indeed Sharon was the only prime minister who came to power through terror-provocation that included provocative visit to some holly sites in East Jerusalem! Conversely Nelson Mandela came to power on account of multi-racial support given his all-inclusive commitment to fairness. Mandela inherited a divided South Africa and bequeathed a united country coping with the challenge of nation building. Conversely Sharon inherited Israeli at war with the

Palestinians and left an Israeli still searching for peace with the Palestinians.

A commentator puts it better that:

> "A day will come when it will be recognized that leaders such as Sharon, and those who have shared his vision of Israel as a fortress state rather than one that can attain peaceful relations with its neighbours, have done their own people the greatest disservice."

Once upon a Solidarity*

Last Tuesday, precisely on the 13th February 2014 at the Yar'Adua Centre, Abuja, hundreds of veteran activists against Apartheid in racist South Africa organised a day manifestation in memory of the life and times of Nelson Mandela. True to expectation Mandela memorial has become a metaphor for a nostalgia for the best of human solidarity against racism and injustice the defeated system of Apartheid represented. My friend and Comrade John Ejoha Odah who spoke on behalf of Abuja Collective which commendably put up the memorial remarked that the date also marked the anniversary of the 1976 assassination of General Murtala Mohammed whose short reign as Nigeria's Head of State was of special importance in the liberation of the Southern African sub-region citing Murtala famous "Africa Has Come of Age" speech at the OAU Summit on Angola which categorically mobilised African Heads of State for the recognition of the Popular Movement for the Liberation of Angola (MPLA) as the authentic government of the Angolan people., contrary to the preference of United States of America and the West in general. Indeed Mrs. Aisha on behalf of the Murtala Mohammed Foundation delivered a fraternal address which extolled the virtues of courage, pan Africanism and commitment that distinguished great African leaders like Murtala Muhammed, Kwame Nkrumah and Amilcal Cabral. The occasion paraded notable African anti-Apartheid activists like Comrade Jay Naidoo, the founding General Secretary of South African Trade Unions (COSATU), Comrade Ali Chiroma, former President of Nigeria Labour Congress, Dr Yima Zen among others. The messages of Prof Ben Turok, Member of Parliament

* Monday February 17th, 2014

(ANC) South Africa entitled "Commemoration of the Life and Times of Nelson Mandela" and that of Dr Patrick Wilmot on the YUSSA, the Youth Solidarity on Southern Africa, were read on their behalf. One of the reflections, namely that of Ali Chiroma former President of NLC captured my imagination and refreshes the memory about the historic fact that the Nigerian labour movement and civil society in general have rich heritage of solidarity. Witness Ali Chiroma:

> "By the time COSATU was formed in 1985, it was only the very brave and courageous that accepts the huge responsibility to lead mass organisations like trade unions, as they were targets of assassination attempts by the dirty tricks unit of the rampaging Apartheid regime. For us in the Nigeria Labour Congress, when we reorganised in 1978, we realised that part of our solidarity responsibilities to the South African workers was to strengthen our ties with the anti-Apartheid groups, as well as the predecessor to COSATU, which was South Africa Congress of Trade Unions (SACTU). When I became President of NLC in 1984, and later became a member of the steering committee of the Commonwealth Trade Union Council (CTUC), we made sure that we were a leading voice on the issue of the Apartheid regime in South Africa. At Commonwealth Heads of Government meetings, either in Vancouver, Canada or Nassau, Bahamas, at a time when Margret Thatcher held sway as British Prime Minister, and main supporter of the Apartheid regime in South Africa, we took the lead among trade union colleagues at international forums in denouncing the self-serving argument she and other like her were banding around that sanctions would hurt the South African workers and poor people much more than it would hurt the racist government.
>
> At the NLC, we used to mobilise for material support for our counterparts in their very difficult task of organising under vicious Apartheid laws. I was privileged to play host at the Olajuwon Street Lagos headquarters of the NLC to many ANC and other anti-Apartheid leaders of the South African people. One such visit I have vivid recollection was the visit of Oliver Tambo, then ANC President in 1986.
>
> Since the Federal Government of Nigeria established the National Committee Against Apartheid (NACAP), the NLC President was one of the institutional members. While I was President, Comrade Salisu Mohammed and, later, Comrade John Odah, the convener of this programme, used to represent the Congress if I wasn't attending. By the time Mandela visited Nigeria in May 1990, three months after his

release from his 27 years in prison, my successor, Comrade Paschal Bafyau, served on the National Organising Committee of the visit.
Perhaps I should conclude my reflection with regard to the anti-Thatcher protest in 1988. The NLC just before we went for the 1988 Delegates' Conference specifically on 7th January 1988, led Nigerian people in Lagos and Kano in a huge demonstration against Margret Thatcher, when she visited Nigeria that year, to demonstrate the revulsion of Nigerian people against her wrongheaded support and backing for the Apartheid regime. After the servile courtesy she got when she visited Kenya, under Arap Moi, where she was given 40 gun salutes instead of the customary 21, she was told in clear terms that she, as a friend of the Apartheid regime, was our enemy and therefore not wanted in this country.

It is our hope that the ANC government in South Africa would uphold the legacy of Nelson Mandela and do all in its power to curb corruption and bad governance which is the bane of most post independent African countries."

Africa, the collapse of Dignity*

"We come from a people who, because they would not accept to be treated as subhuman, redeemed the dignity of all humanity everywhere." - Nelson Mandela *Address to the Parliament of Canada, Ottawa, Canada 18 June 1990*

After a "successful" first U.S.-Africa Leaders' Summit last week attended by as many as 50 Presidents and Prime Ministers, my interest is purely as usual academic. According to the host President Barack Obama, the summit was premised on "...a new model of partnership between America and Africa -- a partnership of equals that focuses on your capacity to expand opportunity and strengthen democracy and promote security and peace ". With such "partnership of equals" in which one partner (read; United States of America) could confidently host and almost talk at as many as 50 partner-countries of Africa, the world certainly needs a redefinition of equality/partnership equation in which one equals fifty. Certainly Africa (Sorry; 50 Presidents and Prime Ministers from Africa) needs urgently a new "Idiot's Guide to (In)equality". And that Guide can certainly not come from United States of America. For one America is the most unequal country on earth. Studies indicate the richest 1 per cent in the United States now own more wealth than the bottom 90 per cent. Indeed in recent times economic inequality has reportedly worsened significantly in the United States and some other countries. Thus USA cannot offer what it does not have at home (I.e. Equality) which perhaps explains why its President Barack Obama Joyfully equated one country of his to 50 African countries. It is also instructive that three or so African countries were not invited to the

* Monday August 11th, 2014

Washington historic summit. The countries included predictably Zimbabwe and Sudan whose Presidents are far from being partners of America anyway, even if America has not said they are enemies to it either. At least America in line with the principle of transparency and accountability guiding any partnership should have made it known that the concluded Summit was with Africa minus those countries not invited, in which case it would be clear to an alien from the outer space that this "partnership" was with some countries in Africa not necessarily with the Africa union! Also observers of global events wonder aloud why did the first "historic" summit between Africa and US hold in Washington and not on the African soil? Of course President Obama had an answer when he said it was "....the largest gathering any American President has ever hosted with African heads of state and government." Certainly what we had was a "gathering" of unequals rather than a summit of partners.

The US meeting undoubtedly went the way of the familiar "summits" in which African heads of states were summoned to Beijing (Africa/China summit) and Ankara (Africa/Turkish summit). This year marks the 57th anniversary of the Independence of Ghana from British colonial rule as well as 51st anniversary of the formation of OAU/AU. It is certainly a collapse of dignity that Africa would be literally shut down by its leaders for a summit in faraway Washington. The promise of Independence is that those who would engage with Africa must engage with it on the African soil.

It is debatable if the likes of Kwame Nkrumah and late Nelson Mandela were to be alive any foreign power (sorry; partner) would have dared to "gather" for an engagement outside the continent as our contemporary Africans uncritically did last week. Certainly everybody knows that there is no free lunch in Washington. But that African leaders were treated to free square meals for a week long further created the bad impression of dependence which the struggle for independence once put an end to. The devils are in the details of the benefits of the concluded summit some of which included some promissory notes of billions of dollars' worth of investment. Some of these details further reinforce the dependency of Africa which in a "partnership" keeps on receiving rather than giving. Or better still a dependency in which Africa through capital flight, corruption and now uncritically unidirectional visits of its Presidents and Prime Ministers keep on under developing the continent.

By the way, it was refreshing that President Obama promised to hold the next YALI (Young Africa Leaders Institute) on African soil next year. He also changed YALI to Nelson Mandela young Leaders Institute. But must African young leaders discover Nelson Mandela in Washington instead of Abuja or Cape Town and Cairo?

No Lesson from Scottish referendum*

"We prefer self-government with danger to servitude in tranquillity."
Kwame Nkrumah

It is interesting how detailed result of the Scottish referendum according to which 55 per cent of Scottish voters said no to Independence in a historic vote has become another source of so-called lesson for Africa. When will Africa be tired of some unhelpful received wisdom and received "lessons" from Europe? Or better still when will Africa proactively show that it has a lot to offer the world from its historic struggles and accomplishments, despite the current challenges? Certainly Africa is more quotable on Independence than any country in Europe including Scotland. Still better put it is Scotland that must learn from the struggle of Africans for independence from colonialism and slavery (with Scottish connections!) and not the other way round. The historic facts are in support of Africa. The late Julius Nyerere of Tanzania once rightly observed that "Ghana was the beginning, our first liberated zone. Thirty-seven years later - in 1994 - we celebrated our final triumph when Apartheid was crushed and Nelson Mandela was installed as the president of South Africa. Ghana won Independence in 1957, after 100 years of British colonialism and almost a decade before Martin Luther King made the prophetic speech "I have a Dream" in America. Freedom and liberty to Ghana and indeed Africa was a fall out of series of struggles and pressures led by the late Dr Nkrumah, who was imprisoned several times by the British. Mandela noted that the events of 1957 in Accra which led to the historic pulling down of the Union Jack and its replacement with Ghana flag were sources of

* Monday September 22nd 2014

inspiration against Apartheid which was courageously defeated in 1994. The point cannot be overstated therefore that Africa has a lot to teach the Scott's on how to struggle and attain Independence and not the other way round. Many have rightly venerated pastor King's dream speech, but the first dream speech was that of Nkrumah who prophetically declared that "Our independence is meaningless unless it is linked up to the total liberation of the African continent." Since that historic speech colonialism, Nigeria fought and got independence in 1960, Angola in 1976, Zimbabwe in 1980, Namibia in 1990 and in general liberty rains from Cairo to Cape Town. There is no doubt that last week's Scottish votes counts signified deep democratic/Self-determination aspiration for freedom, some 1,617,989 YES (45%) votes for independence compared to the NO 55% 2,001,926 votes. However Scottish liberty aspirations is nothing compared the democratic enthusiasm of South Africans for freedom in 1994 when African National Congress had a Popular Yes vote of 12,237,655 for democracy and abolition of Apartheid.

The Afenifere Renewal Group, ARG, reportedly said: "Nigeria's disintegration can only be averted if the wisdom now on display in the United Kingdom on devolution of power and self-determination is urgently brought to play in the Nigeria's governance model." In a press release, signed by Olawale Oshun, its National Chairman, the ARG asked for "full devolution of power to the constituent units in Nigeria, including corresponding fiscal powers and resource control." Certainly Nigeria does not need Scottish referendum before it appreciates that it must return to genuine Federalism. Please note; return (genuine Federalism) because until the military intervention of 1966 Nigeria once devolved powers to the functioning vibrant federating regions. Afenifere compares 'like' with "unlike" when it points to Nigerian reality to draw attention to a non-existent "lesson" from Scotland. The truth is that Nigeria is already a sovereign state compared to a dependency, Scotland. What the latter desired is not some devolution of powers contained in the political promissory notes of Prime Minister David Cameroon already a subject of acrimony with the Labour Party opposition leader, accused Ed Miliband. Indeed United Kingdom, (inclusive of the disappointed Scotland) may have to learn from the imperfect federal structure of

Nigeria. Nigeria's national conference (with the signatures of Afenifere delegates!) preceded the Scottish referendum. To this extent the search for a functioning Federal Republic of Nigeria does not depend on the outcome of the Scottish referendum. There are enough policy recommendations in the National Conference's reports to make our Federation work better.

But lest we forget, David Livingstone (19 March 1813 – 1 May 1873) was a Scottish missionary and an explorer in Africa. He was also an imperial reformer and anti-slavery crusader, and advocate of commercial colonial empire. But that was after 200 years of slavery perpetrated by both the Scots and English in West African countries including Nigeria. Following the 1707 Act of Union between Scotland and England, Scottish merchants joined the English trade routes. The notorious Trans-Atlantic slave trade worked like this:

> "Goods such as cloth, copper and guns were shipped from Britain to West Africa to be sold or exchanged. There, captive Africans were bought and taken to the West Indies or America and sold as slaves. The enslaved people worked on the plantations, producing raw materials such as sugar, rum, tobacco and cotton, which were shipped to Britain. Two major trading ports in slaves were Port Glasgow and Greenock."

Germany, Russia and China had rightly reacted to the Scottish referendum based on their historic experiences and interest. Africa must do the same instead of imagining some "lessons" in a referendum in which Africans and African interest never counted anyway.

Cuba and America; the Audacity of new relations*

"In the most significant changes in our policy in more than fifty years, we will end an outdated approach that, for decades, has failed to advance our interests, and instead we will begin to normalize relations between our two countries."
-American President Barack Obama

"We can't pretend that by improving ties with the United States, Cuba will renounce the ideas for which it has fought for more than a century"
-Cuban President Raul Castro

In its cover story of November 23rd last year, the British Economist weekly magazine dubbed President Barack Obama as the "The man who used to walk on water" . The cover picture actually said it all; a sinking President in coat and tie in a deep sea! The impression according to *The Economist*, was that President Obama had lost credibility at home, citing what it dubbed "the chaos of his health reform" and abroad it claimed that the 44th American President " is seen as weak and disengaged". But well before The Economist bully hysteria cover, President Obama and the author of The Audacity of Hope has shown that far from being weak and disengaged, he was capable of a number of commendable innovative activist domestic and foreign policies which previous American Presidents could not have contemplated for fear of being smeared with the establishment political incorrectedness. In November this year, President Obama frontally took on the hostile Congress which had shut down the administration more than once. He bypassed it and took direct executive actions to reshape the nation's immigration system which

* Monday December 22nd, 2014

had kept the fate of millions hanging. By the singular 15-minute address to the nation, Mr. Obama announced executive actions on immigration policy which prevented as many as five million people from deportation and allow many to work legally if they passed some background checks and pay their taxes. President's Obama's executive action on immigration complimented the earlier executive actions through which he audaciously increased the federal minimum wage from $7.25 to $10.10 per hour despite the opposition of the Republican lawmakers!

However the most far-reaching important bold foreign policy decision of President Obama was contained in the December 17, 2014 speech in which he disclosed he had instructed the Secretary John Kerry to immediately "begin discussions with Cuba to reestablish diplomatic relations that have been severed since January of 1961". In addition he added that "Going forward, the United States will reestablish an embassy in Havana, and high-ranking officials will visit Cuba." In return speaking on Saturday in the National Assembly in Havana, President Raul Castro hailed Mr Obama's speech that terminated 50 years of bilateral Cold War between the countries following the Cuban revolution of 1959. The major highlights of Obama's Cuba new policy include reviewing the designation of Cuba as a state sponsor of terrorism, the notorious policy of president Gorge bush. Obama rightly argued that "Terrorism has changed in the last several decades. At a time when we are focused on threats from al Qaeda to ISIL, a nation that meets our conditions and renounces the use of terrorism should not face this sanction." Others are easing travel ban for US citizens, easing financial restrictions, increasing telecommunications links and most importantly, efforts to lift the 54-year-old trade embargo. The new audacious relations between USA and Cuba show that international relations is desirable for all nations notwithstanding the ideological differences. President Obama put it rightly when he exposed the hypocrisy of maintaining ties with far away Communist China while keeping far away Cuba at arms length. He said America would directly engage Cuba on issues related to "democracy and human rights in Cuba". Conversely Cuban President Raul Castro disclosed that Cuba was open to discussing a wide range of issues with Washington but stressed that Cuba would not give up its socialist principles: “In the same way that we have never demanded that the United States change its political system, we will demand respect for ours.” The new diplomatic relations between America and Cuba is a victory for Africa and progressive forces of the world that have conversed and demanded for this era of new relations in the past decades. All African governments and trade unions such as NLC (of which I belong) have always demanded for the lifting of trade embargo on Cuba. Cuba is a country that has sacrificed much in terms of humans and financial resources in spite of modest prosperity for the liberation of Angola, Namibia and South Africa from the clutches of colonialism and apartheid. The recent practical solidarity of Cuba with Africa is seen in the ongoing medical battle against Ebola in which Cuba has sent hundreds of doctors and medical personnel. The past 50 years of Cuba America relations has been characterized by dramatized power games including the Failed Bay of Pigs invasion by CIA-backed Cuban exiles in 1961, the year Obama (like me!) was born, Soviet Union deploys ballistic missiles to Cuba, prompting Cuban Missile Crisis in 1962, the jailing of Cuban Five , in Miami for spying in 2001, and the detention of US citizen Alan Gross detained in Cuba in 2009 accused of spying and recently in Dec 2013: US President Barack Obama and Raul Castro historic hands shake at Nelson Mandela’s funeral - the first such public gesture since 1959.

The latest new relations was made possible by the commendable intervention of His Holiness Pope Francis in the release of US citizen Alan Gross. As President Obama acknowledged in his historic speech, the world can be better off with improved Cuba-America relations. Witness him;. ”It was a Cuban, Carlos Finlay, who discovered that mosquitoes carry yellow fever; his work helped Walter Reed fight it. Cuba has sent hundreds of health care workers to Africa to fight Ebola, and I believe American and Cuban health care workers should work side by side to stop the spread of this deadly disease”. The world hails Obama’s global statesmanship!

Index

www.ingramcontent.com/pod-product-compliance
Lightning Source LLC
Chambersburg PA
CBHW060032030426
42334CB00019B/2289
* 9 7 8 9 7 8 5 3 3 2 1 1 7 *